PRAISE FOR LINDA WOLFE'S
DOUBLE LIFE

"LONG BEFORE THE NATION BECAME TRANSFIXED BY O. J. SIMPSON, NEW YORK HAD ITS OWN SHOCKING JEKYLL-AND-HYDE TALE, starring Sol Wachtler. . . . and Joy Silverman . . . a sleek, striking brunette who could give a few lessons to Susan Lucci's Erica Kane."

—Maureen Dowd, *The New York Times Book Review*

". . . as recounted by Linda Wolfe. . . . a fascinating and disturbing tale. . . ."

—Katha Pollitt, *Washington Post*

"I found Linda Wolfe's book engrossing and staggering in the magnitude and scope of the research entailed. It will, I suggest, ripen into the definitive work on this most baffling of all scenarios I have encountered in my thirty-six years in the criminal justice system. It reinforces my belief that the human heart has depths and dimensions beyond the dreams of our philosophy."

—Edwin Torres, Justice of the Supreme Court of the State of New York and author of *Carlito's Way*

"Set in a world that many only dream of, a world of politics and wealth. . . . *Double Life* . . . is stranger than fiction. . . . author Wolfe has penned an exceptionally well-researched study on the unexplainable aberrations of the human psyche. And, filled with sex, lies, and audiotape, it contains all the needed ingredients to keep the reader riveted."

—Glenda Eckert, *Tulsa World* (Oklahoma)

A Literary Guild Selection

Books by Linda Wolfe

Wasted: The Preppie Murder
The Professor and the Prostitute
    and Other True Tales of Murder & Madness
Private Practices (a novel)
The Literary Gourmet
Double Life: The Shattering Affair
    Between Chief Judge Sol
    Wachtler and Socialite Joy
    Silverman*

*Published by POCKET BOOKS

DOUBLE LIFE

THE SHATTERING AFFAIR BETWEEN CHIEF JUDGE SOL WACHTLER AND SOCIALITE JOY SILVERMAN

LINDA WOLFE

POCKET BOOKS

New York   London   Toronto   Sydney   Tokyo   Singapore

POCKET BOOKS, a division of Simon & Schuster Inc.
1230 Avenue of the Americas, New York, NY 10020

Copyright © 1994 by Linda Wolfe

Photo insert researched, edited, and designed by Vincent Virga

ISBN: 0-671-87481-0

First Pocket Books paperback printing June 1995

10 9 8 7 6 5 4 3 2 1

POCKET and colophon are registered trademarks of
Simon & Schuster Inc.

Front cover illustration by John Stephens; Sol Wachtler photo by Julia
Gaines/*Newsday*; Joy Silverman photo by Terry Ashe/*Time* Magazine

Printed in the U.S.A.

For R. S. B.

Both sides of me were in dead earnest; I was no more myself when I laid aside restraint and plunged in shame, than when I laboured, in the eye of day, at the furtherance of knowledge or the relief of sorrow and suffering. . . . I thus drew steadily nearer to that truth, by whose partial discovery I have been doomed to such a dreadful shipwreck: that man is not truly one, but truly two.

—Robert Louis Stevenson
Dr. Jekyll and Mr. Hyde

ACKNOWLEDGMENTS

There were many people without whose help I could not have brought this book to fruition. First and foremost were those who granted me interviews. I'm grateful to them for permitting me entry into their lives and for sharing with me their individual perspectives on the events recounted here.

I'm also grateful to my two researchers—Naomi Bernstein, whose skill at digging up elusive facts was extraordinary; and Jack Bourque, whose persistence in tracking down elusive individuals was exemplary—and to my brother, Alan Friedman, who read an early draft of the manuscript and offered invaluable suggestions.

In addition, I want to thank Michael Kelly, who patiently transcribed the tapes of my interviews; Risha Rosner, reference librarian of the Great Neck Public Library; and Cathryn Lopiccolo, executive editor of Washington and Lee University's newspaper, *The Ring-tum Phi*.

ACKNOWLEDGMENTS

Friends kept me going and provided me with precious leads. Among those who were especially helpful were Pat Baer, Mary De Bourbon, Judith Ehrlich, Lee Gruzen, Mike Kandel, Thelma Kandel, Dr. Helen Kaplan, Dick Laupat, Deborah Mitchell, Tully Plesser, Caroline Stoessinger, and Jo Thomson. But there were many others without whose contacts, insights, and encouragement this would have been a far less worthy book.

Finally, I want to thank my husband Max Pollack, who unstintingly shared with me his psychological wisdom.

AUTHOR'S NOTE

Most of the information in this book was obtained from interviews. In the back of the book, there are detailed notes identifying and commenting on sources, and the reader is urged to consult them.

The use of dialogue in conversations comes from at least one participant or from written documents. In the narrative, when someone is said to have "thought" or to have "believed" something, that assertion has been obtained from the person in question or from some source who gained direct knowledge of the person's thoughts and beliefs from a conversation with that person.

PROLOGUE

On Monday, October 5, 1992, handsome, youthful Sol Wachtler, chief judge of New York's highest court, parked his distinctive Lincoln Town Car in front of a gas station a few miles from his home, attached a voice-altering device to the receiver of the station's pay phone, and placed a call to a woman named Joy Silverman. But just as she came on the line, Sol realized that his voice disguiser had slipped off the receiver. Quickly, he hung up, got back in his car, and drove away.

Two days later, with the voice device functioning properly, he phoned the woman again, this time making the call from a hospital less than a mile from his home.

"Mrs. Silverman? Don't you dare hang up on me," he warned gruffly when she answered his ring. "And don't you record this call. You hear me?"

"I'm sorry, but I don't understand you," Joy stalled for time.

"Yeah, I know you can't understand me," Sol growled. He was hoping to make Joy think he was not himself but a private detective named David Purdy. "Well, goddamn, you better understand me. You're gonna get a letter from me, and you better listen to every word of it, and do what it tells you to do, or you're gonna be in serious deep trouble, and you're not gonna

1

see your daughter again. You hear me? I'm a sick and desperate man. I need the money. And you'll be hearing from me.''

"What is it that you want?" Joy asked.

"Twenty thousand in hundreds and fifties," Sol said. "The instructions will be given to you. The delivery will be made November seventh."

Joy attempted to prolong the conversation. She'd told the FBI she'd been receiving ominous phone calls, and they'd instructed her to keep her caller on the line as long as possible so they could trace his calls. "What assurances do I have after this, that this is over?" she asked.

"You'll know that it will be over because I need the money and I'm a sick man," Sol said.

"Well, what are you giving me for this?" Joy asked. "What am I going to get for this?"

"Right after you give me the money, you'll get the photographs. You'll get the tapes. You'll get information that will blow your mind. Do you hear me? I'm gettin' off now, because I think you might be tracing this."

She didn't want him to know she was. "Well—*ahh,*" she said, but couldn't quickly enough think of anything else to say.

"You'll be hearing from me," Sol cut her off. "You'll be hearing from me."

"Well, I, what kind of—I don't understand," Joy stammered. "What assurances do I—"

But the phone had gone dead. Sol had hung up.

"Remember the Silverman case?" Victor Ashrafi, chief of the criminal division of the U.S. Attorney's office in New Jersey, said on the phone later that day to his boss, Michael Chertoff, who was home with the flu.

"Yeah," Chertoff snuffled.

"You'll never believe who the caller is."

"Who?"

"Sol Wachtler."

Chertoff was incredulous. "Victor, you're kidding me!"

"No," Ashrafi said. "The FBI's got evidence. They'll lay it

2

out for you when you come in. There's a call from his car. There are calls from places he could easily have been.''

Chertoff grimaced. *Could have been!* Garbage. Hanging up, he phoned Jere Doyle, the acting head of New Jersey's FBI. ''Jere,'' he expostulated, ''if you traced the call back to Chief Justice Rehnquist, it couldn't be more ridiculous.''

Judge Wachtler had been asked to address a judicial conference in Reno, and on Thursday, October 8, he flew from his home in New York to Nevada. He checked into Harrah's Hotel and Casino and spent the evening catching up with friends he hadn't seen for a while. In the morning, before going to one of the conference's panels, he found a pay phone in an isolated corridor of the hotel and, attaching his voice disguiser to the phone, once again called Joy. ''You're not tracing this call?'' he asked her at the start of the conversation. ''You're not going to trace this call, are you?''

Joy said no, and he decided to accept her denial. ''All right,'' he said. ''You deserve an answer to your question about how you can trust me—can you hear me now?''

''Yes, I can. Just talk slowly.''

''I was hired a year ago. To shake you down. I thought the fat pig who hired me was from New Jersey.''

''The what? The who?'' Joy interrupted him.

''The fat pig. A fat pig hired me.''

''A fat pig?''

''Yes, hired me, and I thought she was from New Jersey.''

''Right,'' Joy said. ''Did she give you a name?''

''I know her name, but I'm not giving it to you,'' Sol said. ''She gave me a lot of shit about toxic waste and your boyfriend.''

''Right.''

''And she paid me to find out the rest, and I started calling you a year ago to track you.''

''Talk more slowly,'' Joy demanded, in order to keep him on the phone. ''It's hard for me to understand. I don't want to make you impatient. I'm just trying to understand you and to hear you.''

3

Sol found talking to her slow going. She asked him to speak more slowly or more loudly after virtually every sentence he uttered. He had to struggle to convey what he wanted to say. But after a while he managed, telling her about his compromising pictures and tapes. "Now, when you see and hear what I got," he said, "it's gonna blow your mind."

"Why is it going to blow my mind?"

"Because you know you thought I was a big fuckin' joke. You don't know shit. You understand me? You don't know shit."

On her end of the phone, Joy was shaking. But she tried to keep her voice steady and, remembering that the FBI had told her to try to get her caller to be specific about any harm he planned to inflict on her or her fourteen-year-old daughter, Jessica, led the conversation to the subject of menace. "Why are you threatening my child?" she asked.

Sol wasn't ready for the question. He wanted to tell her the sort of man David Purdy was. "Now, listen to me," he directed her. "I got diabetes, all right. I lost one kidney and I'm losing another one. That's why you didn't hear from me, and that's why I didn't visit Jessica this summer—you understand that? Yeah. Now, listen to me. I'm wearing a diaper."

"You're what?" Joy said. "You're wearing what?"

Sol made her be still and went on limning Purdy, his imaginary private eye from Texas, making him sound like a grotesque straight out of the fantasies of movie director David Lynch. "I'm wearing a diaper now. I've lost my teeth. I weigh over two hundred pounds." Then, at last, he told her what he wanted. "I want only twenty thousand dollars. I'm not asking for a hell of a lot from you."

"And what will you do to me, what will you do to me and my child, if I don't give it to you?" Joy persisted dutifully.

"If you don't give me, I'll tell you what I'm gonna do," he answered. "The first thing I'm gonna do is, Jessica is going to spend Thanksgiving with me. Okay? That's only one thing I'm going to do to you. Number two, what I'm going to do to you is, I'm going to take the material that I have and I'm gonna send it to people that—I'm gonna send it all over creation. You understand that? You won't be able to walk down the street, lady. You understand?''

Joy had been so well coached that she didn't express any emotion when she heard ''Purdy'' threaten her with exposure. She just asked again what specifically he had in mind doing to her child.

But Sol wouldn't answer that question. ''I'm sending you instructions out now,'' he said, changing the subject. ''November seventh is the date. You understand that? Now, listen. I'm a desperate man. I told your doorman I was going to get new teeth. I can't get new teeth because my gums are—I can hardly walk now. I'm dying. I'm dying.''

Joy kept on trying to find out just what he was planning to do if she didn't comply. ''I wanna know what you are threatening me with my child,'' she said.

Sol turned ugly. ''Why don't you fucking find out, lady? Why don't you just fucking find out? Why don't you just not pay me, and see what goddamn happens?''

''To whom?'' Joy, still following her instructions, asked.

But once again, Sol terminated their conversation. He hung up the phone and began circulating among the judges and lawyers who were attending the conference. He was, some of them would later remember, affable, friendly, charming.

''There's been another call,'' Victor Ashrafi said to Michael Chertoff the next day. ''It was from Reno.''

''Where's Wachtler?'' Chertoff asked.

''In Reno. Giving a speech.''

''Anyone from his staff go out there with him?'' Chertoff asked.

Ashrafi shook his head.

''It *still* could be someone trying to set him up,'' Chertoff said. But he knew that if asked to put money down on who was calling Joy, he'd have to bet Wachtler.

He and Victor, he decided, had best meet with James Esposito, the new head of New Jersey's FBI. And with Doyle too. And Brzezinski and Fleming and their supervisor, Garey Chin. They'd all better put their heads together and decide what they were going to do about arresting the chief judge of the Court of Appeals of the State of New York.

That same day, Sol Wachtler headed home from Reno on a flight that required changing planes in Denver. When he boarded his plane, he had with him a small, stamped packet. In it were instructions about when and where Joy was to drop off the twenty thousand dollars "Purdy" wanted from her and a manila envelope in which she was to place the money.

When he landed in Denver, he walked to a gate where there was a flight departing for San Antonio. At the gate was a stewardess who would be assisting on the flight. "Would you mind mailing this for me from San Antonio?" he asked her. "It's a gift for a friend. A handkerchief." He was ingratiating, seductive. He wanted, he explained, to have the woman to whom he was sending the gift think he'd purchased it in San Antonio. He'd promised to send her something from there.

The stewardess was accommodating. She took the packet, and when she got to San Antonio, she mailed it for him.

She had no idea that inside it was a letter that said,

Even my assistant, a two bit hore [*sic*] from Queens, knew she was being recorded last Sunday. Don't try that on me or all bets are off.

This is the deal—if you do anything to queer it you will regret it for the rest of your life. Tell the police or put your keystone P.I.'s on it and you'll be sorry. They may be good at deactivating bugs but they'll not outsmart me in this operation. And you can't take a chance that you will beat me. You will lose.

There is a laundry shop called Shanley located at 184 East 84th between Park and Lexington Avenues. Right next door is a cellar entrance. Have your doorman Ramón put the manila envelope which I am enclosing in that cellar entrance stairway. The envelope is to contain $20,000 (twenty thousand in used 100's and 50's).

DOUBLE LIFE

One month later, on the morning of November 7, 1992, Joan Wachtler, blond, slim, and unabatedly beautiful, despite her sixty years, went to Saks Fifth Avenue to pick up some clothes she had ordered. She'd chosen a variety of items, dresses and skirts and tops, but everything was black—she was partial to black because it set off her pale complexion becomingly—and each of the knitted tops could be worn with any of the knitted skirts, some short, some long. She'd put a lot of thought into these purchases, choosing items that not only were interchangeable but would travel well, because this was a terribly special wardrobe. A campaign wardrobe. Her husband, Sol, was gearing up to run for governor in the 1994 election and had asked her to accompany him to the requisite statewide public appearances. She didn't really want him to run—had, in fact, begged him not to run—but he'd had his heart set on it, and at last she'd given in and said she'd do as he asked.

Sol didn't know about the clothes yet. When he came home this afternoon, she was going to surprise him by showing him her purchases and telling him they were her gift to him, the embodiment of her decision to participate in his campaign. But she was going to tell him, too, that if he won and moved up to the state capital in Albany, she wasn't going to leave Long Island, where they lived. She had a job, children and grandchildren, a home, a life of her own, here on the Island.

She heard from him at about one in the afternoon. "Want me to bring some bagels?" he asked, calling her on his car phone. She told him yes, and he said he'd pick them up and be home around two.

Two o'clock came and went, and she was beginning to worry a little about why Sol wasn't home yet, when the phone rang again. But it wasn't Sol. It was some man whose voice she didn't recognize. He didn't know hers, either. "Are you Mrs. Wachtler?" he asked.

She said yes, and he said, "This is the FBI."

She thought it was one of those nuisance phone calls, someone trying to scare her or a kid playing a puerile joke. "Who are you?" she said sternly, hoping to challenge the caller out of his game. But the man on the phone went on insisting he was with the FBI. Unsure, and wanting to check, she said, "Give me your number. I'll call you back."

He gave her the number, and she dialed it, and it *was* the FBI, and this time when the agent got on the phone, he said, "Mrs. Wachtler? We've arrested your husband."

She couldn't believe her ears. She'd just spoken to Sol. Surely he would be walking in the door with a bagful of fragrant, freshly baked bagels any moment now. Yet something about the man's tone made her realize that what he was saying was authentic. "Where is my husband?" she demanded. "I want to talk to him."

"You can't," the man from the FBI said. "He's allowed one call, and he's already made it. To your son-in-law."

She had three sons-in-law, but she knew he must mean her eldest daughter's husband. He was a New York lawyer. *"Why* have you arrested him?" she asked.

"For extortion. You can speak to him in a while from now."

Suddenly, it was as if everything Joan knew and had ever known had scattered and skittered out of her mind. She couldn't even recall what the word *extortion* meant. Dazed, she put down the phone and tried to remember, and then she ran for her dictionary. There it was: *"Extortion.* Illegal use of one's official position or powers to obtain property, funds, or patronage."

That can't have anything to do with Sol, she thought. If there's one thing I'm sure of, it's that Sol is as honest and honorable as the day is long.

Denying to herself that what the man from the FBI had said could contain even a kernel of truth, she waited by the phone to hear from her husband or her son-in-law about what she was sure must be a bizarre mistake.

But by evening she knew there had been no mistake. Sol had indeed written an extortion letter—an ugly, threatening letter filled with filthy language of the kind she'd never heard him speak and demanding twenty thousand dollars from its recipient in exchange for compromising photographs and tapes. Worse, the recipient of the letter was a woman who'd broken off an affair with her husband, an affair that had gone on for four-and-a-half years. Behind her back.

8

Not only that, she knew the woman. It was her cousin. Joy Silverman.

Joan Wachtler was shocked and puzzled by what she learned on that dismal November day. And so was everyone else when news of Chief Judge Wachtler's arrest was broadcast later that night. He had the reputation of being an amiable, dignified, effective, and charismatic man. He also had the reputation of being immensely powerful, one of the most prominent men in the United States.

Why had such a man done the deeds Wachtler was said to have done, people everywhere wondered. Had he been at the pinnacle of judicial power for so long that he had come to consider himself above the law? Or had he been sick, the victim of a plaguing mental illness. And who was the woman who had prompted his tumble from grace? What was it about her that had made him lead a double life, deceive wife, friends, and family, and then turn criminal?

But above all, his arrest sparked a particularly dreadful question: If *this* man could commit the crimes of which he was accused, then how could one ever again trust one's judgment of one's fellows, how could one ever know what horrors might erupt from within them.

The story that follows, a tale of the members of a single family—the real-estate dynasty into which Sol Wachtler married—probes behind the proliferation of headlines and partial information sparked by his arrest in order to answer those perplexing questions.

PART 1

A Family
and a Fortune

CHAPTER 1

Sol Wachtler was born in Brooklyn in 1930 and lived for the first years of his life in a tiny apartment above a cleaning store on a bustling shopping street. He adored his mother, Faye, a warm and indulgent immigrant from Russia. About his father, an American-born traveling salesman who made his living auctioning off the estates of the dead or the failed, his feelings were more complicated. Philip Wachtler was a quiet, strict man with a highly developed sense of right and wrong, and although Sol knew he was a concerned father, he found him cold and unaffectionate.

Times were hard for the Wachtlers in those Depression days, as they were for many Americans. Philip, Faye, and the children had to share their little apartment with an aunt in order to make the rent. But in 1938 Philip began to earn some decent money and was able to move his wife and two sons—Sol and his older brother, Morty—to the South, where he was increasingly doing his business.

They lived in a number of small towns in Georgia and the Carolinas and finally settled down in St. Petersburg, Florida, where Philip opened a small jewelry store and the children went to public schools.

When the war came, the whole family—except for Sol—

started working in the store. There was an Army camp nearby, and soldiers from the camp crowded into the shop all day long to buy trinkets for their sweethearts back home. But although he could have used an extra hand, Philip had other plans for his youngest son. He wanted Sol to stay home and study so he could go to college. So he could be the first person in the family to go to college.

The boy had proved himself to be a go-getter. When he was twelve, he'd talked the local radio station into letting him emcee an afternoon show, a comedy and variety hour. When he was thirteen, he'd started a little mimeographed newspaper, "The Eternal Light," distributing it among the hundred or so Jewish families that lived in town. Philip was certain that one day Sol would make the family uncommonly proud, and told him repeatedly, "You're going to be the professional man in the family. So stay away from the store, and do your homework."

Sol was pained by his father's edict. It was lonely, coming home to an empty house. Taking meals by himself. "Let me work in the store like Morty," he begged Philip one day. "I could help out. Wrap packages." But Philip was adamant. "Stay away from the store," he insisted. "I don't want you tainted by it. By business."

Sol did as he was told, and when he was in his junior year of high school, Philip, who like many businessmen had grown prosperous during the war, decided to bankroll him to a prep-school education, or at least the last part of one, so that he could go, not just to college, but to a *good* college.

He sent him to Milford, a Connecticut school that was reputed to have an excellent record of getting its students into Yale.

Sol arrived at Milford in the winter of 1946. He was a handsome adolescent. His nose was a tad too big, but his smile was ready and ample, and his eyes a remarkable crystalline blue. He was popular—students and teachers alike enjoyed his company. And he was immensely energetic. He flung himself into the life of the school, joining the public speaking club, the music appreciation society, the school newspaper, the varsity basketball team.

In the summer he went home to St. Petersburg and over the

vacation got his nose bobbed. In the fall, he returned to school handsomer than ever and reaped the rewards of his initial popularity, getting elected president of the senior class. By the spring semester, his final one, he'd become such a big man on campus that even though he'd been at Milford only a year and a half, the school decided that, come graduation, they'd give him their principal award, the Wilson Cup, an annual prize awarded to the student who contributed most "to the life and spirit of the school."

He was proud when he heard he would be receiving the award. But there'd been a big disappointment too. Yale had turned him down. The prestigious university had been harder than ever to get into that year, what with all the veterans getting preference, and his grades hadn't been all that exceptional.

Where to go instead? He decided on Washington and Lee in Lexington, Virginia. "It was in the South, and I liked the idea of living in warm weather again," he would one day explain. "It was one of the better southern universities. And my pal Ronnie Levick was going there and having a great time."

In the spring of 1947, he sent his acceptance to Washington and Lee.

That same spring, a woman named Jeanette Fererh, who hailed from Saranac Lake, New York, gave birth to a baby girl. She named her Joy, perhaps for the feelings that holding and cuddling the dark-haired infant inspired in her.

Jeanette was a charmer. Tall and voluptuous, with sparkling jade-green eyes and fine dark hair that she wore in a chignon, she had an irresistible way of relating to people. She'd focus entirely on whomever she was addressing, her stunning cat's eyes glued to theirs, her wide mouth fixed in a radiant smile. And she'd issue lavish praise, compliments that made women feel they were trusted confidantes, men as if they were ten feet tall.

But her marriage to Ben Fererh wasn't a happy one, and soon the two would drift apart.

On a balmy June weekend in 1947, shortly after he'd graduated from Milford, Sol Wachtler traveled to Queens to spend a few days visiting his friend Ronnie. Ronnie had glorious hijinks planned for Saturday night. A bunch of friends, all paired off into couples, would go to Manhattan and spend the evening dancing and drinking at some Broadway hotel, maybe the Astor, maybe the famous Biltmore, where all through the war their older brothers had kissed farewell to their girlfriends beneath the big clock.

But I don't have a date, Sol pointed out.

Don't worry, Ronnie told him. I'll arrange one for you. With a cousin of mine.

She was Joan Carol Wolosoff, a high school junior, and she was rich. Her father, Leon, the son of a cantor, was president of Wolosoff Brothers, one of the big building companies in Queens. Her mother, Elsie, was a daughter of Max Blumberg, a lumber and millwork dealer who had come to America as a penniless fourteen-year-old from Lithuania and quickly amassed so great a fortune that he not only left millions to each of his children but became one of the most generous Jewish philanthropists of his era.

Sol didn't know all this when he first laid eyes on Joan. He just knew that he liked the way she looked. She was blond and buxom—her nickname at the summer camp she had gone to had been "Tits Wolosoff"—and she was very graceful.

On their first date, bobbing and twirling to the hotel band's feverish lindy hops and gliding in each other's arms to romantic fox trots, they knew they wanted to see each other again. On their second date, they went to see *Brigadoon,* the number one hit on Broadway, and when they drove back to Queens, neither of them wanted to get out of the car, so they parked in her driveway and talked for hours about their friends, their families, their dreams for the future. On their third date, they went with a crowd of boys and girls to Jones Beach, where they watched the play of the moon's silver light illuminating the crashing waves, and later the rays of the rising sun. After that, they started going together. Going steady. Except that they both knew that Sol would be leaving for college in the fall.

He was going to be a lawyer, he had decided by then. Washington and Lee had a program that enabled students to receive both their B.A. and LL.B. degrees in just six years.

Sol entered Washington and Lee in the fall of 1947. The school, one of the oldest universities in the South, had a bucolic campus that rolled across a hundred acres shaded by ancient trees and dotted with handsome Greek Revival–style columned buildings. Sol pledged a Jewish fraternity, Phi Epsilon Pi, and, remarkably, in his sophomore year was elected frat president, a position generally won only by an upperclassman. He had won the election, one of his frat brothers would recall years later, because he had an almost instinctive gift for politics. "It was like he was a favorite of some mythological god," the frat brother observed. "Like he'd been given a magic potion to drink or an invisible cloak to wear. Something that always made him win."

His political abilities had paid off in other ways as well by then. He had become the secretary-treasurer of the Washington Literary Society, a group that sponsored roundtable discussions, the secretary and speaker of the Forensic Union, a debating group, a prominent member of the Washington and Lee Debate Team, and a member of the Christian Council and War Memorial Scholarship Committee. His energy in pursuing his interests was extraordinary, and in a reprise of his experience at Milford, in his second year on campus he won an award, sponsored by the university's Inter-Fraternity Council, that was reserved for the student "who has contributed most to campus activities."

He was still keen on Joan Wolosoff, who had graduated from high school by then and was attending Goucher College in Towson, Maryland. Sometimes he made the five-hour drive to visit her; sometimes she came down to Lexington to see him. But they had agreed that they could each date other people, and occasionally, they did. Yet Sol wasn't very interested in girls, not nearly as interested as some of his house brothers were. They broke the frat-house rules—girls weren't allowed above the second floor—sneaking their dates past the watchful eyes of the housemother and into upstairs bedrooms. And they hung out with them at a town juke joint, dancing and drinking beer. But Sol

17

didn't sneak girls into his room, and he rarely turned up at the juke joint.

"He wasn't a big ladies' man," another of his frat brothers would one day recall. "He wasn't a make-out guy. He was very—well, clean-cut. And besides, there was Joan. There was always Joan."

Sol had met her family the previous year—not just her mother, Elsie, and her father, Leon, but her uncles, Morton and Alvin, the one known as Bibbs. Leon was the eldest of the three brothers, a sweet-natured, energetic man who was always running. He'd bound up the stairs to his second-story office on Queens Boulevard, then skip down them, always taking them in twos. Morton, too, had a sympathetic personality and was known as the family peacemaker. But Bibbs, the youngest, was tough, opinionated, convinced that he was always right. Despite his scratchy exterior, Sol hit it off with him.

The three Wolosoff brothers had been in the building business for over twenty-five years. They'd constructed homes right through the Depression and even during the war, when, despite the fact that almost no new housing was going up, shrewd Bibbs had managed to obtain a government contract to erect homes near a naval base. Suddenly, after the war, they started to be immensely successful.

It was that sort of a time. People were clamoring for all the things they'd had to do without during the war years—to get a car, they'd pay a thousand dollars under the table. For an apartment, several thousand. And the demand for houses, houses roomy enough for war veterans who were producing the children of the baby boom, was mammoth. William Levitt began building inexpensive housing for veterans and in a few short years constructed and sold close to eighteen thousand homes. The Wolosoffs, too, began building similar low-cost homes, and they were snapped up as soon as they were erected. Then Leon began building more expensive homes.

The Wolosoffs did not live grandly during those early postwar years. Morton had an apartment in the city. Bibbs lived in a four-and-a-half-room apartment in Queens. Leon, the only one with a house, had a small, attached three-bedroom place, also in Queens.

But in 1949, the year Sol Wachtler was a junior at Washington and Lee, Bibbs decided to build a home in Nassau County for himself, his wife, Sylvia, and their two young sons. Nassau was home to some of the most luxurious houses in the country, an area in which until recently there had been vast open fields dotted with vegetable farms and edged by miles of scrub oak and gnarled pine along an untouched shoreline. It was an area where women whose photographs appeared in the society columns of newspapers attended debutante balls, where men still played polo and rode to hounds. And it was an area where once there had been few Jews but into which, increasingly, newly wealthy Jewish families had begun penetrating.

The North Shore of Nassau County was its "Gold Coast," one of the richest areas in the United States, a region of rolling fields and high bluffs overlooking the majestic Long Island Sound. Land here was expensive, and better deals could be had on the flatter expanses of the South Shore. But he would buy and build, Bibbs decided, in the burgeoning town of Great Neck on the desirable North Shore. He could afford whatever he'd have to pay for the property—and he purchased six acres. He also decided that he would make his home a dream house, a place that would announce to all who saw it that here was a builder with vision and taste.

Perhaps Leon, too, would have decided to build himself a grand home. But in the spring of 1949, while he was running up the stairs to his office, he collapsed. He was rushed to a hospital, where it was discovered he had had a severe heart attack. Hospitalized, the forty-eight-year-old builder showed some improvement at first, but several days later he worsened and died. His daughter, Joan—his only child—became an heiress, inheriting real estate that was not yet income-producing, but that would one day be worth many millions of dollars.

After Leon died, Sol and Joan talked about getting married, but Joan's mother, Elsie, wouldn't hear of it. Sol had no money, he wasn't society, and he was still just a college student. Sylvia

Wolosoff, Joan's aunt, made fun of him. "Elsie," she called out to her sister-in-law one day when she was visiting her house and Sol arrived to pick up Joan for a date, "Elsie, the delivery boy is here!"

Sol and Joan bided their time. But they saw each other whenever they could. Once, in Sol's junior year, Joan came down to Washington and Lee and, looking very much the prototype of the young postwar debutante, her blond hair bobbed and sleekly banged, her neck bangled with three strands of pearls, her smile a wide flash of perfect white teeth, had her picture printed in the school newspaper. Another time, she was named "the sweetheart of Phi Epsilon Pi," Sol's frat. Sol was proud of her and paraded around the campus with her on his arm, a frat brother who recalled Joan's visits would eventually say, "Like a peacock displaying tail feathers." "And why not? She was one of those perfect girls. Poised, self-assured, and with every hair in place."

By 1951, the marriage between Jeanette and Ben Fererh had broken up and Jeanette was raising three-and-a-half-year-old Joy on her own. Jeanette would say that breaking up had been *her* idea, but years later when she was grown, Joy would tell intimates that her father had walked out, abandoned the family.

Joan Wolosoff had, by that same year, transferred to Sarah Lawrence College to be near her grieving mother, and Sol Wachtler was attending law school, where he was elected president of Washington and Lee's Bar Association. He was also trying his hand at being a creative writer, coauthoring a column in the school paper, which ran under the byline "Sacco and Vanzetti." Sometimes the columns were filled with puerile jokes or letters signed with such would-be-amusing names as "Twisted Mind," "Dementia Praecox," or "Chow Hound." At other times, there were short stories.

In one, a girl whose initials, like Joan's, are J.C.W. and who, like Joan, is a psychology major, asks a young man to tell her a dream so that she can interpret the symbolism. Other friends have done her this favor, she points out. But the hero of the story, not wanting his inner self made public, refuses to present a real dream and instead makes up one so zany and so tauntingly overladen with Freudian sexual symbols, including snakes, boxes, umbrellas, and a mace "cunningly hinged to the navel of the bearer," that the poor girl is utterly frustrated. "You're not psychotic," she tells him. "You're . . . just plain juvenile."

In another, a frat man's girlfriend—"Every hair on her head was in place, every gesture correct and assured, and every aspect of her dress had a costumelike perfection"—comes down to Washington and Lee to visit him.

The hero isn't happy to see her. "When Mary was not there," he thinks, "her status was a source of pride" to him, but her actual presence irritates him. Their relationship, he fears, is bland and hypocritical. "Each weekend was another hollow climax, the apprehension of which was its own *raison d'être*. Each weekend for what seemed like years they had analyzed each other under superficial circumstances, and now they dragged themselves as actors to the final scene."

That scene is a kiss. Anticipating it, the hero muses, "Their emotions would become aroused to some degree or another, because it was understood that some passion might be displayed at this appropriate time." But, in fact, very little passion is manifested. Indeed, wiping his mouth after the kiss, the hero notices that so lightly and cautiously have he and Mary kissed that his handkerchief is hardly soiled. He is disappointed and filled with inchoate yearning.

At the time Sol wrote this story, he and Joan had not yet had sex together, although they'd been dating for five years. Restrained and proper, they'd agreed not to make love until they were married.

That they *would* be getting married was definite, and in Sol's senior year of law school, they at last began laying plans for their wedding.

Sol wanted a big one. Joan wasn't sure. She'd never liked large gatherings, and this one was promising to be huge. Still, she went along with Sol's wishes and had her mother book the ballroom at the Plaza Hotel for a date in May. But as the day of the wedding drew closer, she grew increasingly uneasy.

In February, during a school vacation, she went home to her mother's apartment, and Sol came up from law school so they could draw up a final guest list. The two of them, along with her mother and a few favorite aunts and uncles, sat around the living room discussing various relatives, and they couldn't decide whether to ask this one or that, or both of them, or neither of them, or just how many people to invite, or whether to make the whole event bigger, or make it smaller. Joan started feeling anxious. This whole thing's getting beyond me, she worried.

The aunts and uncles were growing vociferous. And then suddenly Uncle Morton said, "What do you need all this trouble for? Why don't you two just go out and get married?"

It was ten-thirty at night. "What do you mean, 'go out and get married'?" Sol asked. "How can you just go out and get married?"

"You could get married tonight," Morton said. "All you need is a rabbi."

It was true, Joan realized. They'd already gotten their blood tests. Why not just go out and get married? A few minutes later, Sol was on the phone to a rabbi and she was borrowing a navy blue satin dress from her mother and a ring from one of the aunts. And then she, Sol, and her mother, with Uncle Morton along to serve as a witness, raced off to the rabbi.

They were married so late at night that her mother always said afterward that she wasn't sure if they'd been married on the twenty-third or the twenty-fourth of the month.

The day after the wedding, Joan and Sol went back to school— she for her final semester at Sarah Lawrence, he for his final semester of law school. Back on campus, Sol found an apartment for them—a couple of tiny rooms in a Quonset hut, one of those corrugated metal units erected right after the war to house married veterans. No refrigerator, but the place had an icebox, and he made arrangements for regular deliveries of fifty-pound blocks of ice.

Joan took the overnight train down to see her new home, and for the rest of the school year, she commuted between Bronxville, New York, and Lexington, Virginia. She was happy with her new life and so absorbed by her handsome, talented spouse that when asked to list her interests for publication in her college yearbook, she cited only two: the scholarship drive and her husband. On her graduation day, she tore off her cap and gown, tossed them to her father-in-law, who was standing in for Sol, shouted, "Give these to my roommate," and raced off to catch a train for Virginia.

That summer, they rented an apartment in Hollywood, Florida, where Sol's parents were living. Sol took a job in a law office and enrolled in a Florida law school to make up three credits he was missing and would need in order to graduate. He also applied for a commission in the Navy. The Korean War was going on, and once he graduated, if he didn't get a commission, he'd be drafted.

One summer's day, he received a telegram from the Navy, eagerly ripped it open, and saw that he'd gotten the commission. He'd be a lieutenant junior grade, the telegram said; he'd be assigned to Naval Intelligence and stationed in Washington, D.C. What could be better? Sol was joyous, except for one nagging little thought. Just a few days earlier, he'd received a draft notice, telling him he'd be called to Army duty in a few months. Well, surely, he decided, the naval commission took precedence. And he promptly made plans to move to Washington. He quit his job and broke the lease on the apartment, his mother went out and bought him a Navy ensign's black raincoat and a handsome briefcase, and his friends threw him a big farewell party. Then he went up to Washington to get his commission and find an apartment for himself and Joan. I'll send for you as soon as I have one, he told her.

In Washington, he went to the Office of Naval Officer Procurement to receive his commission. But a desk officer said to him, "You were sent a draft notice?" And he gave Sol an odd look.

"Yeah, I got it about a week ago," Sol acknowledged, starting to feel uncomfortable.

"Then you can't take the commission," the officer said. "Too bad."

"Why not? I'm not in the Army." He was indignant, stunned. "I've got a Navy commission. Here's the telegram."

"Yeah, but as soon as you get your draft notice, you can't have your commission anymore." And the desk officer walked away to the back of the busy office.

Crushed, Sol realized he would have to return to Florida, return in the Navy ensign's black raincoat his mother had bought, and resume life in Hollywood, where he no longer had a job or an apartment and where everyone was expecting him to come back in a lieutenant's uniform. He was terribly embarrassed. He was also at a loss about where to live and how to manage financially until the Army wanted him. What to do? Resourcefully, he got on a train and went to Atlanta, Georgia, the home of the Third Army in the area, begged to be taken in right away, and got himself sworn in as a private in the Army.

Joan went north and moved into her mother's place, a one-bedroom apartment. She slept on a cot in the living room, and tried to think of what to do next. Maybe she'd go back to school. Maybe she'd get a job. But she and her mother, living right on top of each other that way, began quarreling constantly, and she missed Sol, and after three days she went down to Augusta, where he was taking basic training, and moved into a rooming house. She had to share her bedroom with another Army wife. And she had to share the bathroom with other roomers. But she didn't hate it. She went to the post every weekend, and Sol would come out and talk to her through the gates.

When he finished basic training, they took a little two-bedroom house right outside the post. And then she got pregnant and had her first baby, Lauren, a plump little girl with blue eyes. She was scared of the baby. She had been an only child. She'd never been around infants before. When Lauren cried, she was terrified that something dreadful had happened. But the other women on the post—some of them had had four, five, even six babies—took her in hand, showed her what to do, calmed and cuddled her, just as she calmed and cuddled the baby.

She loved the Army post. The wisdom of the women. The sandy earth. The scrubby pines. At night, she and Sol would go for walks beneath the trees, the baby in her carriage, all wrapped in thick netting to keep away spiders. Or they'd go to the drive-in movie, sit in the warm darkness with the baby in her basket in the back of the car and James Dean and Elizabeth Taylor and Bette Davis and James Stewart moving against the sky like giant, glowing gods. They had no troubles, no worries, no concerns. She wanted them to stay there forever.

CHAPTER 2

To live in Great Neck in the early 1950s was to inhabit a world in which it seemed that nothing unpleasant could ever happen. The roads were uncrowded, the streets were quiet, and everywhere the eye lit there were parklike lawns and sumptuous homes—rambling colonial cottages, spacious Spanish haciendas, stately English Tudor great houses. Great Neck was where life was sweet, especially for the women, who had maids, cooks, chauffeurs, and so much time for beautician's visits and massages and tennis games that, in those days before it was understood that women wanted more from life than just leisure, a popular joke was, "Lord, when I die, let me be resurrected as a Great Neck housewife."

Bibbs Wolosoff's wife, Sylvia, seemed to many of her neighbors the personification of the privileged, happy Great Neck housewife. She was long-limbed, lean, and blond, with smooth tanned skin and a measured smile, had two young sons, James and Van Warren, and a tall, distinguished-looking husband with Prussian blue eyes and a full head of thick, just-graying hair. What's more, he had built her a mansion.

The house, which was in the Kings Point section of the town, was a low-slung, glassy creation that awed the neighbors by its audacity and art. It had more than eight thousand square feet of floor space, much of it expended on a mammoth open living room and an atrium in which there flourished, nurtured by a sprinkler system and Japanese gardeners, a veritable forest of plants and a verdant tree that soared right through the roof. Upstairs was Bibbs's den, which was another large room, as well as a few small bedrooms and a master bedroom appointed with two separate bathrooms and a dressing area that contained hundreds of feet of closets. But it was the amenities and grounds outside the house that were truly spectacular. There was a big pool, a hot tub, a sauna, and a roomy boat dock, all offering views of the glittering Long Island Sound, as well as a long winding driveway that secured the estate's privacy as it twisted upward from the road past gardens, shade trees, and a velvety one-hole golf course.

At night there were frequent parties at that mansion, parties to which the Wolosoff boys and their friends were not invited. "I don't want you guys hanging around the house," Bibbs would tell them. "Go downstairs to the basement, or go outside, go play by the dock." The kids did as they were told, but sometimes they'd creep back into the house and tiptoe down the hallway and listen outside Bibbs's den.

"You hear that?" a boy named Dick Simons said once to Van Wolosoff. "You hear how they're laughing?" From behind the door came sounds of raucous giggles and giddy banter.

"Jeez! They're drunk," another boy said. Glasses were tinkling, ice was rattling.

The drinking noises, Dick Simons would one day say, were the prelude to change, to domestic disruption, the sounds of adults getting ready to explore new directions. In 1960 the marriage of Bibbs and Sylvia broke up. She married a neighbor, Sol Weinsier. Weinsier's wife married a man named Gordon. Gordon's wife married someone else's husband. And Bibbs married a statuesque woman named Jeanette, whom he'd met in the course of pursuing a real-estate deal in Newark.

She was Joy Fererh's mother.

Jeanette had had a hard time after her relationship with Fererh broke up. She'd had to work to support her little daughter—

Jeanette would later tell others that not only didn't Fererh contribute financially to the household, but there were times when she had to help him out with money—and she'd become a secretary in Newark, New Jersey. In addition, she'd had a long series of affairs, some of which had been downright humiliating, and none of which had taken her where she wanted to go—namely into a decent marriage with a man rich enough to afford her cultivated tastes. Once, when she was having an affair with a married doctor of her acquaintance, his wife had come home right when she and the doctor were in his bedroom, and she'd had to hide in the closet like a thief until the coast was clear. But to her relief, after a while she'd succeeded in getting married for the second time. She'd become the wife of a prosperous Long Island builder, a French Jew named Germont.

Germont had installed Jeanette in a pleasant if not luxurious house in Sands Point, a fashionable section of Port Washington, a suburban town just east of Great Neck. He'd bought her expensive jewelry and clothes. And he'd given her another child, a boy they named Bruce. Bruce was six years younger than her little girl, Joy.

Jeanette had been happy with her new husband, but he had leukemia and died prematurely. She inherited the house and some money. But not enough. She could barely meet the mortgage payments. And, strapped for cash, she'd gone back to work. Not as a secretary. She didn't do secretarial work anymore. Rather, working on a contractual basis, she did public relations for the city of Newark. She ran parties, hiring the caterers, supervising the guest lists, and acting as hostess. She was a wonderful hostess—enthusiastic, concerned, chatty. She'd learned that she could talk to anyone—all it took was reading the *Enquirer,* so as to be up on the latest scandal, and following the astrology columns in the women's magazines, so she could amuse people by predicting their futures.

It was at one of her functions that Bibbs had met her. He talked to her briefly and, family legend has it, was instantaneously smitten. The next day, he sent her flowers—ten dozen roses.

After that, they started seeing each other, albeit surreptitiously at first. But after he and Sylvia broke up, Bibbs invited Jeanette for a two-day cruise on his yacht and, during the cruise, asked her to marry him.

Jeanette's little girl, Joy Fererh, reveled in the story of their romantic courtship. Joy was a pretty little thing who looked a lot like her mother. Indeed, sometimes, when she dressed up in her mother's clothes, her mother would say, "You're *me!* You're a carbon copy of me." And while some young girls want to look like anyone *but* their mothers, Joy seemed happy to think that she might have inherited not only her mother's extraordinarily good looks but her remarkable ability to make a man fall—in an instant—head over heels in love with her.

It didn't take Bibbs long to realize that Joy was exceptionally attached to her mother. After he married Jeanette and moved her and her kids into his mansion, the little girl was always getting underfoot. When he'd come home from work, she'd be parked in his and Jeanette's bedroom, chattering away. And at night, after dinner, she'd be sitting cross-legged on the bedroom floor, trying on her mother's jewelry. Jeanette had a passion for jewelry. "Bibbie," she'd say—she always called him Bibbie—"you *are* going to buy me that emerald, aren't you?" Or, "Let's go to Winston's on Saturday. There's a diamond necklace there that'll take your breath away."

"Oh, let's," Joy would say, considering herself part of the plan. And her mother would kiss and cuddle her and promise to take her along.

Bibbs found her an annoyance, a constant interference between himself and Jeanette. He liked Jeanette's little boy. The kid was self-reliant and musically talented. He could sit and play the piano for hours on end. But Joy was always hanging on her mother's skirttails, demanding her attention. And getting it. Bibbs resented the love Jeanette lavished on Joy. "But she needs all that love, Bibbie," Jeanette would say. "The poor little thing, she never had a father. I'm all she's got."

Joan Wachtler, whose father had been Bibbs's brother, was living nearby with her husband, Sol. After the Army, although at first they'd planned to go back to Florida and live there, they'd moved up north.

They'd done it largely at Bibbs's urging. The aging, rich builder had taken a great liking to his niece's husband. He liked educated men, he told Sol, men with whom he could discuss business and ideas. And it was good to have a lawyer in the family, he told friends, especially a good, sharp lawyer like Sol.

Bibbs needed a good lawyer. People were always threatening to sue him. Tenants. Subcontractors. Copartners. He didn't mind being sued. One of his favorite sayings was, "You do what you have to do in business. And if people don't like it, screw 'em, let 'em sue you. The most it'll cost you is twenty-five thousand dollars. That'll buy out any lawsuit."

Still, he needed a lawyer to handle all the threats and keep him on the good side of the government. Only one year before he'd persuaded Sol to move north, he and his brother Morton had been investigated for fraudulent practices by the Federal Housing Administration. They'd been accused of reaching into federal mortgage money and helping themselves to a half million dollars. Bibbs had been cynical about the government's probe. "What's the big deal?" he'd said to friends. "They wanted houses. We wanted money. We both got what we wanted." But he'd had to testify at an unpleasant hearing at which Prescott Bush, the Republican senator from Connecticut, had been caustic and harsh. A smart young lawyer like Sol could have been a boon at a time like that.

After the hearing, Bibbs had corresponded regularly with Sol, and at last persuaded him to rent a little ranch house in the Lake Success area of Great Neck.

Sol took a job with Austin and Dupont, a law firm in nearby Queens, with offices facing the elevated subway. It wasn't the kind of firm he'd dreamed of working at. But that kind of firm, a prestigious Manhattan firm, didn't hire Washington and Lee law graduates. Firms like that hired Harvard men, Yale men. Sol contented himself with his thirty-five-dollar-a-week job—though he never grew used to the rumble of the elevated train. When he was talking to a client on the phone and a train started to roar by, he'd say, "Just a minute. I've got to find some papers," and keep the receiver covered until the noise was gone. But while Austin and Dupont wasn't much, he was practicing law—and although Bibbs didn't let him handle any of his big real-estate deals, he gave him some work, good work, and took him under his wing, made him his confidant, his adviser, his counselor.

Once, Sol even negotiated a land deal for him. It was a family affair. Philip Wachtler had bought a large tract of land near St. Petersburg, Florida. He'd paid thirty thousand dollars for more than three hundred acres, much of the acreage right on the water. The price had been cheap because the land was virtually inaccessible. No roads ran through it and no ferry or bridge connected it to already developed areas. Then, lo and behold, the state decided to construct a superhighway through the land, and suddenly Sol's father was offered two hundred thousand dollars for his property, and then three hundred thousand, and then more and more, until at last he was being offered eight hundred thousand. He didn't know whether to take the offer, and so Sol asked Bibbs, who knew so much about real estate, to come down to Florida and look over the site. The three of them walked what part of the land they could, but much of it was mangrove swamp, so they rented a little boat and motored through the rest, and then Bibbs said to Philip, "This land is terrific! You can pump out the water and double the size. How much were you offered? Eight hundred thousand? I'll give you eight hundred and fifty."

Philip cheerfully said okay.

Two weeks later, a construction company which had developed much of Florida offered him a million and a quarter. Hearing the figure, Sol told his father that he wasn't bound to accept Bibbs's offer—they hadn't yet signed a contract. But Philip stood by his word. "Look," he said, "I shook hands on it."

Bibbs was impressed. "Your father's a man of honor," he told Sol. And he promised to build Philip a beautiful house, right on the most exquisite part of the land, where it would be surrounded by water on three sides. He also told Sol that if he liked, he could be the one to develop the land. All he had to do was put up fifty thousand dollars. But Sol didn't have the money.

31

Joan didn't, either. Her father had left her mother all his income-producing properties and given Joan property that, while potentially worth a great deal, was not yet earning much. Sol let go the offer to develop the land.

It didn't bother him much at the time. He was busy with other matters. For one thing, with Bibbs's backing, he'd begun to try his hand at politics, this time in the real, not the ivy-walled, world. He was a Republican—he'd been one ever since he could remember, having learned at an early age that in the South, the Republican party was the liberal one, the one his father and indeed nearly all the Jewish people he knew voted for. Before he'd moved out to Great Neck, he'd asked one of Bibbs's stockbroker friends to put in a good word for him with the local Republican bigwigs. The stockbroker had called Joe Carlino, a New York State assemblyman and vice-chairman of the Nassau County Republican Committee, and told him, "I got a young guy from a very good family moving out to Nassau. He's a real personable young fellow. I'd like you to meet him."

Carlino never forgot the call. He remembered it because the young man, when he finally met him, really *was* personable, a find, which wasn't always the case when people touted protégés to him. But this Sol Wachtler was unique. Affable, witty, smart. After talking with him, Carlino introduced him to all the Republican leaders in Nassau. And after that, Carlino remembered, "Sol just got going. He joined the Republican Club in North Hempstead, and the first thing I knew, he'd made a whole lot of friends there."

That was in 1956. By 1960, the year that Bibbs married Jeanette, Sol was thinking about entering electoral politics. Joan had an uncle who'd been a state senator. Maybe someday he could be one too.

"Jeanette! Good God, what happened to you?" a friend of the new Mrs. Wolosoff said to her one afternoon shortly after she'd married Bibbs. The two women were sharing a fitting room in a Great Neck dress shop. Jeanette had just removed her blouse, and her friend had noticed that her flesh was flecked with tiny little bruises. Hickeys. From here to there!

"It's nothing," Jeanette said, smiling. "Just Bibbs. You know he can't keep his hands off me."

He also couldn't keep himself from buying her whatever she wanted—which was a great deal. She asked to have the house redecorated, and he gave her free rein to indulge her taste for costly white lacquer furniture and thick white and beige carpets. She coveted jewelry, and he bought her diamonds and rubies, sapphires and emeralds, necklaces so intricate they looked like tracery and earrings that shone on her ears like beacons. He'd pay for the purchases from the wad of crisp hundred-dollar bills pinched together by a shiny money clip that he always carried in his pocket. He didn't use a credit card and almost never wrote checks. Sometimes he'd reach into the safe he kept in his den and take out ten thousand dollars and slide it into his money clip.

Bibbs enjoyed going shopping with Jeanette. She had a way of turning everything, even sitting around in a shop, into an adventure. They'd ride into Manhattan in the Lincoln Continental, driven by Bibbs's chauffeur, John Green. They'd go to Bonwit's or Saks, Jeanette's favorite stores. And then, her eyes glistening with excitement and her hands caressing him, Jeanette would select dresses and suits and furs—a mink cape was his special treat.

Jeanette was a big-boned woman, and she worried a lot about her weight. But she had magnificent slender legs, and when she put on her highest heels and her latest Pucci print, pulling back her fine black hair the better to show off her diamond earrings, she was unforgettable, a presence. At parties men would vie to talk with her, and Bibbs, seeing their avidity, would gloat.

At home, he was happier still. Jeanette fussed over him, brought him little surprises—shirts made of cotton so smooth it felt like silk and ties that looked better with his blue blazers than anything he himself could have picked out. And she ran the house with unique style and largesse. Was Bibbs expecting a visit from a business associate who liked fruit? When the man arrived, there would be not just a bowl of fruit, but platters and baskets of fruit, perfuming the rooms with sweetness. Did Bibbs have a friend who liked chopped liver? Jeanette would order pounds of it. Did one of his business associates crave nothing for lunch but an omelette? Jeanette, although they had a cook, would herself go into the kitchen and whip up an eggy extravaganza. At large parties and dinners, for which she hired waiters who flipped open soft damask napkins and laid them upon the guests' knees, just as it was done in England, visitors felt just as pampered. Jeanette thought of everything, having written most of the guests' preferences down in a notebook. She made everyone feel swaddled in luxury and made all the men feel envious of Bibbs.

The only fly in the ointment was the kids. Bibbs still didn't care for Jeanette's little girl, Joy, who was moody and excitable and talked a blue streak. And Jeanette was none too fond of Bibbs's sons. He understood her antipathy. The boys were spoiled. He had lavished money on them when they were growing up, had spent over a million and a half dollars on them. He'd bought them boats and cars—he'd given Jimmy his own almost brand-new white Corvette convertible when the boy was only sixteen. But Jimmy, who was argumentative and strong-willed, was Jeanette's pet peeve—she was always saying she couldn't stomach him. And Van, well, he'd always been a little odd. He was a handsome boy, with curly blond hair and blue eyes, but he was slow, sweet but slow, and there was something of the rebel about him. He wasn't interested in school. He wasn't interested in business. Or even in money. All he cared about was boats and cars. Taking them apart. Fixing them. Riding them fast. Too fast. Plus he hated to shower, hated to put on clean clothes. He was always so grimy that the other kids in the neighborhood had nicknamed him "the ditchdigger."

It didn't surprise Bibbs that Jeanette started complaining regularly about his sons.

"You must be the new Mrs. Wolosoff's daughter," Dick Simons said to Joy one cool spring evening in 1960. He'd come over to play gin rummy with Jimmy and his friends. She was standing at the door, holding it open for him. And although he'd heard from his father, who had met Joy at a lavish bar mitzvah, that she was a stunning girl and no ordinary thirteen-year-old, Dick Simons, who was eighteen, was astonished at her beauty.

She had pitch-black hair and wide dark eyes and a smile that was so dazzling it made him think of fireworks. She wasn't dressed up. She was barefoot and had on a pair of cutoff blue-jean shorts, a tight little T-shirt that showed the outlines of her already full breasts, and a little black bandanna that was folded around the top of her hair. "You look like Pocahontas," he told her. And that made her brilliant smile even wider.

Throughout the game, she lounged near the cardplayers, serving them beer and crackers, and flashing smiles at Dick. And when the game was over and he was once again standing at the front door, this time wishing her good night, she said, before he realized he wanted to say the same thing, "Are we ever going to see each other again?"

He told her, "Sure."

"Then, why don't we start right now?" she asked. "Why don't we go for something to eat?"

"Yeah, sure," Dick said, and he drove her in his car to Squire's, the local deli, and they talked for a long while, and she wanted to go on talking, and they sat in a booth and kept on talking, and at last he said, "Shouldn't I take you home?" and he drove her back, and when they got there, it was two in the morning, and he wanted to kiss her, but he was afraid, because she was only thirteen, even though there'd been nothing thirteen about her.

Not long after Dick met Joy, Jeanette began asking Bibbs to adopt Bruce and Joy. She asked him repeatedly, but he wasn't sure he wanted to do it. Okay, yes, maybe the little boy. But the girl? *Her* father wasn't dead. He was living God knows where, doing God knows what. But whoever and whatever he was, he was Joy's father. Bibbs told Jeanette no about the girl, but said he'd think about adopting Bruce.

By summer, Dick was at the Wolosoff house constantly, and he and Joy had become boyfriend and girlfriend. They'd listen to music together, or she'd come to the baseball field and watch him play ball with his buddies. At night, after the games, he'd take her to dinner. And on weekends, they'd go out on his boat.

Her mother seemed amused by their relationship. Dick had felt peculiar in Jeanette's company the first time he met her. He'd been used to Sylvia's being the woman of the house, and now there was this new woman, Jeanette, sitting on Sylvia's couch and offering him a cold drink from Sylvia's refrigerator. But Jeanette had apparently understood his awkwardness, and she'd tried to make him more comfortable. She seemed to know about his father, a successful retailer who imported, manufactured, and sold furniture, and about his mother, who was so close to the Shuberts, of theatrical fame, that many people who knew his family thought she *was* a Shubert, and she chattered away, asking him about the sports he played and telling Joy she was lucky to have an athletic boyfriend and saying that someday she'd like to see him play ball too.

Later on, Jeanette got even more complimentary. She said he was a good influence on Joy, and she showered him with praise about his looks and his easy charming manners. "You're not like Jimmy and Van," she'd tell him. "They're impossible, the two of them." And she'd joke with him and touch his arm, acting for all the world as if he were *her* boyfriend too. And sometimes when she had to get ready to meet Bibbs for an evening out, she'd invite both him and Joy to come into the bedroom and talk to her while she got dressed, changing her clothes right in front of them. In front of them.

Joy didn't seem to mind. She was in love with her mother, Dick thought. So there was nothing her mother could do wrong. The trouble was, he was a little in love with her mother too. He'd never met a woman who was so flattering, so interested in everything he said. Joy was wonderful. They'd taken to petting heavily every night, and he loved that. But there was something about Joy that made him think she wasn't herself, that most of the time she was putting on an act, trying to be just like her mother.

In 1962, when Joy was fifteen, the Wachtlers bought a two-story colonial-style house in Kings Point, very close to Bibbs's mansion. The house cost them about eighty thousand dollars and had an acre of land and a little goldfish pond, as well as a big kitchen, a screened porch, and lots of bedrooms. They needed the bedrooms. They had four children by now, three girls—Lauren, Marjorie, and Alison—and a son they'd named Philip, after Sol's father, who had died a couple of years earlier, without ever getting the house Bibbs had promised to build him.

Sol was working hard, and his law practice was flourishing. He'd switched to a new firm, Hoffman and Altamari, in Mineola, the county capital. But whenever he was at home, he devoted a lot of time to the children. He helped them with their homework, did magic tricks at their birthday parties, and with his own hands crafted special toys for them, toys their friends didn't have. Once, when Lauren was going through a shy period at a new school, he made her a big wooden boat and set it in the schoolyard, where all the other kids ran over to see it, asking Lauren if they could please, please sit in it and in short order making her feel like the most popular girl in the school. And always, every weekend, he took the four children to Kiddie City, an amusement park in Long Island City.

On the way home, when they were tired and cranky, he told them stories. There was one with a hero whose adventures he kept going for months. The hero was a little boy named George Raft. He didn't tell the children that George Raft was the name of an actor who played bad guys in the movies. All he told them was that *this* George Raft was a really bad little boy, who was always doing something nasty. He made the stories so suspenseful that invariably the kids didn't want to get out of the car when he pulled into the circular driveway in front of the house. "Oh, Dad, go on! Tell us the end," they'd cry. But he always said, "No. To be continued," and promised that next weekend he'd pick up George Raft just where he'd left him off.

He was living with a certain amount of suspense, himself. A vacancy had come up on the North Hempstead Town Council, and he wanted to have a go at the job. If he did, it would be his first stab at running for electoral office. But Norman Penney, the Republican leader of North Hempstead, didn't think it was a good idea. North Hempstead was a political grouping that drew together a handful of actual towns, and its population was very conservative. Sol wasn't. He'd allied himself with the liberal wing of the party, had supported Jacob Javits and Nelson Rockefeller. He was also Jewish, and North Hempstead, despite some pockets where there were heavy concentrations of Jews, was largely Italian. Penney said there'd never been a Jewish candidate elected for any office in North Hempstead, and that it wasn't likely there ever would be one.

Still, the party agreed to let him fight for the nomination in a primary. It would be the first primary the Nassau Republicans had held in their two-hundred-year history on Long Island, and Sol, convinced that they were holding the contest simply because he was the first Jew who had ever wanted to run for office in the area, was bitter about it. Nevertheless, he campaigned. And to the surprise of many of the local leaders, he won the primary.

Joe Carlino took it upon himself to reassure Penney. Going to see him, he sang Sol's praises. He told him Sol was a very active guy who'd campaign tirelessly. He told him he was a guy that people would like the looks of. He told him Sol loved the political life. And he said, "Sol won't have any money problems— his family has substantial funds."

Penney was still reluctant. "That's a big order," he said. "To put up a Jewish guy over here."

"No," Carlino told him. "It's the best thing you can do."

After that, Sol threw himself into trying to win the seat on the town council. He turned up at school auditoriums, fraternal organizations, women's clubs. He shook thousands of hands at commuter stations. And he attended scores of campaign parties.

Some of the parties were thrown by Bibbs and Jeanette. "I wanna see Sol go all the way," Bibbs told Dick Simons one day. Dick thought Bibbs's enthusiasm had something to do with the fact that he needed some land rezoned, and the town council decided zoning matters. But he didn't ask Bibbs about it. With Bibbs, he had learned, the best policy was never to question why he was for or against anything.

Joan and her children didn't come to the parties at Bibbs's house. Joan and Jeanette had never hit it off, perhaps because Joan had been fond of her aunt Sylvia, and Jeanette seemed like an interloper to her. Moreover, Joan didn't want her children associating with Jeanette's children. The boy, Bruce, was rumored to be part of a fast crowd. And the girl, Joan would one day say, "had this *reputation*." Joan didn't want the members of *her* family to come under her influence.

That fall—it was 1963—Sol won his seat on the town council. But he did more than just get elected. He won the seat by the biggest victory margin either before or since the election. "He's a great campaigner," Penney acknowledged to Carlino.

"He's gonna be one of the stars of the party," Carlino prophesied.

Van Wolosoff had a crush on his stepsister, Jeanette noticed that year. And Joy seemed to like him too. Or did she just feel sorry for him? Jeanette wasn't certain, but one thing she was sure of: she had to discourage their friendship. Van wasn't just slovenly and eccentric. He had no sense of propriety. Or of money. If you gave him money, he was apt to give it away to any friend or beggar who asked.

Jeanette was always having to scold him. He'd come into the house after one of his marathon sessions under the hood of a car, and he'd be barefoot and shirtless and covered in grease. And as if that wasn't enough, he'd march over to the refrigerator and start looking for something to eat, handling the food with his filthy hands. She'd shout at him, "Get out of here! Go and get washed!" But he never seemed to learn from her scoldings or show any improvement. He was, Jeanette began to feel, a total fool.

Ordinarily, she'd have expected Joy to agree with her. They agreed about so many things. But Joy had a soft spot for Van. She was sixteen now, and like so many sixteen-year-old girls, she had a passion for misfits and rebels. It made Jeanette uneasy, so uneasy that she wasn't sure she wanted Joy growing up under the same roof as Van.

She hadn't liked having Joy grow up under the same roof as Jimmy, either. But at least Jimmy was grown now and living away from home. Jeanette wished Van was out of the way too, and after a while she began badgering Bibbs about sending him to a private school, someplace where he could learn to be more like other boys. But Bibbs said no, and Jeanette decided that, under the circumstances, she'd best send Joy away.

The school she picked for Joy was an exclusive and expensive finishing school in Bridgewater, Massachusetts. It was called the Howard School for Girls, and it taught young women manners, deportment, French, and the social graces. Joy was miserable when she first arrived, but she soon adjusted, becoming a cheerleader and an active member of the drama club. But although she tried her best, her grades were terrible. "I hate to study," she told her old boyfriend Dick on one of her visits home. "I hate to *read*."

There was something else she hated. It was the way her stepfather looked at her. There was something sexual about it. He *wanted* her, she began to think. And one day, sure enough, he grabbed her and tried to kiss her. He forced his tongue between her lips and began to fondle her breast. She pulled away and screamed at him and told him if he ever came near her again in that way, she'd tell her mother.

Dick didn't know that Bibbs had made a pass at Joy. Had he known, he most likely would have been furious, because he and Joy had become lovers. They had sex whenever they could, sometimes in the house when Jeanette and Bibbs were out, sometimes, when they were home and asleep, in Dick's green Corvette.

To their chagrin, one night Jeanette caught them. It was four in the morning, and they were in the car, their bodies half-naked, their limbs groping for comfort in the tight space, when suddenly she appeared out of nowhere, dressed in her nightgown, and began banging on the window. Joy adjusted her clothes and ran from the car. Dick, flustered and embarrassed, blurted out how sorry he was. But to his surprise, Jeanette didn't act angry or even astonished. "You *should* be sorry," was all she said. And then, "I'll talk to you in the morning." But when she saw Dick the next day, she said nothing further.

After that, Dick concluded she didn't hold it against him that he'd been making love to Joy. In fact, what he'd done seemed to make Jeanette treat him in a different, closer way, as if he were family. She took him along with her when she rode up to Massachusetts in the chauffeured limousine to visit Joy. And she called him frequently, inviting him to spend the day with her. "Come on," she'd say. "Let's take the car and go into the city. John will drive us, and we'll go shopping and have some lunch."

Dick looked forward to her phone calls. And when they got in the car, they'd laugh and talk, and it was sort of as if *they* were dating. Dick wasn't sure why she acted so cozy with him—whether it was because she wanted him to marry her daughter, or because she liked him for himself, *really* liked him, even though he was twenty-two and she was in her forties, or because it was just her nature to be flirtatious, because she couldn't be around a man, any man, without trying to make him feel he was everything in the world to her.

Whatever her reason, Dick enjoyed their expeditions. They'd go to Bonwit's or to the Park Avenue shop of David Webb, one of the finest jewelers in the country. At Bonwit's, Jeanette would try on clothes, and he'd tell her, "You look really gorgeous." And at David Webb's, she'd look through the showcases and ask the clerk to take out whatever caught her fancy. "Let's have a good close look at that one," she'd say. And she'd study it, turning it this way and that.

"Like it?" She'd hold it up to her throat or her ears. "How about this one?" she'd ask. "Or this one."

"Pretty terrific," he'd say. And when he liked something, she'd say, "Bibbie is going to buy me this, Dick. You'll see, Dick."

And Bibbs always did.

He did almost everything Jeanette asked him to do. But he wouldn't adopt her children.

Early in 1965, while Joy was still away at the Howard School for Girls, Sol Wachtler began entertaining hopes of running for town supervisor of North Hempstead.

As a member of the town council, he had made many powerful friends among the party leadership, and they had not only accepted his being Jewish but even come to see it as an advantage—or at least an advantage just now, when the Democrats, fresh from Lyndon Johnson's landslide victory in the recent national elections, were riding high. Most of the communities that made up the township of North Hempstead could be counted on to vote Republican, but there were by now two areas in the township, Great Neck and Roslyn, that were predominantly Jewish, and Jewish voters tended to vote Democratic. Sol had convinced the Republican leadership that a liberal Jewish Republican like himself might prompt many Jewish Democrats in the crucial towns of Great Neck and Roslyn to vote Republican in the upcoming town supervisor's race.

There was only one problem. Sol wasn't the incumbent, and as everyone knew, his being the incumbent would give him the best shot at winning.

In the spring, the man who *was* the incumbent, a Catholic named Clint Martin, was called into a meeting by one of the Republican leaders, a lawyer named David Holman. "You've got to step down, Clint," Holman told him.

"What the hell for?" Martin said.

"Because we've got to do something about Roslyn and Great Neck," Holman told him.

Martin dug in his heels. "I'm the supervisor and the leader, and I'm not stepping down. Nohow."

"We've got another job lined up for you," Holman said. "Commissioner of elections."

Martin went white. "Commissioner of elections!" It wasn't even a plum. It was a job that paid some three thousand dollars less than the town supervisor's job.

He continued to argue. But his protests got him nowhere. Without the support of the party, he was dead meat. And it was clear to Martin that Sol, with his suave social and political skills, not to mention his wife's and his uncle Wolosoff's money, had won the support of the party.

When the meeting with Holman was over, Martin resigned, and Sol was appointed to replace him.

In Kings Point that summer, something happened between Joy and her stepbrother Van.

There would always be two versions of just what actually

42

occurred. There was the one Jeanette told Bibbs—that Van had attacked her daughter. He came into her room by stealth, she said, and forced himself on her. There was also the story that Dick Simons said Joy later told him—that she had for years harbored feelings of love toward Van, and that one night she told him so. When she did, Van said he'd always loved her too. After that confession, they'd become inseparable—much to Jeanette's dismay. They'd even spent a night together on a little cabin cruiser that belonged to Sol Wachtler, who kept his boat tied up at Bibbs's dock.

Whatever really happened, in an effort to break them up, Jeanette went to Bibbs with her story about Van's attack on Joy, and a short time later, Van was sent away from home. He was placed in a private school in Westchester County and he returned to Great Neck only once every other week, when Bibbs and Jeanette would drive up and get him.

Jimmy wasn't welcome at the estate, either. "I can't stomach either of your sons, Bibbie," Jeanette told Bibbs. "They're ruining my life." And at last, she prevailed upon Bibbs to make up to her for all she was suffering by adopting *her* son.

By the time the grass on Bibbs's lawns had turned a brilliant summery green, Bruce Germont had become, officially, Bruce Wolosoff. When the lawns began to fade, and the leaves on the shade trees began to turn gold and red, Joy entered the University of Maryland as a freshman who would be studying the liberal arts. And in November, when the leaves had fallen from the trees, Sol was elected town supervisor, receiving a plurality of twenty-three thousand votes, the highest plurality ever achieved by any candidate who had run for the office.

CHAPTER 3

"Why didn't Bibbs adopt *you?*" Dick Simons asked Joy after Bruce had become Bibbs's third son.

"Because he hates me," she told him.

Dick figured it must be true and tried to comfort her when she told him how angry and envious she was. He didn't know that Joy, who went by the name of Joy Germont, had a different father from Bruce, nor that her father was still alive somewhere. Joy never mentioned it, and neither, until many years later, did Jeanette.

Dick was still seeing Joy now that she was at the University of Maryland, but only from time to time. Mostly it was when she came home for school vacations. At Maryland, she dated other men.

Dick was jealous. But he tried not to think about the other men in her life and to maintain as much of a connection with Joy as she would permit him. He called her frequently and, several times, drove down to Maryland to see her.

Jeanette also visited Joy in Maryland, and one weekend, she suggested that she and Dick drive down together. But she didn't want to make the whole trip in a single day. "We'll stop somewhere," she suggested. "Have dinner, sleep over in a motel."

A motel? Dick wondered about that.

They set out in Dick's new burgundy Jaguar, with its black top and smooth black leather interior, and when they found a motel, Jeanette said, "We might as well share a room."

What did she have in mind? Dick, who had been to see *The Graduate* with her, kept on wondering. He tried to put the question out of his head. We're buddies, he told himself. And, hey, she's Joy's *mother*, for Christ's sake.

That night, they shared the room. Dick undressed in a hurry while Jeanette was out of the room in the bathroom. He tried to pretend everything was normal. Maybe it was. At least for Jeanette. Anyway, they had two beds. He got into his.

Jeanette, in her casual way, wandered about for a while in her nightgown. Was she being provocative? Or was she just oblivious to his presence? Unwilling to put the matter to the test with a woman so much older than himself, and his girlfriend's mother to boot, Dick shut his eyes.

Nothing happened between them. And in the morning, they had breakfast and continued on to Maryland.

Much later, thinking about that night, Dick concluded that Jeanette couldn't stop herself from being seductive. Seduction was second nature to her.

Sol had been a progressive town supervisor. He'd built public housing, sponsored parks and recreational facilities, and paved the dirt roads that were still common in areas of North Hempstead where the black people who were the servants to the rich lived.

His public-spirited efforts had brought him acclaim, and early in 1967, he was asked by the leadership of the Republican party in Nassau if he would be willing to run for Nassau county executive, the premier job in the county. Nassau, with close to a million residents, was more heavily populated than many American cities, and its county executive administered what was then a princely budget of two hundred and fifteen million dollars. He determined ten million dollars in personal service contracts that were awarded without competitive bidding. He was the boss of fourteen thousand county employees, and he controlled nearly six thousand patronage jobs. It was an important and powerful job. Moreover, if Sol won, he would be his party's fair-haired boy, in line for even higher, statewide office.

But Sol wasn't sure he wanted to run. The man he would be up against was the incumbent, Democrat Eugene Nickerson, one of the most popular Long Island politicians ever to hold office.

Suppose he lost? He didn't want to be a loser, and there were those who said that Nickerson was unbeatable.

Uncertain what to do, Sol discussed his dilemma with State Senator and Republican County Leader Edward Speno. Take the gamble, Speno advised him and promised that if he lost, the party would be grateful and he could have any job that was available. Sol decided to say yes.

In February, he was endorsed for Nassau executive by the Nassau Republican Executive Committee, after which Speno held a press conference and called Sol "one of the most dynamic, young, articulate figures in the Republican party in the state and throughout the nation." In March, at a raucous convention in a hotel ballroom in Garden City, he was officially nominated.

He stood on the platform and saw surrounding him nearly two thousand committeemen, flourishing banners and balloons and shouting his name. He had been participating in political conventions, some mock, some real, ever since his college days and had come to love the push and surge and glitter of those extravaganzas. But now, the screams and chants were for *him*. When his name was put forward and the crowd began to stamp and cheer, a vision of his future, of political conventions that would blazon his name for ever higher and higher office, seemed to sweep over him, and he looked down upon the crowd with an expression of undisguised euphoria.

The party leaders who had been instrumental in selecting him to run were euphoric in their own way. Politics was being played differently that year. For virtually the first time in history, local candidates were addressing voters not just through public appearances and print and radio advertising, but through the volatile medium of television. Sol seemed to his party's leaders ideal for television—so good-looking, so youthful and energetic, and so sincere in manner. Shortly after he was nominated, they announced they would spend the then startlingly high sum of five hundred thousand dollars to try to elect Wachtler and that the bulk of the expenditures would go for putting him on television.

Sol was taken in hand by an army of political public-relations experts. He was advised by one, Don Kellerman, who was in charge of marketing him, to be less meticulous in his appearance. "Be more informal," Kellerman told him. "Don't come on as such a gentleman." And following Kellerman's advice, Sol stopped wearing cufflinks and took to dressing without a tie or with a tie that was amusingly askew.

Joan, too, was subjected to Kellerman's scrutiny. This was no doubt harder for her than it was for Sol. She was a more private person, reserved where he was outgoing, deliberate where he was breezy, and she hated the glare of publicity. Still, she went along with the public-relations man, cooperatively allowing him to help her select clothes to wear at public appearances. But when he jokingly suggested she try to gear her outfits to making her look as if she was thirty years old, the median age of Nassau's voters, she couldn't help saying, in a somewhat brittle voice, that she'd seen that age already and wasn't going to be seeing it again.

What was Joan's image? Kellerman limned it. "Joan's image," he said, "is that of partner."

And indeed, she felt like a partner. She had been restless the last few years, as the children had begun to grow older, had been dissatisfied with just keeping house. Sol's campaign gave her a chance to engage in political work, and while she didn't like being in the spotlight, she thoroughly enjoyed working behind the scenes. She organized public appearances for Sol; she planned his calendar; she ran the campaign office. "I loved the political life," she would one day recall. "I wasn't just the candidate's wife. I had a *job*."

Sol didn't spend all his time campaigning. He still did some legal work, and one morning he drove with Bibbs to Mineola, where the Nassau courthouse was located. Bibbs's stepdaughter Joy, now a young woman of twenty, was in the car too. Sol had met her years before, when she was around thirteen and had first become a member of Bibbs's household. But she'd made no impression on him. Nor did she this day. But she was impressed with *him.* She listened to him discuss his campaign with Bibbs and, although she wasn't much interested in politics, found what Sol was saying fascinating.

"He's very bright," she told Dick after she rode with Sol in the car. "And handsome."

By early September, Sol's campaign was in full swing. He was greeting potential voters not just at commuter stations, but even on the rails themselves, riding the trains into the city, then back out to the suburbs, then into the city again, then back out to the suburbs again.

Meeting the public, he stayed calm, no matter who attacked him. But Joan, who was quick to anger, occasionally lost her temper. One day when they were standing at a commuter station, a man came up to Sol and said in a gruff voice, "Are you Wachtler?" When Sol acknowledged that he was, the man said, "Well, I hope you lose." Joan, standing at Sol's side, snapped, "Well, I hope you don't make it into New York!"

Sol was also visiting shopping centers, attending kaffeeklatsches, and addressing enthusiastic supporters at fund-raising barbecues, cocktail parties, luncheons, and dinners. He told reporters, "It's a great embarrassment to have to ask friends for money," but he proved exceedingly adept at it. At one luncheon alone, he raised what was then the munificent sum of a hundred thousand dollars.

The liberal Jews of Great Neck were particularly attracted to him. They liked Nickerson, but Wachtler had a special appeal. "He was the Great White Jewish Hope out on the Island," a woman whose parents worked in Sol's campaign recalled. "He was on that beautiful bandwagon of Javits, Lindsay, and Rockefeller, but he was one of us. There was talk about him becoming president one day—the first Jewish president."

But as the campaign proceeded, trouble began brewing. Sol was using dirty tricks, the opposition charged. He was employing false images in his television commercials and campaign leaflets. One of his ads accused Nickerson of wasting public funds by having six photographers on the county payroll, and it showed a group of photographers busy doing nothing except snapping photos of the Democratic county executive. But the photographers in the ad were actors, posing as photographers. Moreover, as Nickerson was quick to point out, *he* hadn't hired any photographers. His Republican predecessor had, and he'd been stuck with them. All six of them. Another Wachtler ad showed a large crowd of people milling about in front of a building that bore the signs "County Assessor's Office" and "Grievance Day." The copy beneath the picture said that taxpayers were groaning under Nickerson's fiscal policies and that as a result, "every day is Grievance Day in Nassau County." But no such crowd had ever gathered in front of the county assessor's office. The photograph was, in actuality, a picture of an intermission crowd at a Broadway theater in Manhattan. Wachtler, Nickerson raged, was running "a slick, scurrilous campaign of distortion, appeals to fear, and outright misstatements."

The accusations didn't prevent Rockefeller from campaigning for him. One autumn day, he crisscrossed Nassau County with Sol in a chartered bus, praising, promoting, and puffing him for a marathon twelve hours. And one autumn evening, he came to a party at Sol's house.

Alison Wachtler was only nine years old, but she would never forget it. She and her brother and sisters stayed upstairs while the party swirled and eddied below them. She saw men with big cigars, women in gorgeous dresses, and the expansive, exuberant governor. "We kids weren't supposed to come down," Alison recalled, "but we stayed awake and kept sneaking downstairs to get hors d'oeuvres."

Then, later in October, the Nassau County Democratic chairman accused one of Sol's chief aides of paying one of Nickerson's secretaries three thousand dollars to supply him with confidential information about Nickerson. Sol denied having any knowledge of the affair, and the aide resigned. But a cloud had begun to gather over the campaign.

On Election Night, November 7, 1967, Sol and Joan went to the Garden City Hotel, where the campaign had started and where, on this night, three thousand Republicans were assembled. It still seemed to Sol that he had a good chance of winning, and indeed, as the election results started to pour in, he was often ahead of Nickerson. At 11:30 P.M., he was winning by three thousand votes. But at 11:50 P.M., with ninety-four percent of the vote in, the trend began to change and Nickerson pulled ahead.

Ed Speno, who was receiving constant tallies, took Sol aside and whispered to him that the unofficial result was that Nickerson had won, though only by some thousand votes. For a moment, Sol became serious, downcast. But a second later, he composed himself. Smiling, and speaking in an upbeat tone, he said to Speno, alluding to the fact that at the beginning of the race neither of them had really thought they'd come anywhere close to knocking off Nickerson, "That's a win, right?"

Speno nodded. "That's a win for all of us, and it's a beginning for you, fella."

Sol kept the positive words flowing. "We got a county clerk. We got a controller."

Speno played the game too. "I think all the other candidates won." Then he hugged Sol. "You put up a tremendous fight. A great campaign."

His body locked in Speno's embrace, Sol let no sign of disappointment show on his face. And a moment later, he was buoying up Speno. "Keep a smile on," he said. And Speno promised he would.

Joan was sitting nearby, a sad expression suffusing her pretty face. But Sol continued to betray no sign of authentic emotion. It was as if he had learned, in that moment of defeat, how to wear a mask.

Joy, by this time, had dropped out of the University of Maryland and taken a job in Manhattan with the film company MGM. She was a receptionist. But she was hoping that, with a little luck, she might be able to become an actress. Someone might discover her.

She'd also taken an apartment. It was on East 63rd Street, and she shared it with a roommate, a young woman named Karen, who was studying nursing. Dick Simons was once again her steady boyfriend. And one of his friends was her roommate's boyfriend. It was a convenient arrangement. Each evening they could, the two young suburban men would drive into the city together, have dinner with their sweethearts, and spend the night.

One evening, however, when Dick and his friend arrived, only Joy was in the apartment. "Come into the bedroom," she said to Dick, drawing him away from his friend.

He followed her, wondering what was going on.

"Karen's met another guy," she said. "A doctor. She's going to marry him."

Not long after that, Joy began talking about giving up her job and her apartment and marrying Dick.

He should become a judge, Speno had told Sol after he lost the election against Nickerson. There was a seat on the New York State Supreme Court in Nassau that was going to be vacated in January by a judge who was retiring. It would be a perfect spot for Sol.

"What do you think?" Sol asked his old buddy, Joe Carlino. Sol was down in Florida, trying to get over the disappointment of his defeat, and Carlino had called him up to see how he was doing.

"Don't do it," Carlino advised. "You get on the state supreme court and you die. You're never heard from again." He suggested that, instead, Sol should go after a congressional seat. "Take on Wolf," he said, naming a Democratic congressman. "You'll knock 'em dead. And you'll be *alive*."

But Sol didn't want to listen to him. The more he thought about the judgeship, the more appealing it was. He wouldn't have to run for the seat. He'd just have to be appointed by Rockefeller. The idea of not having to start in on another electoral fight was bliss. He was worn out, exhausted from the Nickerson race.

Back in New York, he told Speno he wanted the judgeship, and one day when Rockefeller summoned him to his office to ask what reward he wanted for having undertaken the grueling fight against Nickerson, he told the governor too.

"You want to be a judge?" Rockefeller said, with disbelief in his voice.

"Yes."

Rockefeller, who didn't think much of the judicial profession, shook his head. "After three years, you'll be bored or alcoholic," he said. Then he sat back, sure of himself. "Think it over and tell me tomorrow what other job you would like."

But Sol had made up his mind.

He went back to see Rockefeller the next day, repeated his request, and this time Rockefeller acquiesced and agreed to recommend him for the opening.

After that, Sol thought things would go smoothly, but they didn't. It wasn't Rockefeller's fault. The problem was politics—local politics. It was customary in Nassau for a potential judge to receive the endorsement of his party's local executive committee, but the committee to which Sol belonged, the North Hempstead Executive Committee, had already endorsed someone else for the judgeship he wanted. They'd endorsed David Holman, who several years earlier had helped Sol become town supervisor of North Hempstead by getting Clint Martin to resign.

Holman was a former district attorney, and he had many powerful friends in North Hempstead. "Maybe you should go after a different job," one of them said querulously to Sol on the phone one day. "What about deputy commissioner of state taxes? There's an opening for that slot, up in Albany."

Sol got angry. "I've been *supervisor*," he snapped. "I'm not going to be deputy anything." And subsequently, refusing to take no for an answer, he went to the executive committee of a different Long Island town, the nearby town of Hempstead, and got *their* endorsement.

Holman's supporters were furious. Sol went behind our backs, they muttered. Worse, he treated his old friend like dirt, like a bug he could crunch under his feet.

Rockefeller wasn't aware of the mounting anger in Nassau against Sol. Early in December, he announced that he was recommending him for the judgeship. But as he had made it his practice to appoint only those judges whose bar associations approved them, it was necessary for Sol to do one more thing, to appear before the Nassau County Bar Association's judiciary committee and gain their approval.

52

A routine matter. Shortly before Christmas, Sol spoke to the committee. He told them he'd represented six major corporations, that his job as supervisor of the town of North Hempstead had been quasi-judicial, and that he'd argued cases before several courts, including the Supreme Court of the United States. When he was done, he left, and the committee took a vote.

It went against him. With three of its seventeen members absent, the bipartisan group voted ten to four not to approve him. He wasn't qualified to be a judge, they said. Not that there was anything wrong with his character, learning, or background. No, the problem was he had too little trial experience.

The bar association's rejection of him was a blow for Sol, another blow. Two in a row, not even two months apart. But he didn't fold up. He went before the judiciary committee again, and this time he talked to them for an hour and a half. When he was done, they held a five-hour closed-door session and then took a second vote. But once again, the vote went against him.

Up in Albany, Rockefeller was enraged. "You guys have embarrassed the hell out of me!" he screamed at Speno, who had just stepped down as county chairman and been replaced by a new chairman, Joseph Margiotta.

Perhaps it was Rockefeller's fury, or perhaps, as one supporter of David Holman insisted, it was because Holman begged the bar association to stop tearing itself asunder, but in the end, the question of Sol's endorsement was sent to the bar association's board of directors. Both Rockefeller and Sol had many friends on the board, and the directors voted to overrule their judiciary committee and declare Sol qualified. He had been bloodied in the battle, but at last, he had won. In mid-January 1968, he became a judge.

"Is it all right with you if I marry Joy?" Dick Simons, who was working as a furniture salesman in a company owned by a colleague of his father's, asked Bibbs one night that year. Joy had insisted he do things the old-fashioned way and ask Bibbs for her hand. But Bibbs was diffident. "I'm not Joy's father," he told Dick brusquely, and not mentioning that Joy's real father was still around somewhere, he went on, "I'm just a stepfather."

Still, Bibbs lent his energies, and his money, toward ensuring that the marriage got successfully underway. He gave Jeanette seven thousand dollars so that she could buy Dick a gold Piaget watch as an engagement present. He paid for Joy's engagement ring too—a hundred-and-ten-thousand-dollar diamond ring from David Webb that Jeanette had decided was just the right thing, but that Dick had said was way beyond his means.

Bibbs also gave the happy couple a place to live once they were wed. Joy wanted to live in Manhattan, and Bibbs, who had been one of the developers of the stylish Brevort apartment building just off Washington Square Park, in Manhattan's Greenwich Village, presented her and Dick with a large co-op apartment there.

He also threw the engagement party, which was held on his back lawns that rolled down to the edge of the silvery Sound. He and Jeanette invited hundreds of guests, among them some of the most prominent real-estate developers in the New York area. Sam Lefrak, who had built Lefrak City, was there. So was Sol Atlas, the developer of the Manhasset Miracle Mile.

Jeanette had seen to it that Dick, a casual dresser, dressed properly for the affair. She'd gone out and bought him a double-breasted blue blazer, red-and-white houndstooth checked trousers, and a pair of white Gucci shoes. "No one had the right to be that tall, that handsome, that charming," one of the party guests thought when she saw him.

Sol Wachtler was at the party. And although, on the previous occasions when he'd met Joy, he'd taken no notice of her, today there was no overlooking her. Years later, he would date his first encounter with her to this festive evening.

She was wearing a long white summery dress with a cluster of pink carnations pinned onto the bodice. Her dark eyes were sparkling, her smile was radiant, and she had the ecstatic air of a princess about to ascend a throne.

Many of the guests toasted her, wishing her a long and happy marriage. Dick Simons recalled that Sol, glass in hand, toasted her too and that Jeanette thought his gaze too admiring. She nudged her future son-in-law. "Keep an eye on Sol Wachtler," she teased. "He's got eyes for Joy."

54

"Oh, come on," Dick objected. "You can't be serious."

"But I am," she insisted. "I've seen eyes like that before."

Dick shook his head. Jeanette was always trying to stir things up, trying to create little dramas.

But she didn't let up. "Those aren't just the eyes of a friend."

During the time Joy and Dick were engaged, Bibbs made several trips to Florida to check on the land he'd purchased from Sol's father. He'd had it dredged, and now it needed a sea wall, and it needed roads. But once those things were put in, whoever developed the site could build three hundred, maybe even four hundred houses on the land, and sell them for a fortune.

Theoretically, he no longer owned *all* the land. He had transferred the best piece, a hundred acres of prime waterfront property, to an irrevocable trust he had set up for Jimmy and Van. He'd charged the trust $575,000 and explained to the boys that in exchange for the money, *they* would own the land. But he hadn't given them legal title to it, hadn't presented them with a deed or contract. And they hadn't asked for it. Van had no head for business, and Jimmy, to whom Bibbs had frequently said that the things one gets from a father can just as easily be taken back, had learned not to question his father's decisions. So when he'd told Jimmy that the trust should buy the St. Petersburg waterfront lots, Jimmy had just said, "Dad, if that's what you think we ought to do, I leave it to you, and you go ahead and do it."

In January 1969, Joy and Dick were married. The marriage started off inauspiciously. Just before the wedding, the young couple had a fight—Dick had arrived late for the prewedding rehearsal. And after the ceremony, they had another. It started while they were driving to Kennedy Airport, where they were planning to spend the night in an airport hotel in order to board a flight for France early the next morning. Halfway to the airport, Dick realized he'd left their tickets and passports behind. Joy became upset, and even though Dick's brother promptly retrieved the documents and brought them out to the hotel, the new couple, their tempers strained, didn't make love that first night of their marriage.

Nor did they make love the next night, although by then they were staying in romantic quarters in Paris's elegant Plaza Athénée hotel. They began to quarrel because right after they arrived in France, Joy called an old Great Neck friend who was living in Paris and invited him to dinner. Then, after dinner, she suggested to her friend that since it was late and he lived far away, he spend the night in their suite. Dick had a tantrum, stormed out of their hotel room, and spent the night walking the streets of Paris.

When he returned to the hotel in the morning, the friend was gone. But Dick was still angry. When Joy said she wanted to go shopping, he refused to accompany her.

By the time they reached Rome, their next stop, they were reconciled. Now, when Joy said she wanted to go shopping, which it seemed to Dick she said all the time, he went with her. But as they made their rounds, stopping at Gucci and Pucci and Bulgari, he worried that the rest of his life with her might turn out to be nothing more than a shopping spree.

Things were better when they got to the south of France, which was their next honeymoon stop. But something puzzling occurred there. Joy had told Dick that she'd made arrangements for them to visit her grandmother, who lived in the area, and explained that she'd never met her before. On a windy afternoon, they set out on the visit, maneuvering the hilly roads in a rented car and stopping at last at the home of Mme. Germont, Jeanette's mother-in-law by her previous marriage. That Mme. Germont wasn't actually Joy's grandmother, Dick didn't know at the time. He'd always assumed that Joy was a Germont and she'd never told him differently. But today, he was perplexed. The woman Joy had called her grandmother seemed singularly uninterested in either him *or* Joy. She spent hardly any time with them. And although she spoke some English, she barely talked to them.

"What's with her?" Dick said to Joy when, after the tedious visit, they were on the road again. It had occurred to him that perhaps Mme. Germont was angry with her former daughter-in-law, Jeanette. But even if that was the case, was the way she had behaved any way to treat a granddaughter she'd never met before? Dick said this to Joy and observed, "She didn't seem much like your grandmother at all."

Joy changed the subject.

In New York, when the honeymoon was over, Joy and Dick settled down to married life. Jeanette had decorated and furnished their co-op, buying imported furniture and choosing a pale pink-and-white color scheme for all the rooms. Dick went back to work selling furniture, this time at his father's big shop in Queens. Joy bought herself a dog, not just any dog, but a pricey Lhasa apso, and spent her time strolling with her new pet in Washington Square Park or lunching and shopping with her mother.

Jeanette and Dick were still good friends, and one day when she was visiting and Joy was in another room, Jeanette told Dick there was something she wanted to tell him. "Joy's not a Germont," she said. "Her father was a man named Ben Fererh."

Dick was stunned.

"I married Fererh when I lived at Saranac Lake," Jeanette went on. "I was miserable. We broke up."

"What happened to him?" Dick asked.

"He lives near Miami. Miami Beach. I used to send him a hundred dollars here, fifty dollars there. He still calls sometimes."

When she had finished her tale, Jeanette asked Joy to come into the room and said to her that she'd told Dick what he needed to know.

Dick felt sorry for Joy after that. And when he and she fought, which they kept on doing more and more often, he would tell himself that it was no wonder Joy was so quarrelsome and acted at times as if she hated him. The poor kid, he would tell himself, she had one father who walked out on her and another who died on her and a third who refused to adopt her—though now he felt he could understand *why* Bibbs hadn't adopted her. She *had* a father. Still, no matter how you looked at it, each of her fathers had let her down. There'd never been a single one who'd really cared about her and looked after her and made her feel safe and protected. It was enough, Dick thought, to make a woman hate not just a husband but all men.

Some months later, the phone rang and Dick picked it up to hear an operator's voice. A Mr. Ben Fererh was calling collect, the operator said. For a Mrs. Joy Simons.

Dick put Joy on the phone, and she and her father talked to each other for the first time in Joy's adult life. Fererh told Joy that Jeanette had asked him to call. Joy told him that she'd just gotten married, that she adored her husband, and that they'd just had a great trip to Europe, where they'd seen and done the most marvelous things. And that was it. As far as Dick knew, she never spoke to her father again.

CHAPTER 4

The first day Sol took the bench, striding to his high-backed chair in an airy courtroom of the Nassau County Supreme Court in Mineola, a court stenographer eyed him suspiciously. The man was aware of the criticisms that had been leveled against Sol by the local bar association, and he expected a judge who would be at best confused, but more probably ignorant and incompetent. Nevertheless, within hours, as he sat there taking notes, the stenographer came to the conclusion that this new young judge had an unusually clear way of crystallizing issues and sizing up cases. He liked him, liked him a lot.

So did many of the people who met Sol in his new capacity, and he quickly became a highly respected trial judge. He handled civil cases—negligence and matrimonial disputes, contract and business controversies, and land use and zoning arguments (he had great familiarity with both these latter matters as a result of his years as town supervisor). Plaintiffs and defendants were impressed by his fairness, lawyers by the felicitous way in which he moved them and their cases along, appellate division judges with the intelligence and clarity of his decisions, and court personnel with his friendliness. Right away, or so it seemed, he knew the names of all the court officers and court stenographers in the Mineola courthouse. ''It was the politician's ability,'' the

59

court stenographer who had worked with him on his very first day often thought. "But still, you never failed to be impressed."

About eight months after she and Dick got married, Joy became pregnant. Jeanette was overjoyed and asked Bibbs to set up Dick, the father of her future grandchild, in business. She didn't like Dick's being in the retail trade, she said. There were too many late hours; there would be too many parties and dinners Joy would have to attend alone. And besides, she urged Bibbs, if he put his mind to it, surely he'd come up with an occupation for Dick that would enable him to make a great deal more money than he was making now.

Bibbs came up with the idea. He proposed to Dick that he and his father develop the St. Petersburg land that he'd bought from Sol's father and promised to his sons, Jimmy and Van. He was more generous with Dick than he'd been with Sol, to whom he'd also once proposed developing the land. He didn't demand any money up front, but said magnanimously, "You won't have to pay me for the lots until you've sold the houses."

It was a good deal, but Dick was worried that Joy wouldn't like the plan. "We'd have to live there while we're building," he told Jeanette. "And Joy's so into Manhattan. Maybe she won't like it in Florida."

Jeanette thought Joy could be brought around. "She'll like your making good money," she said. "And once you've made your fortune, you and Joy can do what you want to do, live wherever you want to live."

In due course, she and Bibbs and Joy and Dick, accompanied by Dick's father, made a trip to St. Petersburg to check out the area. Dick loved the weather and the dream it evoked of endless summer and perpetual golf games. Joy was unenthusiastic. "Where can you shop here?" she said, and turned up her nose disdainfully. But Jeanette told her it wasn't all that far from Palm Beach, and maybe someday she could live *there*. Joy seemed reassured. So in short order, Dick agreed to Bibbs's deal. (Sol, when he heard about it, was upset. It rankled that Bibbs had wanted fifty thousand dollars from him for something he'd given Dick Simons for nothing.)

Plunging into becoming a real-estate developer, Dick took an apartment for himself and Joy in St. Petersburg. But although Joy lived there with him for a while, she soon decided she wanted to be with her mother during the remainder of her pregnancy and went back up to New York.

In May 1970, the child, Evan Marc Simons, was born at New York Hospital. Dick flew up for the baby's birth, and then he and Joy, with Evan in tow, returned to St. Petersburg. For a few months they were happy, buying a boat and exploring the local bays and channels, but soon their marriage began to show further signs of strain. They quarreled about money. No matter how many clothes and pieces of jewelry she bought, Joy always wanted more, Dick felt. They quarreled about sex. Joy, it seemed to Dick, wanted sex "by the numbers," something automatic and abrupt and unspontaneous. But most of all, they quarreled about where they were living. Joy hated St. Petersburg more and more and said she was languishing there, while back home her mother and Bibbs were having the time of their lives, dressing up and going out to fabulous dinners and parties, where sometimes they even rubbed shoulders with people who got written about in the society columns.

She missed not only the opportunity to meet such people but even the habit of reading about them in New York's gossip columns, and every morning she would call Jeanette and ask her to report the latest dish about New York socialites and celebrities. Jeanette would fill her in and then, because just summarizing the gossip wasn't enough, would read her entire entries from columnists like Suzy and Leonard Lyons and Eugenia Sheppard.

Later in the morning, Joy would call Jeanette again, or Jeanette would call Joy, and they'd talk about the baby. Or clothes. Or their horoscopes. Jeanette was a big believer in astrology. They were on the phone with each other for hours on end. They even called each other to discuss what had happened in their favorite soap operas, which both women watched religiously day in and day out. Bibbs complained to Dick that his phone bills had gone up hundreds of dollars a month since Joy had had her baby and moved back to Florida, and that maybe he'd better buy a place to live down there as soon as possible.

Jimmy Wolosoff had also gotten married and had a child, a little girl. Bibbs liked being a grandfather and began spending time with his son's family.

Not Jeanette. She refused to have anything to do with them. She didn't trust Jimmy's wife, she told Bibbs. And he was a fool if he did. Sure, Jimmy's wife acted sweet and devoted. But she was only interested in his money. Her and Jimmy too. And if Bibbs was fool enough not to see that and went on spending so much time with them, she'd leave him one of these days, walk right out.

"My parents just bought a condominium in Palm Beach!" Joy told Dick one day in 1971. She was speaking to him long distance, for she had once again gone up north to stay with Jeanette and Bibbs. She couldn't bear the dullness of St. Petersburg a second longer, she'd told Dick, and taken the baby and gone home. They'd fought about it, of course, but now she was making peace. "The condo's right on the ocean," she trilled. "And there's something even better. Bibbs has bought land right across from the condo. He wants *you* to develop it, to put up apartments. Oh, Dick, we're going to move to Palm Beach!"

Dick was reluctant to take on the new project. His work in St. Petersburg was going well, but it wasn't finished. He had a hundred people working for him, and he was in the middle of construction on several houses, and besides, he *liked* St. Petersburg. But he agreed to drive down to Palm Beach and meet Bibbs, Jeanette, and Joy there on the weekend.

When he did, Bibbs told him he'd already arranged financing through the Chase Manhattan Bank for the Palm Beach apartments. "We can build a hundred and twenty-nine units," he said, "and we'll be partners in it."

Jeanette, taking Dick aside, urged him to agree. "This will save your marriage," she said. "Joy will have her shopping and her social life, and we'll all be together."

Shortly afterward, Bibbs and Jeanette began living in their new

62

condo, and Dick and Joy rented an apartment in the nearby Sun and Surf, one of the most fashionable apartment buildings in Palm Beach.

Sol Wachtler had been out of the public eye for several years. "You get on the state supreme court and nobody ever hears from you again," Joe Carlino had told him, back in sixty-eight. "You get on the state supreme court and you might as well be dead."

Sol hadn't agreed with Carlino back then. But now, after more than three years on the court, he had come to see what his old friend had meant. He was out of things. Sidelined.

His life was pleasant enough. At home, the children were growing up, and he had assumed a new role with them, not just that of entertainer and caretaker, but of adviser, counselor, and rescuer. The kids had always come to him, not Joan, when they got into scrapes. She'd been the disciplinarian. He, on the other hand, had always been indulgent. Now the kids worshiped him, and he was reaping the rewards, the admiration and adoration, for having played the softy in the familial version of good cop-bad cop.

At the courthouse, too, he was enjoying himself. A New York State Supreme Court judge wields a lot of power, is a man before whom lawyers stutter and defendants quake. Courtrooms are like little fiefdoms, and judges are like barons, expecting—and generally receiving—deference. But Sol knew that his power was not comparable to that wielded by judges in the state's higher courts, the four appellate divisions and the mighty court of appeals. He was ready for a change when Joe Margiotta, Ed Speno's successor as Republican county chairman, proposed to him that he run for a seat on the court of appeals.

Margiotta was a pudgy man who wore rings on his fingers like a Borgia pope and reveled in receiving the news and tribute from his minions over a gold-plated telephone with which they'd presented him. In an era when party bosses were almost becoming as extinct as dinosaurs, he flourished. And in a time when county political organizations were weak and divided, he ran one that was superbly disciplined and amazingly well financed. Under Margiotta, the Nassau Republicans were raising a phenomenal two million dollars a year. There was controversy about the way this money was gathered. Margiotta, it was said, tithed the salaries of party workers and took kickbacks from people doing business with the county.

But Sol got on with Margiotta. There was something about power that was seductive to him, and Margiotta had plenty of power. When he told Sol that he would be helping the party out if he ran for the court of appeals and that, because of this, the party would show its appreciation by giving him extensive and unusual support, Sol said yes.

The party needed help in the election because it had been double-crossed by the Democrats. Generally, court of appeals seats weren't contested. The two parties mutually put up the required number of candidates, thus guaranteeing that whoever was nominated would be elected. But this year—it was early 1972—although there'd been an understanding between the leaders of the two parties that two Democrats and one Republican would be nominated for the three available seats on the court, at the last moment, and after everything had been arranged, the Democratic state chairman had refused to go along with the plan. He'd insisted the Democrats put up all *three* candidates. The Republicans had balked and said that, in that case, they, too, would nominate three candidates. Three strong candidates. Sol, who had put up such a good fight against Nickerson, had come immediately to mind.

When he said he'd run, Margiotta told him that the party would give him four hundred thousand dollars to spend on television ads. Such a costly media campaign was unheard of in a judicial race. Sol would be making history.

Palm Beach, where the Wolosoffs and the Simonses were trying to put down roots, was still, just as it had been for more than fifty years, the favorite winter playground of the very rich. The twelve-mile sandspit was chockablock with third-generation millionaires married to women thirty years younger and twelve to sixteen inches taller than themselves, as well as with Social Register hostesses who employed their own personal publicity agents, and with business tycoons, world-renowned entertainers, international diplomats, polo players, philanthropists, princesses. Consuelo Vanderbilt had a home there. So did Marjorie Merriweather Post Close Hutton Davies. And the Pulitzers. And the Kimberlys. And the Kennedys. In glamorous mansions, some of which had over a hundred rooms, the celebrated rich entertained one another, as well as the titled and royal from Europe and the Mideast, among them the Duke and Duchess of Windsor, Prince Alfonso de Bourbon-Asturias of Spain, and King Hussein of Jordan.

The United States had had a recession in 1971, and the recession had struck Palm Beach. But it had primarily affected people like the stock and bond salesmen who peddled to the celebrated rich and the architects and developers who built modest homes for those who yearned to live in proximity to their glamour. It had hardly touched the celebrated rich themselves. At worst, they were finding themselves forced to live, as one writer put it, "on the interest rather than the interest on the interest." Unaffected, they continued to give their champagne and caviar cocktail parties, their stone crab and lobster Newburg dinners, their charity balls.

The heady lives of the socialites did not often intersect with those of Palm Beach's less affluent, albeit very well-to-do, newcomers, who, like the Wolosoffs and the Simonses, occupied the banks of glistening new condominiums that had sprung up on the island in recent years. But in the breasts of many of these occupants—Joy and Jeanette among them—soared the perpetual hope that, in time, paths would cross, invitations would be proffered, friendships would be formed.

The Palm Beach aristocracy mocked the aspirations of the newcomers. In March of 1971, just before the Wolosoffs and Simonses arrived, Palm Beach art gallery owner George E. Vigouroux told *The New York Times* the sad story of a woman who had a husband worth a hundred million dollars, a collection of very elaborate jewelry, and a white Rolls-Royce in which she made a grand entrance into Palm Beach, only to find herself shunned by the social crowd for a good several years until she "found out finally what was expected of her."

Nevertheless, Jeanette followed the path of her unhappy predecessor. As soon as she arrived in Palm Beach, she bought a white Rolls-Royce, and she began sporting the expensive jewelry that over the years she had gotten Bibbs to purchase for her at Cartier and David Webb. But although she was properly be-coached and begemmed, and properly outfitted in Pucci prints and Gucci shoes, it was difficult for her—and for Joy—to make the right connections, to be invited to the right parties. Joy, whose moods were mercurial and whose temper was turbulent, took Palm Beach's social snubs badly. Once, anticipating being invited to a particularly desirable ball, she purchased an ex-tremely stylish and expensive gown. When the invitation to the ball never came, in a fit of rage, she tore up the gown.

But gradually, after Joy met and became friendly with several young women who were at the very nexus of Palm Beach's party-primed life, their social standing improved. Her new friends included Jacquie Kimberly, whose husband, Jim Kimberly, forty-three years older than she, was one of the heirs to the Kimberly-Clark tissue fortune, and Roxanne Dixon, who would soon be married to Herbert "Peter" Pulitzer, Jr., one of the heirs to the Pulitzer newspaper fortune. Jacquie and Roxanne would eventu-ally be at the center of one of Palm Beach's most scandalous divorce trials, during which Roxanne would accuse her husband of, among other things, turning her on to cocaine and requiring her to make love in his presence to her best girlfriend, Jacquie. When the trial was over, both Roxanne and Jacquie would no longer enjoy the place in Palm Beach's highest social circles that they had held in the early 1970s.

But at the time Joy became friendly with them, the scandal was still in the future, and with the support of her new friends, she—and through her, Jeanette—was at last able to crack Palm Beach's social scene. Getting to know the notorious, like Gregg Dodge—who had been accused in divorce papers of brutally beating her alcoholic husband, automobile heir Horace Dodge, Jr.—and the exquisite, like Susie Hutton—who had given up a career in modeling to marry brokerage heir Willie Hutton—swimming and watching their husbands play golf at the Breakers Country Club, dancing at the Kimberly estate and at Pulitzer's mansion, and even dining with King Hussein—not just once but several times—Joy and Jeanette began at last to live the life they had always read about in gossip columns.

Still, it seemed to Dick that Joy wasn't altogether happy, for her exciting new social life required costumes and jewelry that were costly, and he and she were, as always, having fierce battles about money. She complained to him that he was denying her things he could easily afford. He complained to her that she was insatiable when it came to material objects. And when he told her that they couldn't afford them, she'd say the hell with him, she'd get the money from her mother, for Jeanette was always willing to slip Joy an extra thousand or two, or even five or six. Once, she even sent Joy an envelope with ten thousand dollars in cash in it, a gift to enable her to take a Caribbean cruise with Dick on the *QE II*.

Jeanette's generosity irked Dick. He felt her largesse was ruining his marriage, and one day when he and Joy were having a particularly fierce fight over something she wanted to buy, he told her, "You're not going to get it from me. And if your mother buys it for you, you might as well kiss good-bye to our marriage." The next day, Bibbs called Dick and invited him to have lunch at the local delicatessen with him and Jeanette.

While they were eating their corned beef sandwiches, he tried to talk Dick into letting Joy have her way. "It's only money," he said. "With women, you gotta give 'em what they want. That's the only way to keep peace in the house."

"But I don't have that kind of money," Dick said, and he stopped eating. "Joy goes through money as if it were water."

"I'll give you the money," Bibbs said.

Just then, Dick felt Jeanette's hand on his leg. She was slipping him something. An envelope. "Here," she said, as his hand closed on it. "Just buy Joy whatever she wants. Be happy. Relax."

Dick put the envelope on the table and opened it. Inside was twenty thousand dollars. The bills were crisp. "These just come out of your safe?" he asked Bibbs.

"What do you care?" his father-in-law said. "Just take it. For Joy's sake."

Shaking his head, Dick looked in dismay at his mother-in-law.

"You take the money back," he said, "or I'm going to embarrass you and me both by getting up and throwing it right on the table and walking out."

"Well." Jeanette reluctantly took the envelope. "You're making a mistake."

"You're being a fool," Bibbs said.

"No, this is crazy." Dick went on eating. "When Joy spends the way she does, and you guys pay for it all, it makes me feel like I'm not the man of my house." But he couldn't eat anymore. His heart was burning. "Like I'm a nothing, like I'm, I don't know, just a chauffeur who sleeps with Joy."

For a while after that, Bibbs and Jeanette made no more offers of cash to Dick. But the fights between him and Joy continued. He was despondent. She was edgy. And although she was seeing a psychiatrist and receiving tranquilizers, sometimes Dick made her so mad she threw things, not caring what she threw. Once, she pitched a Lalique ashtray across the room. Once, a Steuben-glass vase.

There was something else that was unusual about Joy when she got angry. She didn't brood on her injuries. She took action. Her father-in-law, Alexander Simons, noticed this one day. He'd been to Italy on a business trip, and he'd promised Joy that while he was there, he would buy her a certain Gucci bag in Milan. But in Italy, he forgot to buy the bag and when he returned and went to visit Joy, he arrived empty-handed. She was furious. He apologized, but she wouldn't accept his apology and, giving him a belligerent look, reached for the telephone, dialed Gucci in Milan, and ordered the bag.

In Great Neck, Sol had begun to worry that his TV commercials were too low-key. It was 1972, a presidential election year—Nixon was running on the Republican ticket—and Sol had been advised by his handlers that, with a presidential race at the top of the ticket, a whole slew of other races beneath it, and the court of appeals race all the way down on the bottom, he needed to do something to focus attention on himself. He was advertising, but his ads weren't having enough impact.

One day he met with Sheila Kelley, a political consultant and advertising specialist, to discuss a different direction for his commercials. "What about concentrating on crime?" he asked. "Crime's on everyone's mind." It was true. Nixon had declared a "war on crime," and a number of national magazines had taken up the chant, pointing out that crime rates were rising, jails becoming overcrowded, and judges growing demoralized. "We've got to address this," Sol said to Kelley, and urged her to find a dramatic way of doing so.

The commercial she came up with was powerful. Sol, wearing his judicial robes, was filmed touring a corridor of cells at the Nassau County jail, slamming a cell door shut with a loud clang and earnestly pledging he'd "get the thieves and muggers and murderers into these cells."

When the commercial was aired, there was a tremendous outcry from the Democrats. Sol was accused, just as he'd been accused in the Nickerson campaign when he'd employed doctored photographs in his ads, of misleading the public—this time by erroneously suggesting that court of appeals judges dealt directly with criminals. The Bar of the City of New York, a nonpartisan organization, also became enraged and issued a series of ethical guidelines to control future advertisements for judgeships—candidates shouldn't pose in judicial robes, they recommended, and they shouldn't run ads that appealed "directly or indirectly to the fear, passion, or prejudice of the electorate."

Despite the criticism, Sol kept the commercial running. But as the criticism mounted, he began to have second thoughts, and at the end of October, just before the election, he dropped the offending ad.

His change of mind came too late for his critics to forgive him, and afterward a movement to change the way judges got onto the court of appeals began to flourish. Judges shouldn't run for the top court, influential people said. They should be appointed. Chosen on the basis of their merit. Eventually, this view prevailed and the system was changed. But in the meantime, Sol had been successful in his efforts. In November 1972, he was elected to the court of appeals by a small margin.

In December, Margiotta tried to take all the credit. When a reporter mentioned to the powerful county leader that he'd heard that Sol might someday like to run for a state position such as attorney general, Margiotta said, as if to demonstrate that he and he alone pulled all of Sol's strings, "Sol has to sit there in that judgeship for a while."

If Sol was troubled by this, he kept it to himself. In politics, keeping things to oneself is essential, and Sol had mastered that art.

"We should never have left St. Pete," Dick kept saying to Joy. "We should never have come to Palm Beach." The tensions in their household were coming to a head, and when Dick's brother, Steven, announced that in June 1973 he would be getting married, they exploded. The catalyst was Joy's search for a dress to wear to the wedding, which promised to be very lavish— Steven was marrying a Houston petroleum heiress. Joy went shopping, and one day returned from a foray to the fashionable Martha's on Worth Avenue to inform Dick she'd found what she wanted. It was a great dress, but it would cost them five thousand dollars.

Dick did a double take. "Five thousand dollars!" he exclaimed. "For a dress to wear to a wedding!"

Joy looked at him archly. Then she said, "Well, Dick, I have to tell you something I haven't told you. The dress has to be custom made. Because by the time I wear it, it's going to be a maternity dress."

Dick was astonished. He hadn't known she was pregnant. "Why didn't you tell me sooner?" he asked.

"Because you've been in such a bad mood lately. My mother and I thought I should let it go until you were in a better mood."

He was glad about the baby and told her so. But he was stubborn about the dress. "Cancel it," he said. "It's too much money to spend. Especially now that we're going to have another child."

The next day, Jeanette called and asked Dick to have lunch with her at Chessler's, and during lunch, just like the time she'd tried to give him twenty thousand dollars, she pressed an envelope on him. Inside was five thousand dollars. "Joy's going to *have* to be in a maternity dress by the time Steven gets married,"

Jeanette said, "so you might as well let her have the dress she wants."

Dick refused. "You're making me feel like nobody, like a piece of shit," he said. "You're ruining my life with your money."

Jeanette's response was to tell him that he was ruining Joy's life by being such a pinchpenny with her and that Joy was convinced he was having an affair. He said he wasn't, but that he was at his wit's end in the marriage. "Maybe Joy and I should have a trial separation," he suggested. "Maybe I should go back to St. Petersburg for a few weeks and we should each try to think things through, figure out what we can do to make the marriage work."

Several days later, he did just that, driving back to their old house in St. Pete. But he wasn't there an hour before Joy called to say she missed him, and after he'd been gone a few days, she flew up to see him.

They stayed at the Hyatt in Tampa and made love for the first time in weeks and it was good, and afterward Dick thought that maybe they *could* salvage their marriage. So he returned to Palm Beach. But right away, they started fighting again, and at last, he decided to leave for good.

Before he left town, he went to see Bibbs. "I'm going back to St. Petersburg again for a while," he said, "and when I come back, Joy and I won't be living together. We're separating."

"You're making a mistake," Bibbs said. "You should have told Joy, 'I'll give you anything you want.' That's all she wants. Other than you. She loves you."

"She can't love me," Dick said. "All she wants is money." Then he said, "I hope this doesn't ruin our building project here, Bibbs—you know, I'm going to fulfill all my obligations on the job. But I gotta get away for a while. It's really best for all of us."

Bibbs smiled at Dick affectionately. "I've known you since you were a boy," he said. "Since before I met Jeanette. Or Joy. Whatever happens between the two of you, you and I will still be friends. And partners."

Reassured, Dick left town. And ten days later, Bibbs served

him with nine lawsuits, charging him with abandoning their business in Palm Beach and leaving all their financial obligations in his lap.

Joy filed for divorce. She said in court papers that marriage to Dick had been so stressful that she'd become emotionally ill, and at a court hearing she explained that she was a fragile person who'd grown up filled with "insecurities" because her parents weren't the same set of parents as those of her brother. "My childhood growing up wasn't exactly a normal one," she said, and comparing her existence to the entertainments she had always watched so avidly, she asserted, "My life is like a soap opera."

It had certainly become a soap opera of sorts. Not only was she suing Dick for a divorce, but he and her stepfather were suing each other over their business ventures—not just the Palm Beach condominiums, but now, even the St. Petersburg property. Bibbs had decided to refuse to sell Dick the final plots of land he had promised to him.

Joy was on Bibbs's side in the disputes, and Dick, to whom she was still speaking occasionally, was surprised at this. "How can you stand behind your stepfather, who hated your guts for so many years?" he asked her one day. "How can you lie for him and stand behind him when you know he's doing what he's doing just to hurt me?"

"Hurting you is the *idea*," Dick recalled her saying. "We're going to hurt you. And you won't be able to fight us. We're the Wolosoffs."

"Aw, come on," Dick said. "You're not a Wolosoff."

"Oh, yes I am," Joy said. "I'm a Wolosoff because my mother is a Wolosoff."

Infuriated by her response, Dick sought out Jeanette, whom he still considered a special friend. He wanted to talk to her about Bibbs, but she wanted to talk about the split between him and Joy. "Maybe it was all my fault," she said. "You and Joy breaking up. But if it was, it was unintentional."

He knew she was talking about the money, and he felt bad. She had tears in her eyes.

"I thought I was helping," she went on. "I just wanted my

daughter to have whatever she wanted. I just wanted her to be the Queen Bee.''

Dick forgave her. How could he not? But there was no way he was ever going to forgive Bibbs.

"I loved Bibbs," he said. "He was like a second father to me. And I was like a son to him. But he's a sneaky, no-good shit, and you can tell him that I said so. And tell him this: I may be younger, and I may not have the money he has, but I'm gonna prove that I'm right and he's wrong, and I'm gonna get him for what he's done to me.''

Jeanette was diplomatic. "May the man who's right win," she said.

Joan Wachtler, for all her blond beauty and her good Sarah Lawrence education, had been eclipsed by her husband, who cast an enormous shadow. When they went out together, he was the person to whom everyone wanted to talk, he was the funny one, the lively one, the *important* one. She was the auxiliary, the supporting player, the helpmeet. It had been this way for years. But it wasn't just their friends and acquaintances who bathed him in admiration. It was the children too. As they'd scrambled through the thorns of adolescence, they'd grown even closer to him than they'd been before, telling him their hurts, their hopes, their secrets, vying with one another to gain his attention. She was often left out in the cold.

She was left out in the cold in another way too. After Sol's campaign against Nickerson, when she'd discovered she enjoyed the details of politics and was a superb office administrator, she'd begun doing political work, volunteering in the campaign headquarters of Senator Javits and other candidates. She'd adored the work and reveled in the feelings of pride and identity it gave her. But one day someone had called Sol and said it wasn't right for his wife to be doing political work, what with his being a judge. And that had been the end of her career. She'd had to give up the work she loved.

Now she was realizing that she'd better find something to do with her life. Something that was hers and hers alone and didn't have anything at all to do with Sol. After a while, she began thinking about social work. It suited her. One of the reasons she'd liked working in politics was that she was interested in social causes, in women's issues and poverty issues. If she became a social worker, maybe she could put those interests to work. Maybe she'd be able to help others at the same time that she helped herself.

Inspired by the possibilities, Joan decided to get a graduate degree in social work.

Once her divorce from Dick became final, Joy went up to New York. There, in New York Hospital, the same hospital in which she'd given birth to Evan, she had an abortion. It was very late in her pregnancy and the abortion required an operation.

Jeanette called Dick and told him that Joy blamed him for her having had the abortion. She wouldn't have had it, Jeanette said, if she hadn't been worried that because of all the tranquilizers she'd taken during the stormy days of their marriage, the child would be abnormal. "If I were you, I'd prepare myself," Jeanette warned Dick. "I don't think she'll ever forgive you."

And she didn't. She stayed in New York, even though according to the terms of their divorce agreement, she wasn't supposed to move away from Florida. And she wouldn't speak to Dick anymore except when it was absolutely necessary that they confer so that he could arrange a visit to Evan.

Dick hoped she'd get over her anger at him. And he hoped her move to New York was a temporary thing. That she'd soon come back. In the meantime, he was busy with his litigation with Bibbs.

A new figure had entered that litigation. He was David Paul, a thirty-three-year-old real-estate developer who would one day be a major figure in the savings and loan scandal that rocked America in the late 1980s. A man who adored extravagance, he would be accused of siphoning more than twenty-five million dollars from CenTrust, a bank he controlled, and of using the money to pay for his pleasures, among them a nine-million-dollar estate, a ninety-five-foot yacht with gold-leaf ceilings, and an art collection that included priceless paintings by some of the old masters.

In the early 1970s, however, David Paul did not yet have an art collection, nor own a kingly yacht and palatial home. Nevertheless, for a man in his early thirties, he was already immensely successful. The son of a Great Neck businessman, Isadore Goldstein, who had lived not far from Bibbs and owned a chain of cleaning stores, Paul, who had changed his name, had already built three strikingly modern apartment developments and started a real-estate investment company.

He was something of a liar, fond of inventing distinguished educational credits for himself. And he had a titanic temper. Nevertheless, Bibbs was willing to do business with him, and when Dick began countersuing his father-in-law, Bibbs sold Paul all his stock in the company he and Dick had owned. Then he and Paul set up a new company for the building of the selfsame Palm Beach condominiums that had once been Bibbs and Dick's venture.

Establishing such a firm might have seemed, to a different investor than Paul, a foolhardy project. Palm Beach real estate was in decline. It had by now been heavily hit by the recession, and story upon story of luxury apartments and condominiums were standing empty. Their prospective buyers had canceled their contracts, and the banks that had lent the money for their construction were getting tough. Indeed, Chase, which had given Bibbs and Dick a three-million-dollar loan, was demanding the return of its loan. And there was no money with which to repay Chase. It had all been spent. But Paul saw a way out. He arranged for a new, five-million-dollar bank loan, then paid Chase back its three million. But once he and Bibbs had the additional two million, they didn't go forward with the building of condominiums. They terminated the project.

Dick Simons hired one of Palm Beach's most noted lawyers, Joseph Farish, to represent him against Bibbs. Farish alleged that Bibbs and David Paul had each helped themselves personally to a million dollars from the new bank loan. One humid day in a Palm Beach court clerk's office, Farish took a deposition from Paul and asked him why, in view of the recession and the cancellations, he had been willing to take a financial risk that the Chase bank had shied away from.

Dick was sitting in the clerk's office. He listened while Paul began his answer, explaining that he had confidence in Bibbs because he knew him, had grown up in the very same town that Bibbs lived in back home. And then he heard Paul say that he was even dating Bibbs's stepdaughter.

Dick was astonished. Joy dating David Paul! He had known David Paul for years and had always disliked him, always considered him untrustworthy. When the session ended, he made his way over to Paul and said to him, "You're scum. You were scum when I knew you back in Great Neck, and you're scum now. You must be as interesting to Joy as a dead worm on the street."

But although he'd spoken as if he didn't believe Joy would go out with David Paul, he knew it was probably true. Paul was a liar, but he wouldn't lie about a thing like that. Dick went home miserable and tried to talk himself into not caring about what Joy did and whom she saw. It wasn't his business any longer.

Joy married David Paul. It was a hurry-up, perhaps even a spur-of-the-moment, thing. She and Paul went to the Las Vegas county courthouse, where marriage licenses were issued all day and all night long, and they took their vows in a wedding parlor, the kind of place where the aisles are banked with artificial flowers and the windows covered with imitation stained glass made out of paper.

After the abrupt ceremony, at three in the morning, Joy telephoned Dick. "It's me," he recalled her saying, when he picked up the phone. "It's the love of your life."

"What do you want?" he asked her shortly.

"I just want to tell you I got married tonight. To David Paul."

He sat up in bed—too quickly. He tried to act disengaged. "You mean you called me at this hour to tell me you got married—like I really care who you marry?" He laughed. "Or is it just to make me feel bad?" He knew that was why.

"Yeah," she said from Vegas, but it was as if she were there in the room with him, still. "To make you feel bad. And I want you to know how I'm going to fuck him tonight."

"That's nice, Joy." He got a grip on himself. He lay down and listened.

"Don't you miss it?" she asked. "Don't you miss doing all those things to me, and me doing all those things to you?"

"No," he managed. "I really don't think about it, you know." But then he couldn't control himself any longer. "Why'd you marry a fat pig like David Paul?" he demanded, almost shouting. "Why'd you do it?"

"Business is business," Joy reminded him. "Obviously, if he can bail out my father and fuck you over too, then I'll marry him." She paused. "For a while."

Dick never forgot those calculating words, the icy sound of her voice that night. She had come a long way, he decided, from being the little "Pocahontas" with whom he'd fallen in love.

CHAPTER 5

Once he was on the court of appeals, Sol began traveling to Albany and residing there, a hundred and fifty miles from Joan, for two weeks a month. He didn't seem to mind. He and Joan had been married twenty years, and whatever passion had once existed between them had begun to evaporate. They still made love on occasion, but the sex they had was workmanlike, unspontaneous.

In any event, sex was apparently not a high priority of Sol's—and perhaps it never had been. A friend who'd known him since college noticed when he went to a party with Sol, not long after he began serving on the high court, that although many of the women present were flirting with him, his libido seemed to be totally bridled, so that he was sending off no sexual signals whatsoever. For a moment, the friend thought this odd, but then his mind wandered back to the way Sol had been in college. Not so different from the way he is now, he thought. Articulate, witty, polite. But not sexy. It's as if, the friend decided, all of Sol's inner energies are channeled, and had always been channeled, into one thing only, a passion for worldly success.

He was having that success in spades now, making a name for himself not only as a hardworking judge but as a far more liberal and open-minded one than those who had worried about

his law-and-order television commercials had ever imagined he
might be. In his first year on the court, in a case involving two
prisoners sentenced to death for having shot a prison guard, he
wrote the majority opinion, overturning the sentence on the
grounds that the trial judge had allowed a steward of the prison
guards' union to sit on the jury. In that first year, he also dis-
sented from the majority when they upheld a strict law on ob-
scenity and pornography, and he wrote such a thoughtful and
socially sensitive decision in a negligence case that an Albany
law professor told the press, "I think we've got a new Cardozo
on the court."

In his second and third years, he wrote other important opinions, one a dissent when the court voted to uphold the state's
right to penalize striking workers without first giving them hearings, and another a majority opinion ruling that people who suffered psychological injuries as a result of job-related traumas
should be as eligible for workmen's compensation benefits as
those who suffered physical injury.

People who worked with Sol in those days were struck both
by his energy and his unusual, and sometimes contradictory,
characteristics. He was exceedingly responsible, working long
hours, replying to virtually every letter he received, answering
virtually every phone call. He was exceedingly kind—he never
spoke haughtily to staff members, not even the lowliest, and
when friends came to him with their personal, financial, or health
problems, or even the problems of their family members, he
was indefatigable in trying to help them. Additionally, he was
exceedingly supportive of the lawyers who came to argue before
him and the court. Once, when a colleague railed at a pair of
opposing lawyers, "Both of you have given me briefs and arguments that are useless," Sol sat forward and said compassion-
ately, "I'm new to the court. I don't have the knowledge and
experience of law that my colleague has—but I found your briefs
and arguments very helpful."

But although he was dependable, accessible, and kind, and
although he didn't like to take part in or even witness public
humiliations, he nevertheless liked tricking people, putting something over on them. He especially liked tricking Jacob Fuchsberg,

a court of appeals judge who came onto the court two years after he did, and whom he disliked intensely. Sol's chambers were on the second floor, and Fuchsberg's on the third. On occasions when he and Fuchsberg boarded the elevator together on the ground floor, Sol would stand near the elevator buttons, press number two for himself, and then, as if to do a courteous service for Fuchsberg, poke out a finger toward the button for the third floor. But instead he would press the button for the basement. When he got off the elevator on the second floor, it would head down instead of up, and he would come into his chambers laughing gleefully and saying, "I did it again! I tricked him again!"

He had other amusements. He enjoyed coming up with one-liners to convey complex judicial ideas—his most famous, expressed in opposition to the grand jury system, was that if a district attorney pushed for it, "a grand jury will indict even a ham sandwich." But tricks were his special joy. He loved going unprepared to judicial conferences, getting a clever idea while listening to the discussions, and swaying others to his viewpoint. When this happened, he would say, "If you've prepared for a conference and people listen to you, there's nothing special about it. But if you haven't prepared and they listen to you—that's executive talent!" He also got a large kick out of pulling the wool—almost literally—over people's eyes when it came to matters of appearance. "Whadya think I paid for this suit?" he would ask staff members, who, invariably, would guess a high figure. This would make him cackle and say that the suit had been dirt cheap, but he'd fooled them by wearing an expensive tie. Then, he'd give them his sartorial advice—if you bought your ties at Saks or Brooks Brothers, you could buy your shirts at K mart and your suits at Syms, because no one would ever suspect a man in a Brooks Brothers tie of wearing a cheap shirt and suit.

If there was something of the trickster about him, there was also something of the comedian. He could imitate peoples' accents and postures to a tee, could "do" his fellow judges so convincingly and so humorously that his staff would erupt into gales of laughter. He also loved telling jokes. But not sexual jokes. He abhorred those, preferring silly and often juvenile stories of the type that mocked cultural characteristics. He'd tell Jewish jokes, Polish jokes, Italian jokes—he loved the one about the Italian immigrant who sadly tells the judge examining him for citizenship that he doesn't know the name of the man who shot Lincoln, only to have his friends and neighbors yell, "That's-a-good, Luigi. You ain't no informer." But he never told a dirty joke—and he disliked it intensely when staff members did. He even disliked their using obscenities. Once, when a staff member in the throes of frustration did so, Sol snapped at him, "Watch your language, sailor!"

Nor did he like it when people on his staff made light of marriage. Marriage was sacred, he would say, so sacred that wedding ceremonies should really not be performed by judges like himself, but by priests, ministers, and rabbis, as they were the only people who could give such ceremonies the weightiness they deserved. Above all, he frowned on philandering—a common activity among certain legislators, who had wives back home in their districts and mistresses up in Albany. So many married people conducted adulterous affairs in Albany that there was even a joke about the city's frequent liaisons. Infidelity was okay up in the capital, went the joke, because the legislators had passed a law, the Tappan Zee Rule, that said that anything goes once you're north of the Tappan Zee Bridge. Sol disapproved of that sort of thing, he let it be known. And the people who worked with him were sure he not only meant it but never gave adultery a thought.

Joy's marriage to David Paul hadn't gone smoothly. "If I'd lived with him two days," she told an intimate, "I'd never have married him." They'd taken a lavish apartment on Park Avenue, living there with little Evan and Paul's two sons from a previous marriage—he'd gotten custody of them after a bitter fight with his former wife. But the couple quarreled constantly, and within two months of the wedding ceremony, they got an annulment in the Dominican Republic.

Six months later, Joy began to be seen with a friend of Paul's, a businessman named Jeffrey Silverman who had just left his wife. Slim, handsome, and debonair, thirty-year-old Jeffrey was the son of an exceedingly wealthy Wall Street conglomerator. With his father's aid, Jeffrey had become a member of the New York Stock Exchange when he was only twenty-one years old and had quickly established himself as a prescient private investor. At the time Joy started dating him, he had just gotten in on the ground floor of the soon-to-skyrocket business of cable television, having established his own cable company.

Jeffrey and his wife, Pamela, had not separated amicably, and there were rumors that Joy was responsible. She'd set her sights on Jeffrey, Dick Simons heard down in Florida, and then she'd provoked or inspired him to leave Pamela. Whether or not this was true, Jeffrey and Pamela, who had two children, a boy and a girl, began to haggle over the terms of a divorce, and Joy, who badly wanted to marry her attractive new suitor, settled in for a long courtship.

Joan Wachtler had been concentrating on her career. She'd been extremely scared when she'd gone back to school. She hadn't been near a classroom in over twenty years, and she'd forgotten what it was like to have to memorize information, write papers, take tests. She hated tests. One day, sitting in a restaurant with Sol, she'd got so panicky over an upcoming exam in statistics that she broke down and sobbed. Sol was concerned. He drove her to school and sat in the car in the parking lot until she emerged from her ordeal. He helped her in other ways too. He gave her emotional support and sometimes, when he was down from Albany, he even assisted her with her homework, just the way he used to help the children with theirs. By 1975, Sol's third year on the court, she was doing so well in her studies that she won an internship at the National Center for Urban Ethnic Affairs, in Washington, D.C.

When Sol was in his fourth year on the court, and Joy and Jeffrey were still waiting to marry, Dick Simons won his lawsuit against Bibbs. His lawyer had been able to prove that Bibbs had illegally and for personal reasons devalued the Palm Beach corporation and denied Dick the last of the St. Petersburg lots that were supposed to have been his. One day in 1976, a Florida judge informed Bibbs that he would have to pay Dick a large settlement and all of his legal fees. Dick walked over to Bibbs in the courthouse that morning, tapped him on the shoulder, and said, "See, you never offered me the twenty-five thousand dollars."

Bibbs turned around, confused. "What are you talking about?"

"The twenty-five thousand dollars," Dick said. "Remember? The money you always told me would buy off any lawsuit."

That afternoon, Jeanette took Dick to lunch. He told her what he'd said to Bibbs, and she laughed out loud. "That's priceless," she said. She, too, had heard Bibbs say a hundred times, maybe a thousand times, that you could buy off any lawsuit with twenty-five grand.

"He made a mistake," Dick said. "He coulda settled with me, Jeanette."

"No." And no longer laughing, she turned serious. "Bibbs never offered to settle with you," she said, "because he didn't want to give you *anything*."

It was Dick's turn to laugh. "He shoulda known better," he said. Then he, too, turned serious. "What gets me," he said, "is that I was like a son to Bibbs."

"I think," Jeanette replied, "that Bibbs thinks of sons as dispensable."

Whether or not Bibbs thought of sons in general as dispensable, he was certainly beginning to think of his elder son, Jimmy, that way. He and Jimmy were not getting on at all. They were too alike, people who knew them both thought. Each of them was stubborn, contentious, fiercely competitive. But their unfortunate similarities might not have driven them apart, had it not been for Jeanette. She had been trying to alienate Bibbs from Jimmy ever since she'd married into the family. In the early years, she'd complained about Jimmy's habits and personality, and in recent years she'd repeatedly insisted that Jimmy was interested in one thing only, and that was Bibbs's money.

Bibbs's money. Everybody wanted some of it, more of it, as much of it as they could get. Dick Simons had gotten a chunk. So had Jeanette herself, largely in the form of jewelry. She had cost him so much, Bibbs would one day confide to Sol, still his trusted counselor and adviser, that she was spending him into an early grave. But the person who was greediest, he began to think, under Jeanette's tutelage, was his son Jimmy. Jimmy had reneged on an agreement the two of them had made concerning some trusts he'd set up for the boy. Bibbs had put close to $1,500,000 into the trusts—it was a way of sheltering money from the IRS—and in return, Jimmy was supposed to pay him a tax-free annuity of $180,000 a year for the rest of his life. Jimmy had paid the annuity for a while, and then he'd stopped, saying that the trust wasn't producing $180,000 a year. What kind of son was that? It wasn't as if the boy didn't have any other money. Bibbs began demanding that Jimmy pay up.

Jimmy took him to court. He sued his father for lying about the annuity payments due him and also for having dealt fraudulently with him in dozens of business transactions—one had to do with the St. Petersburg land Bibbs had bought from Sol's father, promised to Jimmy and Van, and then sold piece by piece to Dick Simons. "My father," Jimmy told the court, "was the dominant, persuasive, and elemental force in our family life," a man who controlled every aspect of the family's affairs, down to the minutest details. He did so, Jimmy asserted, because he was convinced that he *deserved* to do so, in view of "his phenomenal financial success."

Accusations came tumbling out of Jimmy's court papers. Bibbs, he asserted, had intimidated and terrorized his children. Bibbs had even tried to defraud the IRS.

Bibbs hit the roof when he read Jimmy's assertions. He countersued him and vowed he would fight him until he'd driven him into the ground.

Jimmy's lawyer, Allen H. Weiss, a good-natured, compassionate man, didn't comprehend, at first, the extent of Bibbs's rage. He believed he could bring about a rapprochement between father and son. After all, he reasoned, Bibbs had only two sons. Two natural sons. And one of them was a troubled fellow, a misfit. But Jimmy was exactly in Bibbs's image. An intelligent, tough, well-spoken businessman. Surely Bibbs didn't mean to destroy him. Even if he did have Van and the adopted son, Bruce. Blood was blood. Maybe, Weiss reasoned, if he could get Bibbs to see his grandchildren, Jimmy's daughters, he'd come around, settle the suit.

Weiss called Bibbs, and the two of them went to lunch at Stark's in Great Neck. He begged him to see his grandchildren— the two little girls were about three and six, and he hadn't seen them in close to a year, not since the litigation had begun. He told Bibbs he owed it to his own father—a cantor—to see his grandchildren, his descendants, his only true lineage.

Bibbs was surprisingly affected by Weiss's entreaties. He not only paid the whole lunch bill, but he promised he'd see the little girls. Take them out somewhere. He'd have to take them out, rather than have them visit, he explained, because his wife didn't want them in her home.

Not long afterward, Weiss heard about the visit—not from Bibbs, but from his lawyers. Bibbs, they said, had spent an afternoon with his granddaughters. But he hadn't enjoyed it. He'd felt a wall between them.

Weiss shook his head. Bibbs made that wall, he thought. How could two little girls erect a barrier against a grandfather? But Bibbs hadn't considered his own culpability in the building of the wall, or he'd chosen not to consider it. He'd simply decided that his granddaughters had become strangers to him. It was sad. And sadder still was the fact that Bibbs said he didn't think he'd care to see them again. Not ever.

The lawsuit between Jimmy and Bibbs dragged on for months and months, but in the end, Jimmy was the victor. He won release from having to pay the annuity. Bibbs was frantic, furious, besotted with rage. He told Sol that he rued the day that Jimmy had ever been conceived. And he began to focus whatever fatherly feelings might be said still to beat in his steely breast on Jeanette's children. Not just Bruce, but Joy too, despite the fact that for years he hadn't cared for her. He would show Jimmy, he decided. He would cut him out of his will. Him and his daughters too. They were dead, as far as he was concerned. He didn't need them, He had Bruce. And Joy.

She'd gotten married again, at last. Jeffrey and Pamela had

finally divorced, and Joy, after a small and simple wedding, had become the new Mrs. Silverman.

The year that Joy married Jeffrey—it was 1977—Joan got her master's degree in social work and immediately became the director of the mental health and geriatric clinics of the Little Neck YM-YWHA. That same year, some New York Republicans who were beginning to think about the next year's upcoming gubernatorial race started to bandy about Sol's name.

Sol had acted differently from other judges on the court of appeals. Whereas they tended to settle down to their fourteen-year terms, eschewing further politicking, he had continued to court the spotlight and make himself politically known. He had regularly attended dinners and fund-raisers and had become a much-sought-after speaker at these functions. It was easy to see why. His speeches were always a perfect blend of down-to-earth humor and high-minded inspirational phrases. Audiences loved them and the handsome, distinguished judge too.

Sol, on his part, loved his audiences. He thrived on the sounds of their chuckling when he told a joke, reveled in the way they nodded their heads in solemn agreement when he turned earnest. It was always reassuring to be reminded that he was still popular, that he was still the Great Jewish Hope of the Republican party, the man who embodied all the noble liberal ideals of his mentor, Nelson Rockefeller. Invigorated by his audiences, Sol listened seriously to those who thought he ought to run for governor in 1978.

Joe Margiotta scotched the idea. He wasn't sure Sol could get the nomination. The conservative wing of the party wasn't likely to go for Sol, he said. And besides, the state assembly's minority leader had locked up the nomination months ago. He had so many IOUs out around the state, it would be virtually impossible to defeat him in a primary.

Sol, cautioned, decided not to try for the nomination. But he continued to speak whenever he was asked. He's got an extraordinary desire for praise, one of his staff members thought when Sol went on giving speeches even though he was no longer likely to be a candidate. It's an all-consuming passion. He has to be fed constantly with applause and admiration, or else he goes empty and hungry.

Jeffrey Silverman had made a lot of money in his career as an investor, but he'd lost a lot of money too. He was in one of his down times when he married Joy, and although he still had a limousine and a chauffeur, he couldn't afford the kind of apartment he and Joy both wanted, something big and splashy on Park or Fifth. Instead, he moved into the apartment Joy had been living in for several years, a two-bedroom flat on Third Avenue.

Joy may have been disappointed at having to live as a married woman in the abode of her single days, but the marriage brought her contentment in another area. After her abortion at New York Hospital, she had tried to content herself with just little Evan. But she had yearned for another child, a girl she could costume and pamper the way her mother had costumed and pampered her. In 1978, she was able to attain this heart's desire. She and Jeffrey adopted a little girl, a blond-haired, blue-eyed baby who was so perfect in body and temperament that Jeanette dubbed her "the computer baby."

But apparently Joy wasn't altogether at peace. Apparently a part of her was still on the lookout for adventure, romance, and perhaps even another husband, a more perfect one than Jeffrey. This is the view of a dynamic, exceedingly prosperous financier who met her at a party in the late seventies. According to him, he and Joy talked for a while, and when the party was over, she called a mutual friend to make inquiries about him. Was he available? Was he as successful as he seemed to be?

The friend answered yes to both questions, and soon afterward, when Joy and the financier met at another party, he says he picked up signals that she was sexually interested in him.

The financier remembers getting uneasy. Joy was smiling at him, touching him, telling him he was brilliant. And he remembers thinking, I don't want to fool around with her. She's too aggressive. And she looks like trouble, looks like the type who gets hysterical and demanding.

He tried to discourage Joy's interest subtly, without saying anything that would hurt her feelings. But it didn't work. The next time they met, she was all over him again, and he finally had to let her know, in no uncertain terms, that she wasn't his type.

No, he didn't have a middle name, Sol told a reporter in 1979. The fact that his name appeared with the middle initial *M* on his paychecks and in official state records was all a big mistake. But maybe he ought to accept the error that had been made. "What would be a good impressive name to match the initial?" he asked the reporter rhetorically. And then he answered his own question. "There's always Macbeth," he said.

Why Macbeth? Why the name of a man who had stood high in the opinion of all men, yet ended by reaping their curses and contempt? It was, of course, a joke. But perhaps jokes, like slips of the tongue, can be guides to hidden thoughts.

A number of Sol's friends would eventually postulate this, pointing to certain of his favorite jokes. There was the one he told on himself about how he'd felt proud to sit on the court of appeals at the desk once occupied by the great Benjamin Cardozo, only to be brought up short by Joan, who'd remind him that fifty years from now, it would still be remembered as Cardozo's desk. And there was the one about how, when he first ran for a judgeship, his mother said to him, "You mean they know you, Sol? They know you, and they *still* want you to be a judge?"

But revelatory as Sol's self-deprecating jokes might eventually come to seem, in the late seventies they were taken by his friends as signs of his unassumingness. He's accomplished so much, they would say, yet he can still poke fun at himself, still be humble. And indeed, to all outward appearances, he was a fan of humility. One of his favorite stories was the Yiddish folktale of the porter Bontscha Schvaig, a man so modest that although he is beaten and starved, he asks for nothing, no help at all, his whole life long, and even in death, when angels reward his forbearance by offering him anything in paradise he wants, requests only a roll and butter.

Bontscha, Sol told people, was his talisman. He so loved the story that he hung a drawing of Bontscha on the walls of his chambers.

Joy needed things, things she couldn't get from Jeffrey. But there was always Bibbs. When she wanted extra money, she went to him. And generally, he gave her what she wanted. Years later, she'd tell Sol Wachtler that she'd learned over the years just how to get Bibbs to agree. She'd telephone him and make her demand, and if he didn't say yes right away, she'd get angry, and sometimes she'd threaten to report him to the IRS.

Generally, Bibbs capitulated. He wanted desperately to keep peace in his home and to make Jeanette happy, and the way to keep the peace and make Jeanette happy was to give Joy what she wanted.

He was still in love with Jeanette. But in 1980, he realized he was going to lose her. She had stomach cancer.

She fought the illness with all her strength, doing whatever the doctors advised, and, with the flair she'd always shown, drove around Great Neck in her white Bentley, a dramatic white turban atop her balding head. But after a while, the cancer got the better of her, and she became weak and fragile. Still, she never lost her fierce desire to provide for her children. "It's too bad we can't kill Bibbs a few minutes before I die," she joked to Joy shortly before her death. "That way, you'd never have to worry. His money would go to me and then directly to you and Bruce."

When Jeanette died, Joy was inconsolable. She had been so close to, so intimately connected with, her mother. Her mother had been mother *qnd* father to her, she told friends. Her mother had been not only her nurturer but her protector, the only person who had ever really looked out for her. After her death, Joy put a memorial announcement in the *Times,* saying she would miss her and remember her always, and every year afterward on the anniversary of her death, she declared her love in yet another ad, as if trying to reach Jeanette in the great beyond.

In 1981, Mario Cuomo, the lieutenant governor of New York, began to consider challenging his boss, Governor Hugh Carey, and undertaking his own run for governor in the next year's election. Cuomo had made good friends in Albany, one of whom was Sol Wachtler. The two of them, along with a few other friends, frequently played poker together, and they dined together several times a week. One night early in 1981, they went to a friend's birthday party. The party lasted long into the night, and there were hours of jokes and discussions. Cuomo came away from the party convinced that Sol was eager to run for governor on the Republican ticket. Would the two of them be up against each other? Cuomo didn't know, but one thing he did know was that Sol would make a good candidate.

There were plenty of others—plenty of Republicans—who shared that view. Since the last gubernatorial election, Sol had been adding to the luster of his name by writing major decisions in matters that weren't arcane but affected the lives of many ordinary citizens in the state, and while some judicial experts viewed his decisions as being far too pragmatic and too much influenced by considerations of public opinion, the public naturally applauded them.

In one case, he had written a majority opinion that held that employees who were forced to quit their jobs because of racial intolerance were entitled to back pay. In another, he had written a dissent about a two-year-old boy who had been removed from his foster parents' care and put up for adoption, even though the foster parents wanted to adopt him. The child had to be taken away, the majority of the court had ruled, because that was the arrangement the foster parents had agreed to when they got the boy. Sol, disagreeing, said that in the pursuit of orderliness, the court had overlooked the interests of the most important person in the case, the child—a decision that garnered so much favorable publicity that although the Department of Social Services in Nassau won the case, they reversed their position and let the boy remain with his foster parents.

In another important case, Sol had disagreed with the majority of the court when it ruled that medical life support for a severely retarded man, whose mother had petitioned his doctors to let him die, could be discontinued. Sol was generally in favor of letting seriously ill people decide if they wanted to go on living, but in this case, where the wishes of the patient couldn't be determined, he refused to go along with the court, telling his staff that the case reminded him of World War II and the Nazis.

His staff disagreed with him. But Sol held fast—and again, a large segment of the public approved his decision.

Sol had also once again been courting political attention by making speeches wherever he was asked to talk. "We know where crime is born, where it grows and where it thrives," he had told an audience of lawyers and legislators in December. "It grows in slums amid squalor and poverty. It grows in ignorance and it thrives on hopelessness." And, "The greatest responsibility for our national welfare does not rest with statutes carved in stone," he had told an audience of judges, "but with the principles, conscience, and morality of the individuals who constitute this generation and with the judges who have been charged by them with the responsibility of administering the law, free from the passions of the moment and free from the passions of the crowd."

Some people didn't like his speeches or even his demeanor at legal and judicial conferences. He had a reverent, even a pious, attitude toward the dignity of his profession, they argued. He was pretentious, and false.

But if he had critics, he had far more admirers. And many of those who admired him believed that he would be an exceedingly effective campaigner—especially if the Republicans had to run someone against the Democrats' master orator, Mario Cuomo.

Sol, however, didn't know if he wanted to run. All he knew was that he was restless. He'd been on the court of appeals nearly ten years now, and a certain sameness, a dreadful flatness, had crept into his life. Perhaps part of the burnout he felt was the result not just of doing the same kind of work over and over again but of something deeper, more personal. Perhaps part of his feeling of dullness had to do with the desiccation that was his sexual life. He and Joan had stopped making love. They had stopped altogether.

He didn't go seeking other women in order to relieve his sexual frustration. He was too afraid of scandal for that—although he may have been intrigued by a woman who, he would one day say, "made a play for me." She may have been a waitress. While Jeanette was still alive, her sister-in-law Elsie—Joan Wachtler's mother—told her that her son-in-law was having a dalliance with an Albany waitress named Dorothy, and Jeanette passed the gossip along to Joy.

But according to Sol and those who knew him best, he was celibate, a man who had never put sex at the top of his list of priorities and wasn't about to do so now. Instead, he kept himself distracted by devising pranks, antic little jokes that amused him and brought a smile to the lips of the people to whom he confided them.

Some of his pranks were harmless little things, like his habit of coming to court wearing toe socks and no shoes under his judicial robes, or his jest of naming the cabin cruiser he kept back home on Long Island Sound the *Felony I,* and its successor the *Felony II.* But some of his pranks were not small but elaborate, and not entirely harmless. Like the one he had devised to embarrass Fuchsberg, the judge he had for years detested. Sol and a group of other judges, including Fuchsberg, had been planning to go to dinner, as they often did, at the Century Club in Albany, a club that did not admit women. At the last minute, Fuchsberg had sent word that he wouldn't be coming. Sol and his fellow judges rendezvoused there anyway, only to discover that a group of Manhattan reporters and photographers were present, recording the names of legislators and judges who were dining in the segregated club.

Sol was convinced that Fuchsberg had gotten wind of the presence of the journalists and that that was why he had canceled—and he was annoyed that Fuchsberg hadn't alerted the rest of them. So, then and there, Sol devised a bit of vengeance. He asked one of the waiters to page Fuchsberg. Then he directed an upstate judge whose face was not likely to be familiar to the downstate press to answer the page, passing himself off as Fuchsberg. The prank worked. The reporters heard Fuchsberg being paged. Then after a while, they saw a dignified man get up and answer the page. They reported—just as Sol had imagined they would—that Fuchsberg, too, had eaten that night at the segregated club.

Games like these—a member of his staff called them ''Sol's

little scams"—had kept him entertained in the past few years. But essentially, he was bored and ready to move on, except that he wasn't sure he wanted the strain and stress of being a candidate. Having to beg for money. Having fingers pointed in his face. In addition, Joan didn't want him to run. She didn't want to take time off from her social work job to go campaigning. She had her own life now.

Still, despite all the negatives, he let the courtship by his party proceed. After all, this time around, Margiotta thought he might be able to make it. He'd tried to get Sol to run and promised him his full support. But Margiotta's support didn't have quite the cachet it had had before. The old Nassau power broker had been indicted for mail fraud and extortion. According to prosecutors in the federal district court in Westbury, Long Island, he'd dispensed half-a-million-dollars' worth of Nassau County insurance commissions to politicians who did little or no work for the money.

In March 1981, Margiotta was put on trial. Sol went to court to testify in his behalf, an event that troubled some of Sol's friends, one of whom wondered, "Why does my high-minded friend Sol have such a tolerance, even an appetite, for the Margiottas of this world?"

On the stand, Sol was forced to admit that Margiotta had played a prominent role in getting him his seat on the court of appeals. And when the prosecutor then suggested that the corrupt politician would play a leading role in Sol's life if he sought the Republican nomination for governor next year, Sol must have thought he was in deep trouble, for he said he had no intention of running.

But he did. He still did. And it wasn't until September that he finally announced, firmly and definitively, that he had decided not to seek the nomination but to remain on the court of appeals.

By that time, Mario Cuomo had become fairly certain that he was going to run. He had started conducting polls and raising funds. And, according to a widely circulated rumor, he had promised Sol he would name him chief judge when the present chief stepped down in two years. Whether true or false, the gossip in

Albany held that this was Cuomo's way of keeping Sol, whose liberal views were so similar to his own, out of the race.

Bibbs had been broken up about Jeanette's death, but, in the way of wealthy widowers, he soon enough found solace in the arms of a new attractive woman. Her name was Honey. Tall, dark-haired, and dimpled, she'd been a friend of Jeanette's. The couple's was truly a storybook romance, for Bibbs, despite the lawsuits he'd lost and the money he'd lavished on Jeanette, was still a very rich man, and Honey a woman of modest means. She had almost no money, and even less jewelry. Indeed, Jeanette, who had been a generous friend, had been in the habit of letting Honey borrow *her* baubles to wear to special events. Honey took comfort in Bibbs's strength and generosity. Bibbs took comfort in Honey's familiarity and her pleasant nature. And two years after Jeanette's death, he married her.

CHAPTER 6

Bibbs made a new will shortly after he married Honey. He left $100,000 in trust for Van, for whom he had already established several large trusts, and nothing to his son James or to James's daughters. He left Bruce an outright gift of $103,000, and $2,012,000 in trust. He left Joy an outright gift of $100,000, and $2,800,000 in trust. But Honey was the big winner. Bibbs bequeathed to her his seaside apartment in Palm Beach, two of his automobiles, a $3,500,000 trust, and an outright gift of over $4,000,000. He also made her coexecutor of his estate, along with Sol.

Joy didn't know the terms of Bibbs's will. But she was aware of the attachment that had sprung up between him and his new wife and worried that, as a result, he might decide not to leave any money to her. "Did he love my mother? Did he really love my mother?" she kept asking a secretary who worked in Bibbs's office. But Bibbs *had* loved her mother, and he still cared for his stepdaughter, and when, one day, she asked him to lend Jeffrey a large sum of money so that he could buy some stocks, he agreed to do so.

The stocks were those of a small building-materials company called Ply-Gem. Jeffrey had already invested in the company, but he wanted to take it over. Bibbs lent him the amount he needed to do so, and in 1982, Jeffrey became Ply-Gem's controlling shareholder.

Not long afterward, through a series of clever acquisitions and the development of new products, Jeffrey built Ply-Gem into a major do-it-yourself home-improvement company, and Joy found herself married, at last, to a very rich man.

Van Wolosoff, who had about him some of the saintly qualities of Dostoyevsky's Prince Myshkin, wasn't interested in riches. In 1983 one of the trusts Bibbs had established for him was due to come to its end and deliver to him a sum of more than four million dollars. Bibbs thought his younger son, who was already in his forties, wouldn't be able to handle that amount of wealth and asked Sol, who was still serving as his adviser, to speak to Van about letting the trust be renewed. Sol, inviting Van to his chambers, did as Bibbs suggested. "What would you do with this money if you came into it?" he asked.

Van pointed to a court officer who was assigned to guard Sol, and said, "I'd give it to him."

Sol wasn't sure Van had altogether understood his question. "You'd give *him* four million dollars?" he asked incredulously.

"Yes," Van said. "I just want enough money to live on, a couple of hundred dollars a month. That's all I want."

The rest of Bibbs's children were not eager to live as frugally as Van, and after he'd been married to Honey for a while, Bibbs got increasingly annoyed with the way they were draining his estate. Especially Joy—according to Sol. He remembered Bibbs saying to him in 1984, in a phrase inadvertently echoing what Dick Simons had complained of years earlier, "If you give her a million dollars today, she'll be broke tomorrow." One day that year, Bibbs decided to make yet another new will, this one reducing Joy's share of his estate considerably, and he asked Shea and Gould, the law firm that handled his estate, to draw it up.

The new will was drafted but never signed. On a hot summer's day, not long after he'd given instructions about the document, Bibbs decided to cool off by taking a swim in his shimmering pool. He put on his bathing trunks and headed through the kitchen for the pool. Suddenly he felt something grip his chest. He couldn't stand, let alone walk. A moment later, he collapsed on the kitchen floor. And shortly afterward, a doctor pronounced him dead, the victim of a massive heart attack.

Sol went to Bibbs's funeral, a big one that was held at the Nassau North Chapel in Great Neck. He paid his respects to the grieving widow and said a few comforting words to each of the children. One of them he hardly remembered. It was the girl. Jeanette's daughter, Joy. He hadn't seen her for, to his best recollection, nearly twenty years. She had changed. Grown chic in her middle thirties. Sophisticated.

He saw her again several days later when he went to Bibbs's house to pay a condolence call. He had his daughters Alison and Lauren with him, but he left them downstairs and went upstairs with Van, Bruce, and Joy to tell them about Bibbs's will. They all sat down on the bed in Van's room, and he told them the extent of the estate, what their shares of it were going to be, and that he and Honey would be the cotrustees.

Joy—Sol would one day recall—exploded at the news. "Why Honey?" she cried. "Why should Honey be cotrustee?"

He started to explain, but she interrupted, saying, "That's ridiculous! That's absurd!"

The terms of the will, he started to tell her.

"Why should I have to go to Honey for money!" she exclaimed. *"Honey?* You mean, I have to be responsible to *Honey?"*

He wondered how she would have reacted if the will he was telling her about had been the new one instead, the one cutting her out almost entirely. As it was, his cousin Joy was so upset and excited, she appeared to be hyperventilating. It was only after a while that she calmed down. But at last she did, and went downstairs and made small talk with his daughters about her astrologer.

In December 1984, Lawrence Cooke, the chief judge of the court of appeals, retired from the bench, and Mario Cuomo, now the governor of New York, appointed Sol to replace him. The job of chief judge was an exceedingly important one in New York, and entailed not only presiding over the court of appeals but administering the state's huge court system, in which there were some three thousand judges and twelve thousand nonjudicial employees. Sol's name had been on a list of seven worthy candidates who had been suggested by a judicial nominating commission, but the governor's advisers had given serious consideration to only two of the people on the list—Sol and Milton Mollen, presiding judge of one of the state's appellate divisions.

Both men had been checked out thoroughly, one senior adviser recalled, and nothing but good had been heard about either one, so the advisory team had been at a loss as to which of them would be the best choice. But the senior adviser began pushing for Sol. There was a downside to Mollen, he argued. Mollen was a friend of the corrupt Brooklyn political boss Meade Esposito. Sol was a friend of a corrupt political boss too—the now out-of-jail Margiotta. But Margiotta wasn't as bad as Esposito, the adviser contended. And besides, choosing Sol would make Cuomo look good, because Sol was a Republican, and it would show that the governor was above petty partisan politics.

Cuomo may have been influenced by this view. Or he may have chosen Sol simply because, as he explained in a radio interview, "If you look at the law [governing the requirements for the job of chief judge], it speaks in terms of experience. Judicial aptitude. Character. I think that on every criterion Wachtler scored higher than everybody else."

Whatever Cuomo's reasons, his choice was met with great enthusiasm, and on January 1, 1985, Sol Wachtler became New York State's chief judge.

At the time Sol began heading up the court of appeals, Joy was leading a life that resembled that of the majority of American women in the 1950s, but not that of many women, at least those of her age and economic background, in the 1980s. Daytimes, she shopped, attended to her beauty needs, visited her astrologist and her psychic, lunched with friends, and mothered her children. Evan was fifteen now, Jessica seven. As often as she could, Joy would escort Jessica home from school, driving to her private academy, Nightingale-Bamford, in Jeffrey's stretch limousine and scooping her into the vehicle the moment she was dismissed— rather, the mother of one of Jessica's classmates thought, as if the little girl were a princess or a child film star.

Evenings, Joy went to dinner parties and to the theater with Jeffrey or entertained his friends and business colleagues at home. But Jeffrey was often out of town. When he was, she spent a lot of time in her bedroom, watching TV.

She wasn't happy, and she complained about her life to certain friends. "There are a lot of things I want that I don't have," she said to one, a young lawyer named Kathy Greenberg, who worked at Shea and Gould, where she handled the details of Bibbs's estate.

The two women were lunching at the expensive and exclusive Le Cirque, and amid all the restaurant's posh and plenty, Joy's negativism struck Kathy as unnecessarily self-pitying. "You have everything, Joy," she told her.

"You mean everything money can buy?" Joy responded, gloomy.

"No, not just everything money can buy. You also have all the things money *can't* buy. Children. A husband. Love."

Joy frowned. "Whatever," she said. "I'm still miserable."

Lunch was grand. But Joy's gloom didn't lift.

"I don't want Honey to be the cotrustee of my trust," Joy said to Sol one day around this time. She had come to see him in his chambers in Mineola. He remembers listening to her arguments patiently, just as he listened to legal arguments in court. But his cousin Joy was different from the lawyers he was used to listening to. She was excitable, emotional. She got so mad when she talked about Honey that she became a little breath-less, huffing and panting in indignation. She resented Honey, it was plain to Sol. And she felt that in making Honey cotrustee of her money, Bibbs had played a trick on her. He'd left her lots of money, but he'd put her in the position of having to get it doled out, bit by bit, by someone with whom she couldn't get on at all. "Bibbs hated me," she complained.

It was hard for Sol to see why.

"He always hated me."

To Sol, despite her excitability—or maybe because of it—Joy seemed immensely worthwhile. Charming. He promised her he'd look into the possibility of getting Honey to resign.

"I think Jeffrey's fooling around," Joy told Kathy Greenberg one day.

Kathy tried to reassure her: Perhaps Joy was just worrying, imagining.

"Maybe, but I'm having him spied on when he goes out of town."

And then, a bit later, she asked Kathy, "Does Sol Wachtler fool around?"

Kathy found the question offensive and reported it to Sol's daughter Lauren, who was also a lawyer at Shea and Gould. Lauren had a good laugh about it. Her father, as far as she knew, was the most straitlaced man imaginable. He didn't even like it when his kids told off-color jokes.

What should he call Joy? Sol wondered. His niece? She was the right age for a niece, thirty-eight to his fifty-five, but she wasn't the child of a sibling of his or Joan's. She was Joan's uncle's child. Stepchild. That made her Joan's cousin. Stepcousin. And his cousin-by-marriage. Stepcousin-by-marriage. But that sounded so distant. And so unimportant. A stepcousin-by-marriage wasn't much of a relative, wasn't much of a connection. Perhaps, he decided after a while, he ought to call Joy his ward. It was an old-fashioned designation. Dickensian. It conjured up images of men in tall hats and girls in bonnets and crinolines. But it seemed right. She was, as the word *ward* meant, a person under his protection—his financial protection, at least.

In an effort to make her happy with that protection, he talked to Honey about resigning her cotrusteeship. He could handle all the work on his own, he told her. What did she need the headaches for?

Honey saw the sense to what he was saying. Clearly, Sol knew more about financial matters than she knew. Or cared to know.

She told him she'd be happy to resign and leave everything in his capable hands.

When she agreed to resign, he thought how happy the news would make Joy. And a short while later, he dreamed up a way to make Joy even happier. He'd make a delightful little game for Joy out of Honey's resignation, he decided. He'd *give* her the resignation. Literally. He'd get Honey to sign the proper document, and he'd wrap it up and present it to Joy on her birthday. It would be fun, the kind of fun he used to invent for his girls on their birthdays.

Joy's birthday was April 8. Prior to that date, he got Honey to sign the resignation document, and when April 8 itself came around, he filed it with the surrogate's court. Then he hand-delivered a copy of the document to Joy.

What a gift! She was thrilled. He'd given her the *best* present ever, she said. He'd given her just what she'd wanted.

In the next few months, according to Sol, Joy began asking him for assistance and advice in all sorts of matters. Would he meet her at Bibbs's house—it had better be sometime when Honey wasn't there—so she could collect some of her possessions? There was a set of Porthault tea linens she especially wanted, and a Chinese porcelain figure, and a copy of a Jackson Pollock painting. Should she and Jeffrey buy a new apartment? They'd seen one they liked on Park Avenue in the Eighties, but she wasn't sure they'd get past the co-op board. Could he help them? Recommend them? And while he was at it, could he use his influence to get the board to let her keep her dog, her darling little bichon frise, whom she'd named after the great designer—did he know the clothes of Coco Chanel?

Sol helped her with all her questions and requests. He also began making suggestions to her about her future, about how she ought to be doing something more than just being Jeffrey's wife and Evan and Jessica's mother. "You should go back to school," he told her.

"I don't want to go back to school," she explained. "I hate to read."

"Then you ought to get a job," he recommended. "It'd be good for you."

She listened to him, her big eyes fixed on his, and said she'd think about it.

He liked giving her advice. Advising young people was a role he was used to, a part he'd played in the lives of each of his children. But they no longer seemed to need him very much. They were all off and on their own. Just like Joan.

James Wolosoff had grown used to the idea that Bibbs, against whom he had fought and often won so many battles, was dead, but one thing he couldn't grow used to was the way that, in the end, his father had humiliated him, triumphed over him. It wasn't just that he'd divided up the bulk of his estate among relative strangers—a new wife, children and grandchildren who were not really his—but that he'd left money to all sorts of peripheral people. Ten thousand dollars to his chauffeur. Ten thousand dollars to his secretary. Even ten thousand dollars to the former superintendent of his Kew Garden Hills apartment development. But nothing, just as he'd threatened, to his firstborn son.

Raring to do battle once again, albeit this time with a ghost, a hand from the grave with its middle finger pointed straight up, James consulted with Allen Weiss, the lawyer who had helped him win his lawsuit against his father back in 1979.

Weiss thought they had a chance at overturning Bibbs's will. They could argue, he told James, that Bibbs hadn't been in his right mind when he'd cut him out. He didn't mean that Bibbs hadn't been in his right mind in the way that estate lawyers generally used the phrase. Customarily, he explained, they applied it to people who made their wills when they were senile or demented. But clearly Bibbs had been suffering from a mental problem—"I call it monomania," Weiss said—when he made his will. The monomania, the pathological obsession that had dominated Bibbs's brain, had been a maniacal hate. He had detested James ever since the lawsuit. His hatred for James had become so powerful a psychic force that it had caused him to lack testamentary capacity, had interfered with his ability to think rationally. Not in all areas. Just in this one.

Would he be able to prove it? Weiss, remembering how irrationally Bibbs had behaved about his two innocent little granddaughters, James's girls, thought he could.

He'd start by examining the court of appeals' new chief judge, Sol Wachtler. Wachtler was the executor of Bibbs's estate. Bibbs had been so clever, it was possible he'd appointed Wachtler just because he'd expected that Jimmy would want to contest the will, and he'd wanted to make certain his son's efforts failed. He'd no doubt figured that simply having Wachtler as executor would discourage any contest. What lawyer would have the guts to challenge a will whose executor was a member of the court of appeals!

Well, *he* did, Weiss decided. And if he did, Wachtler would probably have to step down from being Bibbs's executor. There was a provision in the state code of judicial conduct that stated that while a judge could serve as executor for a family member's will, he was supposed to disqualify himself if a will was disputed and he sat on a court that might get involved in the litigation. Which surely included the court of appeals, since any litigation in the state could potentially end up there.

In November, in the Mineola courthouse in which Sol had sat as a judge for so many years, Weiss called upon him to testify concerning Bibbs's testamentary capacity. During the examination, Wachtler didn't seem particularly discomfited by the fact that, as chief judge of the State of New York, he wasn't supposed to serve as executor of a will that was on the verge of being contested. Rather, he volunteered, without even being asked, that back when Bibbs asked him to be his executor, he'd not only checked the law but asked his colleagues on the court of appeals whether they thought he ought to disqualify himself, and neither he nor they had seen any reason for him to do so.

Weiss could have gone after him, could have pointed out that that was *then* and this was *now,* and back then Bibbs was still alive and the will wasn't being contested, whereas now it was going to be. But he let the matter ride. Wachtler was using the politically powerful firm Shea and Gould as his counsel, and Raymond Radigan, the surrogate court judge hearing the case, had a son who worked at Shea and Gould. He was also a friend of Wachtler's. So Weiss just skipped to the meat of what he wanted to get at—that Bibbs had been so consumed by hatred for Jimmy that he hadn't been able to think straight. And on that score, Wachtler's testimony helped him out. The father and son had been so at loggerheads, Wachtler testified, that he hadn't dared mention Jimmy in Bibbs's presence. "You don't speak of rope," he said, "in a hangman's house."

At the end of his examination of Wachtler, Weiss notified the surrogate court that he would, indeed, be filing objections to Bibbs's will, and that they would be based on monomania.

Fathers and sons. Sons and fathers. In December, Dick Simons, who was in New York for a hospital examination, saw his son Evan standing on a streetcorner near the hospital. Although the boy was now fifteen and he hadn't seen him for years, he was sure it was him. Evan played with his sister's children, and sometimes she sent down pictures of him. A lanky kid with dark brown hair and big green eyes. How he missed him!

He hadn't seen him because Joy hadn't let him. At first, he used to call and tell her he wanted to fly up and visit Evan on such-and-such a day and she'd say okay and he'd come north, but then, when he'd arrive at her house, she'd be gone. And the boy too. Vanished. Out of town. After a few bouts of that, he'd taken to writing to Evan, telling him he loved him and wanted to see him. But the boy never wrote back. Dick figured Joy was confiscating his letters. But he couldn't be sure. Maybe the kid just wanted nothing to do with him. So in the end, he'd just stopped trying to see Evan. But now, here the boy was, standing on First Avenue just a few feet away from him. "Evan! Hey, Evan!" he called out, his heart racing. "It's me. It's your father!"

Evan heard him. Dick was sure he heard him. But to his chagrin, the boy started running away. He darted across the street, his lean legs pumping.

"Evan! Wait up!" Dick shouted, his voice soaring above the traffic noises. But he didn't run after his son. He felt unable to move. Felt like he'd been kicked in the stomach. He stood there on the avenue and his heart sank and he told himself, Let him go. Let him go. Clearly the kid wants nothing to do with me.

A moment later, the boy had vanished around a corner.

Dick never saw him again. But there was no question that the fleet youth who had darted away from him was his son. Soon after their encounter, he heard from his sister that Evan had told her children, his cousins, about the incident. He told them his father had spotted him and tried to talk to him, and that he'd run away, run as fast as he could. It was like an instinct, his running. But he was sorry about it now. Or sorry, anyway, that his father had just let him go. He wished, he told his cousins, that his father had sprinted after him, caught up with him. Made him stop running.

At Christmastime Jimmy Wolosoff went down to the Caribbean, touring the islands in a sailboat. Allen Weiss went to Florida.

He'd been there only a few days when he received a call from Judge Radigan. "I think I can settle this case," Radigan said. "Get ahold of your client."

It took a while to find Jimmy. Weiss had no idea exactly where on the high seas he was. But at last, he reached him, and as soon as the holidays were over, the two of them went out to Mineola for a settlement conference. Usually, law clerks preside at such conferences, but at this one, Radigan himself was presiding. "This case should be settled," he said.

It was clear that Wachtler wanted it settled. To make sure that it was, he was offering Jimmy a tax-free settlement of four hundred thousand dollars.

Jimmy didn't want to take it, at least not at first. But Weiss thought he should. He pointed out that they were going to have an uphill battle proving Bibbs's monomania, and that their suit was liable to drag on for a long time. So in the end, Jimmy said okay. And that was that. He took the money. His father had cheated him—but not as completely as he had planned.

"I'm going to get a job," Joy told Sol proudly one day, after the fight over Bibbs's will had been averted.

"What sort of a job?" he questioned her.

"With the mayor of New York," she said. "Picking up dignitaries at the airport." She didn't mention that her mother had done the same sort of thing years ago, when Joy was little, for the mayor of Newark. "I'll use Jeffrey's limo and chauffeur," she explained, "and it'll be interesting. I'll meet interesting people."

Sol remembers thinking it wasn't such a hot idea. "You're going to run a taxi service?" he said disapprovingly. Then he told her, "Joy, you have far too much talent to waste your time doing something like that."

"Then what should I do?" she asked him. "Think of something for me."

"I will," he promised. "I will."

He was still mulling over her future when, in 1986, he bought a house and land in Albany. He'd been living, when he was up there, in a condominium apartment, but ever since he'd become chief judge, he'd been spending more and more time in the capital and the apartment had begun to seem too confining. Having a house would give him greater comfort, he thought, and it would provide Joan and the kids with a destination for their summer vacations.

The house he chose was small, a rustic little place with only two bedrooms, but the land was extensive, nineteen acres of woods and fields. He set up a picnic area and a ball field for the kids, and for Joan, who loved to swim and walk, he put in a lap pool and hiking trails. He also took up gardening, planting rows and rows of bushes and flowers.

Gardening became his passion, satisfied a yearning he had not quite known he had and could hardly put into words. He spent a lot of time at it.

One day not long after Sol had bought the house in Albany, Joan was with him in their home in Manhasset when a present arrived from Joy. It was for Sol—a huge gift basket from Abercrombie and Fitch that was stuffed with domestic items, among them a big woolly blanket and a clunky fireplace set.

106

Joan was used to Joy's sending Sol gifts—she sometimes joked to her children: "It looks like Joy's pursuing your father, she sends him so many gifts."

So at first, when she looked at the basket and realized it was from her stepcousin, she was as amused as ever. It was only when she saw that it came from Abercrombie's that she blew up.

"These are the ugliest things I've ever seen," she said to Sol. "And it's absurd. Buying these kinds of items from Abercrombie's! Where they've got to cost a fortune. Why don't you return them and get yourself a gift certificate and buy something nice instead."

Sol didn't say anything, and Joan shook her head. "You know, Joy really is a stupid little girl."

PART 2

The Affair

CHAPTER 7

On a freezing Thursday in January 1987, Sol gave the keynote speech at a luncheon held by the Long Island Association, an organization that promoted the interests of Island businessmen. When he finished his speech—he'd talked about society's need to remedy the urban blight and poverty that were so often at the root of the crimes judges were asked to rule upon—a crowd of people thronged around him on the dais. He was fielding their questions and listening to their comments when he noticed Joy among them.

He was surprised to see her. She'd come to a number of his speaking engagements, and several times she'd turned up without giving him notice that she planned to attend. But today the weather was terrible. Snow had been circling down from the heavens all morning, and the weather bureau had declared the storm a blizzard. It had taken people considerable extra time to make their way to the luncheon, and it was going to take them hours and hours to get home. But there she was. She'd come despite the blizzard. He felt flattered. But he felt even better when she made her way closer to him and said, "You were *incredible!* You were fantastic!"

She kept him company while he made his farewells, and then,

as he headed down the steps, she took his hand. It was the first time he and she had ever touched.

She had, by then, taken the job with the mayor, and he had, by then, helped her figure out a more ambitious career to pursue. He'd pointed out to her that candidates for the 1988 presidential election were already launching their campaigns, that she and Jeffrey were by now wealthy enough to make major contributions and elicit them from their friends, and that if she played her cards right and backed a winner, she could end up with a job in the next president's Washington administration. Or even with an overseas ambassadorship. "There's nothing that wins the hearts of politicians more than funds," he told her, and promised he'd show her the ropes. "For example, you have to be seen at the right functions. But you've got to get the guest lists in advance so you can decide whether it's worthwhile going. Some you go, some you don't bother. And you never go unless you go with someone of significance, because you don't want to be buried. That's worse than not going at all."

He'd also suggested she put her money on Vice President George Bush.

She'd taken eagerly to his suggestions. And he had enjoyed playing Pygmalion to her Galatea. But he had not thought of her in an erotic way—not until she took his hand on the day of the blizzard.

Still, nothing sexual happened between them. Not for a long while. Only one thing changed as a result of their hand-holding: They began to telephone each other more often than they had before.

According to Sol, Joy was the chief telephoner. She called him every morning when he was up in Albany. She always called at 6:30 A.M., before he left his farmhouse to go to his chambers, and she'd tell him little things about her previous day's experiences or ask him political or financial questions or say again what an inspiring, wonderful speaker he was. He loved it when she did that.

She never called from her apartment. She left the apartment, telling her family she was going jogging, and dialed him from a pay phone on the street or, when the weather was inclement, from a luncheonette. She didn't want her calls to him, she explained, to show up on her phone bill.

Then one day she complained about having to carry change around with her. He gave her his telephone credit card number.

In February 1987, Joy and Jeffrey attended George Bush's first major fund-raiser in Manhattan, a New York Republican County Committee dinner at the Waldorf-Astoria. The ballroom of the hotel was packed that night, and the guests were feverish with enthusiasm for Bush. Joy was dressed to the nines, noticed a woman whose husband was a good friend of Bush's, and she was somewhat overjeweled. The clothes and the jewels were in excellent taste, but somehow the whole package didn't fit together. It's as if, the woman thought, Joy's a little girl playing dress-up in her mother's finery.

Joy wanted to come up to Albany and see him, Sol remembered. She told him this in one of her early morning calls, around the time she'd gone to the Bush fund-raiser. He thought that what she had in mind was observing how the court operated, so he said fine and suggested she bring Jessica and Evan. Kids were always fascinated by the workings of the court of appeals.

On the appointed afternoon, he had already taken his seat on the bench when she entered the courtroom. He expected her to be followed by Evan and Jessica and looked around the room for them, but they weren't there.

That gave him pause. But he didn't think long about their absence—perhaps because she looked utterly marvelous. Her full-bosomed figure was trim, her movements agile, and her lovely, mobile face alive with curiosity. He felt proud of her and turned to his good friend Judge Joseph Bellacosa, who occupied a chair right alongside him on the wide curved bench, and whispered, "That's my ward."

Judge Bellacosa was impressed. Raising his eyebrows, he scribbled something on a piece of paper. Sol glanced down at the paper. Bellacosa had scrawled, "Madonna mia!"

"Joe, I don't want to be alone with her," Sol recalled saying to Bellacosa later that afternoon, when they'd left the courtroom after the day's legal arguments. He'd told Joy he would take her out to dinner, but he was suddenly nervous about doing so. He was nervous because she was making, he believed, "a tremendous, tremendous rush" for him. He was nervous because, he also recalled, "I had never cheated in my life. I was straight as an arrow. And very critical of those men who strayed." He didn't even come on to women. "I never—never with one exception, [that] woman in upstate New York who used to make a play for me—I never, never, never made a pass at a woman." And except for that one woman, they didn't come on to him. "Well, yes, during campaigns. There was once a woman who slipped me a note saying, 'You can put your shoes under my bed any time you like.'" But basically, women were so uninterested in him that he "used to think there was something the matter with me. And then I thought, maybe it's because women *know*. They look at you, and say, 'This guy doesn't play around.' So they leave you alone."

Except for Joy. She'd been calling him all those early mornings and turning up unannounced at his speeches and at his chambers in Mineola.

Sol Wachtler didn't ask himself whether he was now sending out different signals from those he'd sent out all his life, signals that said yes, he was available. He simply focused on Joy's apparent desire for him. And in an odd reversal of traditional roles, seeing himself as a kind of virgin prince and Joy as the bold seducer, he worriedly asked Bellacosa where *he* was having dinner that night, hoping he could eat in the same place and thus preserve his virtue. When Bellacosa said, "Ogden's," which was a good restaurant set on the edge of the vast downtown plaza Rockefeller had built, Sol immediately said, "Look, make a reservation for me and Joy at a table near yours."

It would have been all right, he remembered, except that she didn't like the table. It was just inches from where Bellacosa was sitting with a friend. "I thought we were going to have dinner alone," she objected. "This is like a table for four." And before Sol could say anything, she called the headwaiter over and said, "Could you please get us a private table."

The waiter obliged. He put them at a table in a quiet, dark

corner of the restaurant. It was candlelit, and they ordered wine, and after he'd drunk some, Sol began to relax. They ate and drank, and they both began feeling happy, and when dinner was over, they went walking on Rockefeller's plaza, where he showed her the sights.

It was while they were strolling that they came across Jeffrey's limousine—Joy had driven up in it, chauffeured by Jeffrey's driver, Charlie—and Sol realized it was getting late. "You better get back," he remembered telling her. "You've got a three-hour drive in front of you. It'll be midnight before you get home."

"I can't," she said, "because Charlie is at the movies." She'd sent him there, she explained, so that he'd have something to do while she was dining.

Sol invited her up to his chambers, to pass the time till Charlie got back.

In his chambers, he showed her around the opulent quarters—two rooms for his staff and a vast wood-paneled one for himself, furnished with a leather-topped desk, a soft couch, and a hand-carved table, on which were displayed photographs of Joan and the children.

She admired his view and his furnishings, but his nervousness had returned, and he kept trying to get her to go home. Then he decided to be direct with her. He told her how much he liked her, but that he still loved his wife. He said he'd never been unfaithful and had no intentions of becoming so. "Did you ever read Keats's 'Ode on a Grecian Urn'?" he asked her. When she said she hadn't, he told her about how an ancient artist had sculpted on a vase the figures of a man and a woman, their hands almost, but not quite, touching, and how Keats had used that image to write about unconsummated love. The poet had elevated such love, made it seem the highest kind of love, he explained, for it could survive the centuries. " 'Bold Lover, never, never canst thou kiss,' " he quoted, " 'Though winning near the goal— yet, do not grieve; She cannot fade, though thou hast not thy bliss, Forever wilt thou love, and she be fair!' "

Had Joy understood him? Had she comprehended that he was telling her that he and she had to be like the figures on that vase, destined to go through eternity never touching? He spelled it out.

"That's how you and I have to lead our lives," he said. "Because I don't want to get involved, Joy."

She listened, but she wasn't sure she followed him, because when he finally convinced her to go home, she said, "But aren't you going to kiss me good night?" And although he'd wanted to be like the ancient Greek figure, a lover, yet chaste, a suitor free of the sullying physical connection, he didn't want to disappoint and thwart her, and he took her in his arms and kissed her.

It was a long, rapturous, exciting kiss. "A real kiss," he would say later, with some awe in his voice as if remembering the disappointing kiss he had written about in his school newspaper column so many years before.

The next day, Sol remembered, Joy called him and told him "how wonderful the kiss had been, and how much she'd loved it." But he was having misgivings. They'd started as soon as he and Joy had kissed. "After that kiss," he recalled, "I knew I was in trouble. I felt sordid." Now, he decided, he had to "break up with her." So he asked his secretary to find him a beautiful restaurant in the country, and he said to himself, This is going to be a good-bye restaurant.

His secretary picked a luxurious French establishment in Rye, a suburban town about thirty miles from New York City, and he himself drove all the way down from Albany to Manhattan to pick up Joy and escort her to the restaurant—perhaps because he liked the idea of treating her like a date, perhaps because he didn't want her to repeat her indiscretion of having Charlie drive her to a rendezvous with him.

He did a lot of saying good-bye over lunch. "You're a married woman, Joy," he told her. "And you're getting involved in big-league politics. The last thing in the world you need is scandal." He also reminded her, "I'm the chief judge. I've never—not ever—gone astray before. The last thing *I* need is scandal." Finally, he said, "Let's just cool it. Let's be friends. And let's not *do* anything. Please, Joy."

But Joy didn't seem to think much of his trying to set limits on their romantic future. "She said, 'One day at a time,'" he remembered. "'One day at a time. What's the sense of saying what's going to happen a month from now, six months from now? One day at a time.' "

Still, she agreed that for the time being, they'd just be friends.

Being friends, just friends, lasted only another week or two. Shortly after their lunch in Rye, Joy called Sol and told him she and her friend Paola Cohen were going to a health farm near Albany, and they'd like to drive over and see him. He said fine and asked her where the health farm was.

She said, "Monticello."

He said, "Monticello is nowhere near Albany. But wonderful, come on up."

They came. "What they did was," Sol recalled, "they registered at the health farm. Joy had purposely picked a place with no phones in the room, so Jeffrey couldn't check up on her. They registered there, and then they drove over to Albany and checked into the Susse Chalet, which is a motel near my house. Then Joy called and said, 'Paola and I are dying to see your house.' She'd wanted to see it on her last trip, but I'd kept telling her she couldn't—I just wasn't about to take her home. But now, she says she and Paola want to see the house. Okay. I went over to the motel to pick the two of them up. But only one of them came out. Joy. I said, 'Where's Paola?' She said, 'Paola's sleeping. She's exhausted.' "

He'd feel like a fool if he refused to take Joy to the house. And what, he asked himself, was he so afraid of, anyway? Then, "Okay, come on," he said. "I'll drive you over."

That afternoon, he and Joy made love for the first time. He liked it, loved the feel of her body and the imaginativeness with which she caressed him. He had never made love in the way he had with her. But afterward, his mind was in turmoil. He felt guilty toward Joan and guilty, too, toward Joy. "I felt awful. I felt bad—which shook me. I felt I'd led her on. That this would never amount to anything. And I started getting worried. There was that 'fatal attraction' syndrome out there, and I was worried that Joy—I mean, talk about irony!—I was worried that Joy would start—she was very aggressive. Very aggressive."

But despite his guilt and his fears, he wasn't sorry. That night, he let Joy and Paola check out of the Susse Chalet and move into his farmhouse.

Joy introduced Sol to a whole new world of sexuality, a panoply of pleasures that made intercourse seem dull and pedestrian. From that time on, his affair with Joy would be in the forefront of his mind. But he had other duties, other preoccupations. One that became pressing around the time of the start of his affair with Joy concerned a judge under his jurisdiction. A state commission on judicial conduct had recommended to Sol that the judge, fifty-six-year-old Bertram Gelfand, the Surrogate of Bronx County, be removed from the bench. Gelfand, a long-married husband and the father of three grown children, had been running for reelection when a woman who had worked for him and with whom he'd been having an affair accused him of sexual harassment—he'd fired her when she broke up with him, she said. And he'd made ugly and obscene phone calls to her, and tried to prevent her from obtaining another job.

Gelfand's lawyer, Milton Gould, had argued passionately that Gelfand hadn't done anything so terrible, had merely behaved "as many a jilted lover has before and will again—irrationally, emotionally, and unreasonably." And Gelfand's wife had written a supportive letter to the commission. "Put yourselves into the position of this man," she'd suggested to the panel members, "having to tell adoring children and a loving wife of thirty-one years something you feel will risk all that you hold important and necessary to life.... Sleepless nights, troubled days, and humiliation will remain with you long after the proceedings are over."

Nevertheless, the commission had ruled against the Bronx judge, and in April, Gelfand announced that he would appeal their decision to the court of appeals.

Sol, who knew Gelfand and had been talking to him about his case, didn't want to take part in deciding his fate. But maybe he wouldn't have to, he realized. After all, his good friend, Milton Gould, was Gelfand's lawyer; and his daughter Lauren, who had become a lawyer, was working for Gould's firm. He would recuse himself, Sol decided.

He told this to Gelfand at a meeting between the two of them in his Mineola chambers. "Don't worry," he said. "I know the thinking of the court, and you have nothing to worry about—provided you don't rock the boat." Then, to get Gelfand to relax, he pointed out that the members of the court of appeals weren't all angels and entertained him with some spicy anecdotes about them.

Still, Gelfand wasn't sure he trusted Sol's reassurances. Earlier Sol had promised him that he had sufficient influence with the commission to see to it that they wouldn't even bring formal charges, yet nevertheless, he'd been repudiated. But he was grateful for Sol's attention and concern, and reminded him, "You know the whole thing was politically motivated. I was up for reelection. The commission was responding to political pressure."

"Don't raise that," Sol said.

Gelfand sighed. "But they're applying a new standard to me," he said. "A standard that others on the court aren't being held to."

"Look," Sol said, "just don't rock the boat and you'll be okay."

Gelfand said, "Yeah, I guess that if the court of appeals makes marital infidelity an ethical violation, there'd be a lot of vacancies in the court system—including a few on the court of appeals itself."

Sol's face changed. He looked agitated and edgy. Then, "Look, if you rock the boat," he said, "I guarantee you, you'll be killed." His tone was one Gelfand had never heard him use before. It was cold and harsh.

Gelfand listened to Sol. When his case came before the court of appeals, he didn't rock the boat, didn't accuse the commission of playing politics, or say anything about his being held to a separate standard. But nevertheless the court of appeals eventually ruled, in a decision that he felt was virtually aimed at impugning his credibility, that he had to leave the bench. "Sol clearly used his office," he would say later, "to euchre and browbeat me into not discussing the things that might have helped me—into keeping quiet about both political corruption and marital infidelity in the judiciary.''

During the months the Gelfand case was being resolved, Sol slept with Joy on numerous occasions. They saw each other once every other week and managed to spend at least one weekend a month together. When he stayed away from home on those nights and weekends, Sol told Joan that his work was incredibly pressing, that he was involved in a million things.

She began to feel resentful and, not knowing about his relationship with Joy, blamed his new remoteness on something she had once considered one of his most admirable qualities: his social conscience. He cares about, and cares for, too many ideals, she thought. He cares for them so much that I'm no longer a consideration in his life. The rules of the marriage have changed.

She tried not to let her resentment sour the rare times she and Sol were together, but her anger and hurt were so deep, she couldn't control them, and frequently she exploded at Sol.

People began to notice. The children heard her tirades. Sol's staff members heard them.

The staff members were unaware—as Joan herself was unaware—of the acute rejection to which Sol had subjected her. They were unaware—as she was unaware—that her anger was a response. And among themselves they gossiped that she was harsh and hard to live with. One day, a particularly loyal staff member, who was waiting in a car for Sol outside his house in Manhasset, heard Joan fiercely chewing out his boss and thought, She's got *some* temper. She's eating him up alive.

He was so certain that Joan was the villain of the marriage that he couldn't understand why Sol accepted her abuse, why he stayed passive in the face of aggression. And, unable to grasp—as Joan herself couldn't grasp—Sol's own aggression, the passive aggression that lay behind his conducting a surreptitious affair, he turned to his boss's longtime secretary, who was also in the car, and asked in bewilderment, ''Why does he stay with her? Is it just money?''

The secretary, saddened, shook her head. "They've been together a long time. There's a lot of history there."

Sol had by now begun to take a more active role in directing Joy's flirtation with politics. " 'Go over to the Bush for President headquarters,' " he remembered telling her. " 'Bush is going to run in a primary against Dole, and there's no one that candidates are more grateful to than the people who work for them in primaries, because once you're a candidate, that's something else— you have the whole party machinery behind you. But in the beginning it's only volunteers who are personally committed. So, go over there and volunteer yourself.'

"She did, but about three days later, she calls me up and screams—she's a big screamer—'You gave me terrible advice. Al D'Amato says that Dole's going to win. He's backing Dole. Al D'Amato says Dole's going to win and I'm crazy to support Bush.'

"I said, 'Joy, *Bush* is going to win, and this is great, because now D'Amato is taking all the regular Republicans and putting them on Dole. So you'll stand out even more as a Bush supporter.' "

She *did* stand out. "Who is she?" "How come the limo?" Bush campaign staffers wondered when she first started coming down to campaign headquarters at New York's Roosevelt Hotel. They soon got to know her, for after her first few visits, she turned up almost daily, sometimes doing the most mundane chores such as stuffing envelopes and manning the phone lines. Some of her coworkers found her delightful, a competent and generous woman—she'd send her chauffeur out to buy sandwiches for everyone at her favorite delicatessens. "She was one of the few volunteers you could depend on day in and day out," Russ Schriefer, the state campaign's executive director, would one day say. But others were less kind. "She's a snake," one woman who worked with her decided. Another woman, whose husband was one of Bush's financial advisers, concluded, "She's pushy, and everything she does, she does with an eye toward an appointment." This woman and her husband were working exceedingly hard for the Vice President, with no personal reward in mind, and it irked her that Joy seemed transparently interested in self-advancement.

Still, whatever others thought of her, Joy worked hard, particularly at raising money. She brought in money for Bush from all sorts of sources, from her wealthy friends, from the designers whose clothes she bought, even from a repairman who came to her home to fix her stereo set. "She sucked him up for one thousand dollars," Julie Wadler, the New York campaign's finance director, recalled.

"Today I met someone named Brown," Joy would tell Sol when next she spoke to him. "Today I met someone named Firestone." Sol would check into the backgrounds of the people she'd met, tell her who they were, and, if he deemed them important or thought they might be of future political help to her, compose notes to them for her to sign. "It was a pleasure to meet you at lunch the other day . . ." "I loved talking with you. It's always a delight to talk to someone who's so well informed." She'd put the notes on her own stationery and send them off.

Sol liked writing notes for her. It wasn't so different from what he used to do, when his kids were little and he'd helped them do their school assignments. So sometimes he didn't create just simple glad-to-have-met-you communications, but more substantial letters, comments on speeches given by politicians and statesmen Joy told him she'd encountered, reactions to reports about them that had appeared in the press. "I read your interesting and inspiring closing statement," went a letter Sol wrote for her to send to an acquaintance whose address before a conference on global survival had been reported in a newspaper. "All those present will certainly remember you as well as the leadership you brought." "You done good," went a letter he directed her to send to a friend who had taken a controversial political stance in Congress. "Back where I came from, that was the highest praise of all."

No one to whom she sent his letters guessed that the seasoned New York pol was dictating her correspondence, and Sol threw himself into the task with gusto. "We're sowing seeds," he explained to Joy. "You're casting your bread on the water. This is how you're going to get recognition. This is how you let them know you have some intelligence."

She *was* getting recognition. And meeting more and more interesting people. At a Bush fund-raising luncheon attended by both the Vice President and his wife, Barbara, she met Tania Melich, an influential Republican strategist and consultant. Melich was the organizer of the New York State Republican Family Committee, a committee of Republican women for choice, and Joy agreed to join the group and have her name listed on its stationery. She also met Lawrence E. Bathgate II, a gregarious multimillionaire lawyer and land investor who would soon be named finance chairman of the Republican National Committee. "This is all so exciting," she confided to Bathgate. "I want to become more involved."

Bathgate found her charming. "That's easy enough to do," he told her. "You just have to give us your time, money, resources."

Joy's smile, he remembered, was incandescent.

"How much do you love me?" Joy asked Sol one day. "How much—on a scale of one to ten."

He said, "Three."

She didn't like that very much, and the next time they were together, she asked him again, "How much do you love me? On a scale of one to ten?"

He said, "Four."

Joy had a psychotherapist. Her name was Eleanor Sloan, and she lived in Philadelphia, practicing there and, whenever she came up to New York to visit her daughter, in Manhattan as well. Sloan was a short, heavyset woman in her late fifties. There was nothing chic or sophisticated about her. She wore ordinary clothes, sensible shoes, had about her none of the trappings of affluence that Joy so admired. But Joy swore by Eleanor, liked her so much that she'd been going to her for years, and had even sent friends and family to her for treatment.

Sloan wasn't a psychiatrist or a psychologist. But in order to practice psychotherapy in Pennsylvania or New York, training in such fields isn't necessary. Nor is a license.

Sloan wasn't the sort of therapist who sits back and listens to a patient and only on occasion offers an interpretation or a suggestion. She was a talker, a bright, directive woman, with strong opinions about what would be best for her clients. It was easy to grow dependent on such a woman—she was like a dear best friend. Or a mother. Joy leaned on her, relied on her for guidance, didn't just visit her for treatment but telephoned her whenever she had a perplexing decision to make or an attack of anxiety to fend off. Sometimes she called her four or five times a day. Just the way she used to call Jeanette.

Sol ought to see her too, Joy told him not long after they'd begun their affair. Maybe Sloan would be able to help him, because clearly he needed help. He'd stayed married to Joan—whom Joy didn't think he loved—for thirty-five years.

At Joy's behest, Sol went to see Sloan. "I'd never been to a therapist before," he remembered. "Never thought I was in need of one. But Sloan was going to instruct me in how to leave my wife. How best to do it. She said, 'It will take you two years to leave your wife. That's how long the process takes.' "

The idea of leaving Joan made Sol uneasy, but he liked going down to Philly to see Sloan in her West Evergreen Avenue office. Afraid of scandal, afraid of Joan's learning of his disloyalty, he had told no one, not a single friend, that he was having an affair. The need for secrecy oppressed him, made him feel inauthentic, feel like an impersonator, and it was a relief to be with someone who knew his secret.

Besides, Eleanor, as he soon began calling her, had another beneficence to offer him. "She let Joy and me sleep together in her house," he recalled. "It was a perfect cover for us, because Joy used to say to Jeffrey, 'I'm going down to Eleanor's for the weekend,' and if Jeffrey called, Eleanor would answer the phone and say, 'Joy's out.' "

But they didn't always sleep together in Eleanor's house. Sometimes they'd stay in a nearby hotel, in Germantown. "Eleanor would make a reservation for me under my assumed name. Which was Sloan. I was Al Sloan.''

By this time, Sol and Joy had grown closer, exchanged all sorts of confidences. She had told him the sexual predilections of all her husbands—he hoped she'd never talk about his. She told him, too, about her relationship with her stepbrother Van, which made him surprisingly jealous, even though it had happened so many years ago, when she was just a girl—he thought maybe it was because they'd spent the night together on *his* boat, when it was tied up at Bibbs's dock.

He told her stories about his boyhood and about his father, who'd loved him and wanted to keep him from the taint of business, but who hadn't really been an affectionate man. She told him about her mother and how much she'd loved her, but that she'd hated the way Jeanette had gone from relationship to relationship before settling down. She didn't approve of that part of her mother's life at all, she said, and she didn't want to be like her in that respect.

He was touched by her anxieties. One day, when she asked him again, as she was always asking him, ''How much do you love me, on a scale of one to ten,'' he said, ''Ten.''

When he wasn't with her that spring of 1987, he thought about her all the time, and threw himself into guarding her financial interests. Bibbs had specified in his will that the Kings Point house, where Joy had grown up and Honey had eventually become chatelaine, should be sold and the profits used to bolster his estate. Sol began trying to sell the house. But it had sat empty and unoccupied for several years—Honey was living in Palm Beach—and it had lost the gloss it once had. It needed cleaning, painting, attention. On weekends Sol would go over to the house to see what work needed to be done, and sometimes he hired workmen, but sometimes he did the work himself. He vacuumed the house, and one day he got out tools, crawled outside, and repaired a bit of roof that was caving in. Joan thought he was going to a great deal of unnecessary trouble to spruce up her uncle's mansion. But houses weren't moving, he told her, so he had to make it as inviting as possible to potential buyers.

At last, toward the end of 1987, just after the stock market crashed on Black Monday, but before the bottom fell out of local real estate, he managed to sell the house, getting close to five million dollars for it.

One evening around this time, Joan, who was on the board of Long Island University, went to a fund-raising dinner for the school. To her surprise, her stepcousin Joy was there, and the two of them had been placed right next to each other at one of the banquet tables.

Joan made small talk with Joy, whom she hardly knew and hadn't seen since Bibbs's death.

Joy chattered back and then began gossiping about a woman on the other side of the table, an acquaintance of hers. Most of her comments were derogatory. Had Joan noticed the way the woman walked, she wanted to know. Had she noticed that her arms looked just like lamb chops?

Joan found her remarks offensive. She disapproved of mocking people, but especially of mocking them for physical characteristics, which she considered matters that were generally beyond a person's control. When Joy went on making fun of the woman across the way, she couldn't help thinking, Oh, boy, this Joy is really some piece of work!

Annoyed, Joan turned to the person on her other side, distancing herself from Joy, and as soon as she finished eating, she left the table.

By the spring of 1988, the affair between Sol and Joy was in full bloom, and he was feeling like a new, a young, man. He had for years *looked* like a young man, having banished his wrinkles with facial surgery. But now there was a new youthfulness in his very step and his high, optimistic spirit. He was also funnier than he had ever been. One night in March, he addressed a group of businessmen in Albany and made them laugh so hard that they begged for time to catch their breath between jokes. "We received a letter not too long ago," he began, "from a disappointed litigant who said, 'You judges are stiff-necked, arrogant fools who have no knowledge of the people, and even less knowledge of the law.' "

He paused after that for just the right brief second of time. Then he said, "Well, I say, 'Picky, picky, picky.' "

The audience guffawed, and he went on to tell jokes about his friends and colleagues. He was so funny and so mischievous that when Governor Cuomo, who had also been invited to address the businessmen, got up to speak, he dubbed his chief judge "Mr. Laughs."

Joy, too, was in high spirits. For one thing, her political career had taken off. She had become a chairperson of the New York Jewish effort for Bush and helped coordinate a gala Bush fundraiser at the Plaza Hotel, attended by the Vice President and his wife. Then, in the summer of 1988, she got to play hostess herself to Barbara Bush, throwing a fund-raising dinner for her at Joy's house in Southampton. She invited only forty-eight guests, set up elaborately appointed dining tables beneath a big white tent in the garden, ordered food from the finest caterers, and saw to it that Mrs. Bush changed tables after each course. Joy's guests were enchanted by the balmy setting, the exceptional food, and the opportunity to talk intimately with the Vice President's wife. By the end of the evening, Joy had not only made a friend of Barbara, but raised $135,000.

Her efforts did not go unnoticed. A few weeks after her fundraiser, she flew down to New Orleans to attend some of the preconvention festivities that signaled the start of the Republican convention. One evening she attended a party thrown by the former ambassador to Austria at a hotel in the French Quarter. The party was a festive one—crowds of conventioneers were drinking ebulliently and eating their way through vast platters of creole shrimp, blackened redfish, and spicy alligator—but *her* party, Joy soon discovered, was the one people were still talking about, at least the chosen few who had attended both.

"It was intimate, that was the wonderful part of it," Eric Javits, son of the late senator from New York, Jacob Javits, told her.

"It was the single most successful party for any candidate's wife anywhere. Ever," said Bruce Gelb, Bush's finance cochairman in New York.

Joy was on her way, was becoming a highly visible member of the Republican political community. One night, back in New York, she attended a Bush fund-raiser at the Harmonie Club, a private club frequented chiefly by Jewish businessmen, and she even made a speech. Standing up and speaking in a quavering voice, she said people were always asking her how she had managed to raise all the money she'd collected for Bush but the fact that she'd done it was as amazing to her as it was to them, because she'd never done this kind of thing before. She said she was just a housewife, but her belief in George Bush was so strong that it carried her through the discomforts of having to ask people for money.

"Ugh. The naiveté shtick," William Koeppel, a national Republican party leader, remembered thinking as he listened to her. " 'I'm just this little housewife. I'm doing this for God and George Bush.' If you believe that, you'll believe anything."

Still, her manner impressed some people. Jonathan Bush, the Vice President's brother and general chairman of the New York State Republican Party, was one. He invited Joy to accompany him on the campaign trail to upstate cities.

When the campaign was over and Bush had won, Joy, who by that time had not only raised a great deal of money but, with Jeffrey, given the campaign three hundred thousand dollars and lent one hundred thousand dollars for inaugural festivities, told Sol she'd like to go to work for the Republican National Committee. He remembers disapproving. "You have an opportunity now to get something very significant and very important, and you deserve it," he said to her. "What you should do is try to get yourself an ambassadorship."

"How could I get anything like an ambassadorship?" she asked.

"Very simple. You took French in high school, didn't you? You ask to become ambassador to France."

"You're teasing. They'd never appoint me ambassador to France."

"Of course not. But then you ask to be ambassador to Belgium. Or if Belgium's out, then Luxembourg."

"They won't appoint me to Luxembourg, either," Joy protested.

"That's right," Sol said. "But then you pull out a map of the Caribbean."

She did as he instructed. She asked for Luxembourg. But more than three hundred big contributors to the Republican victory had also submitted requests for ambassadorships, and one of them, an old friend of the President, also wanted Luxembourg. Joy's interest in becoming ambassador to the little European country was discouraged. But sure enough, just as Sol had anticipated, her friends in the administration began discussing the Caribbean with her. Would she like to represent the administration there? If so, there were two possible spots. Bermuda. And Barbados. But the United States didn't have an embassy in Bermuda, just a consulate's office.

So Joy said she'd like Barbados. And, afraid that being identified as pro-choice would harm her chances for appointment, she asked to have her name removed from the letterhead of the New York State Republican Family Committee, although she continued to support the group both financially and ideologically.

She was sponsored for the ambassadorship by two of the many prominent men she'd come to know during the campaign, Bruce Gelb and Jonathan Bush, and Sol promised her he'd help her with her application.

She was grateful and wanted to help him too. Why shouldn't she use her political contacts in Washington to get him a better job than the one he had? Why shouldn't she try to get him named attorney general? Or, better yet, appointed to the Supreme Court!

There weren't any vacancies at the start of the Bush administration. But it was clear that shortly there would be. Joy began spreading the word whenever she met with top Republicans that Sol would be an ideal candidate for the highest court.

William Koeppel, who'd listened irritably to Joy when she'd said at the Harmonie Club that she was nothing but a housewife, overheard her promoting Sol. He didn't know there was a sexu-'

relationship between them. But he knew they were related to each other. Cousins, or something. Relatives of the Long Island builder Bibbs Wolosoff. "Joy's being made into the family political contact person," he thought when he heard her pitching Sol. "It's a family plan to get him to the Supremes. Well, why not. The Rockefellers worked as a family. So did the Kennedys. So now it's a Jewish family. It's the Wolosoffs."

Those were heady days. The two of them working to help each other attain a heart's desire. For his part, Sol peppered Joy with suggestions about how to prevail at becoming an ambassador, helping her develop a résumé, writing out sample questions that might be asked of her at confirmation hearings, and even composing the answers she should make to the questions. "Question: Do you believe that the current situation in Haiti will have a direct effect on the politics of the Dominican Republic? Answer: My study of the region is ongoing. I have not yet focused on that subject. I will certainly do so immediately, and will submit my response to your question as soon as I am able. Question: Do you think ambassadorships should be sold? Answer: Absolutely not! Question: There are those who might charge that you bought yours. Answer: No one with any regard for our president or his judgment would make such a charge. While there are no specified credentials or criteria for ambassadorial designations, President Bush would not designate someone whom he did not consider eminently qualified and appropriate for appointment. Question: How could the President choose someone with no college degree? Answer: He chose Barbara as his wife. She has no college degree. A college degree is not an essential ingredient for good character and wisdom."

Barbados on her mind, Joy wanted to go down to the tropics and check out the island. She'd look over the ambassadorial residence and see if there was a good school for Jessica. She told Sol, who didn't think she should go. Not before she was confirmed. But she flew down, anyway. And she must have come home dissatisfied with what she'd seen, for sometime after her visit, Jeffrey, too, went down to check things out.

He definitely didn't like what he saw. The ambassador's mansion is too small for our family's needs, he thought. And besides, it needs refurbishing.

After seeing it, he arranged with the State Department's help to rent a second residence, a charming little house adjoining the ambassador's mansion. That way, he figured, he and Joy would be able to house Jessica's nanny separately, and they'd have enough space for his children from his first marriage when they came down to visit. He also indicated to the State Department that he'd fix up the mansion, make it more presentable, and pay for the redecoration out of his own pocket.

Joy was still working on the biographical papers she'd need to submit to her sponsors before her nomination could become official. One Monday morning, she traveled to Albany to work on the papers with Sol. He took her to his chambers once again, but this time during working hours, and, explaining to his staff that she was a relative and that she would be sitting at his desk and doing some work while he was at conference, asked the staff to take good care of her.

She looks dangerous, one of the staff members thought. She's so decked out, it's like she's in battle dress for the war of the sexes.

It didn't occur to him that Sol was having an affair with her. Sol, he believed, was the soul of rectitude when it came to marriage. He always said affairs weren't worth it, always joked that the screwing you got wasn't worth the screwing you'd get. Still, there was something troubling about the woman. Her clothes and jewelry fairly reek of money, the staff member thought. Her face and hair and outfit look as if they'd set her back by a fortune. And she was terribly ingratiating with Sol. Fawned all over him.

The staff member was relieved when, at lunchtime, Sol came back to his chambers and he and the woman left.

But then, after lunch, there she was again. In fact, she was there all week. Every morning, she'd arrive with Sol at ten A.M., sit in his chambers while he went to conference, go out to lunch with him, then sit at his desk while he went on the bench. Then, they'd leave together at day's end.

* * *

Was Joy in love with him? Sol thought so. "She gave the impression of total commitment," he remembered. "And total reliance. She didn't write a letter, she didn't go out, she didn't do anything without calling me first and checking to see if it was all right. She used to call me seven, eight times a day. Drove my law clerks crazy—because no one else was allowed to do that. Some days I would take no calls except from Joy or my family. I used to say to her, 'Joy, the one thing that's going to break us up is going to be the telephone.' She'd say, 'Well, I can't help it. I don't get to see you as much as I want, so I have to speak to you on the phone.' " It sounded like love to him.

But was he in love with her? After the day he'd finally answered her familiar question, "How much do you love me, on a scale of one to ten," by saying, "Ten," she'd changed the question, next asking him, "But are you *in* love with me? How much are you *in* love with me—on a scale of one to ten?" The game embarrassed him, made him feel like a silly teenager. But the question began to haunt him. Was he in love with her? Certainly, they were doing the things that people in love did—not just the sexual things, but the romantic ones, the revelatory ones, the things that had to do with nostalgia and loss and history. She'd gotten him to drive her to Lake Hiawatha in New Jersey, where she'd used to visit her grandmother, Jeanette's mother, when she was a little girl. They'd laughed in amazement to discover there was no longer a lake at Lake Hiawatha. He'd taken her out to Brooklyn, to the neighborhood in which *his* grandparents had lived and in which he'd spent his summers when he was a teenager, traveling up from the South to visit aunts and uncles and cousins. He'd shown her the crowded streets on which he used to play and told her how at night, he and the cousins had slept on cots scattered helter-skelter throughout the apartment, and he'd taken her out for cold cuts at a local delicatessen whose spicy smells and pungent tastes he had never forgotten. Had he ever taken Joan to his old neighborhood? Had she ever asked to see it? He didn't think so.

At the end of April 1989, Sol and Joy attended a gala ceremony in Manhattan commemorating the first inauguration of

George Washington. It was held under a sky raining balloons and confetti at Federal Hall on Wall Street, right where Washington himself had once stood, and every dignitary imaginable had flown into town for the occasion. The governor had come. And New York's two senators. And the secretary of the army. And even the President. Joy, who had by then developed a solid friendship with Barbara Bush, had ridden out to the airport to meet the President's plane and be part of his escort into the city. But Sol felt it was *his* show. He was one of the chairmen of the event.

The two thousand VIPs who were to take part in the ceremony—not just politicians but Hollywood stars, world-renowned writers, and the descendants of former presidents— had all been given reserved seats. But as a principal in the event, Sol had one of the best, and he'd arranged to have Joy sit alongside him, right in the middle of the dais. He was feeling splendid that day, proud and happy and complete, as if life had granted him everything he'd ever wanted. Joy seemed exceedingly happy too. When she saw Steve Ross, the chairman of Warner Communications, sitting way off in a corner, she whispered to Sol, "I've got a better seat than he does!" Then she went over to Ross to say hello. Sol saw her standing beside him and saw her take the silk of his tie between her fingers and begin fondling it. But it didn't make him jealous. It just made him think how remarkable Joy was with men. How sensual she was. How sexual.

He wasn't jealous, because she was his. The day was, for him, the pinnacle of their love.

CHAPTER 8

"I *love* George Bush," Joy confided to a woman whose child went to Nightingale with Jessica, not long after the George Washington inaugural commemoration. "I *love* him. He's given me my life."

She had become a frequent guest at the White House ever since he'd been elected. But as the summer of 1989 approached, she began to grow uneasy. Her sponsors for the ambassadorship had begun hinting to her that her résumé, with its lack of a job history or even a college degree, might be a problem. The press had begun attacking her—she was, wrote *The Washington Post*, a "major exhibit" in the Bush team's tendency to name as ambassadors "political appointees with few or no qualifications outside of support for Bush or wealth given freely to the GOP." "I'm caught in a web in Washington," she complained to Andrew Stein, then president of New York's City Council, who advised her to get in touch with Phil Friedman, a political consultant who had helped him out in the past.

Phil Friedman didn't work on Joy's ambassadorship, but he became one of her closest friends. He gave her advice, listened to her worries, comforted and consoled her. He'd heard that George Bush was entranced by her, and he could see why. She's fun, he thought. She makes everything around her fun.

Phil also thought there'd never been anyone in the world quite like her.

She always entertained him in her bedroom, never anywhere else in the apartment, and she'd wander around the room wearing every variety of dishabille imaginable. She preferred not having to get dressed, even though she had a veritable store-load of dresses—there was a wall of walk-in closets in her bedroom that was so big it was like a concourse.

Her favorite item of apparel was jewelry. Once, he went down to Washington with her and stayed in the same hotel, where Joy, who was going to dinner at the White House, had stored her jewelry in a safe-deposit box. She asked Phil to come and have a look at it, and he'd never seen anyone carry on about anything the way she did about the jewelry. "Look at this! Look at that!" she kept saying, flashing one gem after another at him. And her eyes were as bright as the stones.

Often, when Phil visited her at home, she'd invite him to linger in the bedroom and watch TV with her. Her favorite activity was watching old movies. She could watch for hours. But he found the pastime boring and would excuse himself and go home. Even so, she'd want him to watch "with" her. So she'd call him up, and he'd turn on his own set, and they'd talk on the phone a bit, and then watch their screens, and then talk on the phone some more, and then watch some more. Sometimes ten or fifteen minutes would go by without either of them saying anything into the phone, and then one of them would say, "That was great! Did you see that? Did you hear that line?"

One day, Joy told him that she thought her husband was having an affair. "Catting around" was how she put it. She expressed strong indignation at the proclivity of husbands to cheat on their wives and sounded so miserable about her own husband's having done so that Phil was deeply touched by her predicament.

By the fall of 1989, Joy's chances of winning the ambassadorship were looking slimmer and slimmer. She'd become something of a cause célèbre in Washington, where the press had used her lack of a foreign service background, or even a college degree, to beat up on George Bush. They'd criticized her, too, for having complained that the ambassadorial residence on Barbados was inadequate and for having gone out and rented a second residence there. (She defended herself by saying it hadn't been she, but her husband, who'd done these things.) In a last-ditch effort to obtain the position, Joy visited many of the Democratic senators who would have to vote on her nomination.

Most of the time, the visits went well. But sometimes they went poorly, and afterward Joy would get depressed or hysterical. She'd call Sol in New York and say, "I'm lying here in a pool of blood."

He knew the expression was just a metaphor. He knew that Joy liked to imbue her life with high drama and keen tragedy. Still, when she spoke like that, he'd tell Joan he had an appointment with this senator or that, then rush to the shuttle and fly down to Washington to be with Joy.

"I helped her in other ways too," he recalled. "I made calls and wrote letters—one, to an organization of former diplomats. They'd just evaluated Joy's application, and they concluded she wasn't qualified to be an ambassador. After I wrote them, they promised they'd reevaluate her credentials."

He also continued to prepare her for the Senate hearings she would soon have to undergo. "I wrote a statement for her to give to the Senate that would explain why she didn't have a career. The explanation we presented was that because she'd had no proper family—she'd told me her father left her mother when she was three years old—she'd made up her mind that she was not going to do that to her children, and that she was going to stay by them, in steadfast fashion, and if the senators wanted to punish her for that, so be it."

He was still very excited by the idea of his relationship with Joy. He'd even told her that once she was named ambassador, he would start divorce proceedings, and that when her diplomatic assignment came to an end, he would marry her.

But did he really want to marry her? There were times when he wasn't sure. In part, it was because of Joan. In part, it was because he still harbored in his mind the idea that one of these days he would run for governor, and he feared that being a divorced candidate would hamper him. But in part, it also had to do with his feelings about Joy herself. He loved her, he thought. But he didn't always *like* her. "She had a terrible mouth on her," he would one day recall. "Once, I said I'd meet her at the Algonquin, and I was maybe five minutes late, and she started calling me on my car phone and screaming so loudly that I was afraid my driver would hear her. 'How dare you keep me waiting?' she screamed. 'Joy, please,' I said. 'It'll only be five more minutes, for God's sake. The FDR Drive is all tied up.' 'Get off the fucking drive!' she shouted. Jesus, she was terrible."

But on the other hand, he found her fun. He enjoyed "the laughter. And the adoration. She would say things like, 'There's no one, *there is no one,* who speaks like you. You're so brilliant. You're so bright.' " He relished that.

But marry her? Leave Joan after all these years? He just wasn't sure.

Sometimes he felt he was lying to both of the women in his life, lying to Joan *and* Joy. And when he felt that, he experienced a wave of guilt and self-loathing.

In November, Joy's nomination was blocked. Senator Paul Sarbanes argued before the Senate Foreign Relations Committee that Joy had no credentials for the post she was seeking. "There is no there, there," he said of her résumé. And in the end, Joy had to withdraw her application.

She was crushed, and to some extent, she blamed Sol for her defeat. "Whenever you take his advice," she complained to a friend, "it doesn't work." But despite the fact that she was beginning to notice that Sol had feet of clay, she clung to him, for shortly after she withdrew her application, she decided to end her third marriage. She told people she'd gotten proof positive that Jeffrey had been having an affair, and said she didn't want to live with a man who was two-timing her.

"It's absolutely untrue that I had an affair," Jeffrey Silverman would say years later. "I know she told people I did, maybe to justify her affair with Sol."

In any event, Jeffrey moved out, taking rooms in a hotel, and she hired a prominent matrimonial lawyer—an old friend of Sol's named Norman Sheresky. As she'd presented it several times to others, she said to Sheresky that her husband had cheated on her and didn't mention her own adulterous affair.

Once Jeffrey was out of the picture, Joy began to urge Sol to marry her, and she suggested that if he wasn't yet ready for that step, at least they should change the old terms of their relationship and start going out together publicly. She didn't want to be a backdoor woman any longer, she told him. She didn't want to sneak around corners and pretend she was nothing to him but a distant relative.

Joy dearly wanted respectability for a number of reasons. First, she had children, and she didn't want them tainted by scandal. Then, there was her mother, whose voice she could still hear in her mind's ear, saying that what counted with men was getting them to the altar. And finally, there was her career—for by now, she had one. She had a career in politics, and even though she wasn't going to be an ambassador, her future looked bright. The President was her fan.

On January 2, 1990, Bush wrote her a note apologizing for her having had a bad 1989 "because of the spot I put you in" and assuring her that she had been "magnificent, head-high, knowledgeable." In February, he named her to the Kennedy Center board of trustees, a position that did not require Senate confirmation. And on March 16, he wrote her a letter telling her he was sure she would do her "usual great job" in her new position. The letter must have satisfied the yearning for attention and approbation that had haunted her ever since she'd been a fatherless girl growing up as a poor relation on Bibbs's estate, for with eerie foreshadowing, Bush also said he was certain that "the nation and the world have yet to hear the last of Joy Silverman."

If Joy was sick of secrecy, Sol wasn't. For one thing, there was Joan. For another, *his* children. For a third, *his* career. He was more in the public eye than ever, largely as the result of a dispute he was having with Cuomo. The dispute was over the state's financial budget for the judiciary—Sol wanted an increase in the funds allotted to the courts and a ten percent raise for

courtesy Washington and Lee University

GOLDEN BOY. At college, Sol Wachtler, who was always winning prizes and elections, dabbled at being a writer, learning skills he would one day put to a dark purpose. Here he is shown (front row, center) with the Washington and Lee Literary Society, of which he was secretary-treasurer.

"THERE WAS ALWAYS JOAN." Sol was seventeen when he met his future wife, sixteen-year-old Joan Carol Wolosoff. They began keeping company, and they got married five years later.

courtesy Washington and Lee University

"THERE WAS TALK ABOUT HIS BECOMING PRESIDENT ONE DAY." By 1967, Sol was a rising star in the Republican Party. He is seen here on his campaign bus during his run for county executive of Nassau County on Long Island, New York.

"JOAN'S IMAGE WAS THAT OF PARTNER." Joan Wolosoff Wachtler ran Sol's campaign office and organized his public appearances. Here, she awaits election returns with him at the Garden City Hotel.

ROCKEFELLER PROTÉGÉ. Nelson Rockefeller plumped for Sol, and when Wachtler lost the election, his mentor helped make him a judge. Here Rockefeller banters with Wachtler, who has just been sworn in as a justice of New York's Supreme Court. In the middle stands political boss Joseph Margiotta.

"BIBBIE IS GOING TO BUY ME THIS." Jeanette Fererh, Joy Silverman's mother, was passionate about diamonds and furs. She married twice before she met and wedded her third husband, real estate mogul Bibbs Wolosoff, Joan Wachtler's uncle, who bought Jeanette whatever she craved.

"TWENTY-FIVE THOUSAND DOLLARS WILL BUY OFF ANY LAWSUIT." Bibbs, who had a penchant for savvy sayings, refused to adopt Jeanette's daughter, Joy, but he cut one of his own sons out of his will and left Joy millions when he died.

"THERE WAS SOMETHING SEXUAL ABOUT THE WAY BIBBS LOOKED AT JOY." Joy's mother sent her away from home to study at a finishing school in Massachusetts. Later, she attended the University of Maryland, but dropped out to work for MGM, hoping to become an actress. Here she is as a young woman.

"SHE HAD PITCH-BLACK HAIR, WIDE DARK EYES, AND A SMILE SO DAZZLING IT MADE ME THINK OF FIREWORKS," Joy's first husband, furniture heir Dick Simons, said about his initial encounter with Joy. This photograph was taken in 1969, the year they married. Joy was twenty-two.

FUN WHILE IT LASTED. Soon after the marriage, Joy, Dick, Jeanette, and Bibbs began living in Palm Beach, where they hoped for invitations from such local celebrities as Rose and Ted Kennedy, pictured here at a 1972 Red Cross Ball.

WWD / Fairchild Publications

WWD / Fairchild Publications

MAKING IT. It took time, but after a while the newcomers got to know, and associate with, some of the celebrities, among them Jim Kimberly, one of the heirs to the Kimberly-Clark tissue fortune, and his wife, Jacquie.

WWD / Fairchild Publications

ANOTHER FRIEND was Roxanne Pulitzer, who helped Joy and Dick crack Palm Beach's social scene. Roxanne would later be at the center of one of Palm Beach's most scandalous divorce trials.

SITTING HIGH. In 1985, Sol became the chief judge of New York's Court of Appeals, a position that gave him almost unparalleled power in the state. Here he is with his Court of Appeals colleagues.

FORTY-ONE YEARS TOGETHER. Joan and Sol on vacation in the summer of 1988. She didn't know that he had been conducting an affair with her cousin Joy for more than a year.

VIBRANT AND MAGNETIC, Joy never wanted for men in her life.

"SHE CAN'T LOVE ME. ALL SHE WANTS IS MONEY," Joy's first husband, Simons, would say about her in 1972, the year this picture of him was taken. Their marriage lasted three years.

"I'LL MARRY HIM. FOR A WHILE," Joy said of her second husband, banker and real estate developer David Paul, who was later convicted of fraud in a major savings-and-loan scandal. Their marriage lasted only a few weeks.

"JOY FOUND HERSELF MARRIED, AT LAST, TO A VERY RICH MAN." Joy's third husband was businessman Jeffrey Silverman, chairman of Ply-Gem, Inc., and a former Wall Street floor trader.

"HE'S HANDSOMER THAN YOU. AND HE'S RICHER THAN YOU," Joy told Sol Wachtler about the latest man in her life, New Jersey lawyer David Samson. Jealousy began to eat at Wachtler.

"I *LOVE* GEORGE BUSH. HE'S GIVEN ME MY LIFE," Joy told a friend after becoming involved in Republican national politics and getting to know the President. Here she sits on a dais with President Bush (far left) and New York Senator Alphonse D'Amato (far right).

"LIFE HAD GRANTED HIM EVERYTHING HE EVER WANTED." At a 1989 ceremony commemorating the inauguration of George Washington, Sol joked happily with New York's Senator Daniel Moynihan, Senator Alphonse D'Amato, and Mayor Ed Koch. It was a day, he would say later, that was the pinnacle of his life — and his love for Joy.

AP/Wide World Photos

OUT OF CONTROL. By 1992, when this picture was taken, Wachtler and Cuomo were on the outs. They were suing each other over the state's budget for the courts—and Sol was writing scurrilous cards and letters to Joy.

"THE NATION AND THE WORLD HAVE YET TO HEAR THE LAST OF JOY SILVERMAN," President Bush said of Joy in 1990. Here, she attends a Senate hearing on her qualifications to become Bush's ambassador to Barbados.

Sygma

One of the obscene and ominous greeting cards Sol sent to Joy.

Another of Sol's greetings to Joy. A third such card, addressed to Joy's fourteen-year-old daughter Jessica, contained a condom.

Even my assistant, a two bit hore from Queens knew she was being recorded last Sunday. Don't try that on me or all bets are off.

This is/the deal - if you do anything to queer it you will regret it for the rest of your life. Tell the police or put your keystone P.I.'s on it and you'll be sorry. They may be good at deactivating bugs, but they'll not outsmart me in this operation. And you can't take a chance that you will beat me. You will lose.

There is a laundry shop called :Shanley located at 128 E 84 th between Park and Lexington Avenues. Right next door is a cellar entrance. Have your doorman Ramon put the manila envelope which I am enclosing in that cellar entrance stairway. The envelope is to contain $20, ooo. (twenty thousand in used 100's and 50's.

THIS MUST BE DONE AT 10:30 A.M. ON THE DOT -NOT SOONER OR LATER - ON SATURDAY NOVEMBER 7th. I KNOW RAMON IS ON THEN.

If you follow these instructions, I will send you the negatives, some tapes, and a lot of other things which will shock and amaze you. If you fuck up in any way, or have the police or one of you privates involved in this transaction you will regret the day you and Jessica were born.

As soon as Ramon drops that envelope down those stairs, I will be out of your life forever. If he doesn't, I will be with you forever and Jessica will have Thanksgiving Dinner with me.

"IF YOU FUCK UP IN ANY WAY . . . YOU WILL REGRET THE DAY YOU AND JESSICA WERE BORN." This is the kidnap letter that Sol, making strange use of the literary skills he had learned long ago, sent to Joy in October 1992.

MONEY DROP. The Manhattan cellar stairway where Sol directed Silverman to leave the money. Eighty FBI agents were by now involved in the case.

Robert Kalfus, *New York Post*

"THIS CASE CHALLENGED THE VERY INTEGRITY OF THE COURT SYSTEM," said Michael Chertoff, the U.S. Attorney who prosecuted Wachtler, seen here on the steps of a Manhattan courthouse.

"SOL WACHTLER'S PATH THROUGH LIFE HAS BEEN MARKED BY EXTRAORDINARY CONTRIBUTIONS. . . . ALONG THE WAY HE STUMBLED AND FELL," said his defense attorney, Charles Stillman (center, with glasses).

AP / Wide World Photos

AP / Wide World Photos

"THOSE LETTERS JOY'S BEEN GETTING, SHE KNOWS THEY'RE FROM YOU," Norman Sheresky, Joy's divorce lawyer, had told Sol long before the FBI began to track him. Sol ignored his warning.

AP/Wide World Photos

"PRISONER OF PARK AVENUE," a New York newspaper called Joy in February 1993, reporting that because of the scandal, she felt compelled to pass most of her time in her apartment in this luxury building. In fact, she'd recently been to the Caribbean.

"NEXT TIME IT'LL COST YOU MORE THAN ANOTHER TWENTY THOUSAND DOLLARS." FBI agents Bill Fleming and Carrie Brzezinski were aghast at reading Wachtler's final note to Silverman.

New Jersey Newsphotos / Jack S. Kanthal

courtesy Sanford P. Solomon, M.D.

courtesy Louis B. Schlesinger, Ph.D. / Eric Wagman Studio

"WACHTLER *ACTS* AS IF HE CARES ABOUT OTHERS, BUT AT BOTTOM HIS FEELINGS ARE SHALLOW, MANIPULATIVE," said prosecution psychologist Louis B. Schlesinger, who concluded that Sol suffered from a narcissistic personality disorder, a mental condition akin to psychopathy.

"WACHTLER WAS POISONED BY DRUGS," said his own psychiatrist, Dr. Sanford Solomon. "They produced a toxic reaction resembling the symptoms of manic-depressive illness."

© 1993 Don Jacobson, *New York Newsday*

HOUSE ARREST. Before he pled guilty to harassing Joy, Sol was confined to his home in Manhasset, New York, where his movements were monitored by an electronic bracelet.

SHATTERED. Sol and Joan leaving the courthouse on the day Sol entered his guilty plea. "My behavior from late 1991 to late 1992 was foreign to my sixty-two years on earth," he had just told the presiding judge, who later termed his acts "an expression of anger, intimidation, and grotesque control."

Paul Adao, *New York Post*

judges, and the governor wanted to pay for these changes by raising civil court filing fees. "The courts are not for raising revenue," Sol had lashed out at Cuomo when he heard this. "They are for administering justice." "I differ with the chief judge on fees," Cuomo had said. "I differ with the chief judge on raises. You just can't do it this year."

The scuttlebutt in Albany was that Sol had stirred up the clash with Cuomo because he wanted to run against him for governor in the fall of 1990. But that was unlikely. It was clear that in that election, Cuomo was going to be invincible. If Sol had a motive other than true dismay at the governor's plan, it was more likely that he was currying favor with Joy's contacts in Washington. Cuomo was expected to run against Bush for president in 1992, and anyone who took him on would be making himself look good in the White House.

In any event, and whatever his reasons, by the spring of 1990, Sol was at war with his old friend Cuomo. And the fighting threatened to get worse. "There are differences," Sol told one reporter. "And there are going to be more differences."

Yet despite the attention that was increasingly being paid to him by the press, he at last acquiesced to Joy's yearning to feel more like a sweetheart and less like a shameful secret. They would, he agreed, go out on dates with other people.

There were several who already knew about their relationship. There was Joy's friend Paola, of course. And the psychotherapist Eleanor Sloan. There was also Eleanor's daughter, Heather, in whose New York apartment Eleanor occasionally practiced and in which Joy and Sol had occasionally spent the night together.

Additionally, Joy had told her brother, Bruce, and Sol had told his brother, Morty. He had told him because Morty had gone into the jewelry business, just like their father, and Sol needed to buy jewelry. He needed to, Sol said, because Joy had made it clear that she expected gems from her admirers. Unabashedly, she'd presented him with catalogues from Van Cleef and Arpels and other stores. He hadn't wanted to shop retail, so he'd gone to Morty to make his purchases.

Now Sol and Joy enlarged the circle of those who knew their secret. Joy told two women friends, Carol Palin, whose father had been an owner of the Sands Hotel in Las Vegas, and Faith Golding, Ron Perelman's first wife. She also told Phil Friedman and her divorce lawyer, Sol's friend Norman Sheresky. And soon, she and Sol started going out with some of these chosen friends and relatives.

One night, they went to dinner in a restaurant in Greenwich Village with Phil Friedman. Throughout the meal, judges, lawyers, and political personalities came over to the table to greet Sol. He knows everyone, Phil Friedman thought. And everyone knows him. But later, when he got to know Sol better, he was struck by the fact that although Sol knew hundreds of people, maybe thousands of people, he didn't seem to have any real friends. Any close friends. He'd told Friedman, whom he'd just gotten to know and who was young enough to be his son, that he and Joy were going to get married, and that when they did, he wanted him to be his best man.

On another occasion, Sol and Joy went to dinner with Sheresky and his wife at the celebrity hangout Elaine's. Sheresky found the evening extremely uncomfortable. While they were eating and randomly discussing politics and law, Joy suddenly demanded of Sol, "Do you love me?" Sol didn't answer her. He seemed embarrassed to be asked to talk of love in front of friends. But Joy wouldn't let him off the hook. "Do you love me?" she asked again. And when, still, Sol didn't answer, she repeated the question yet again. Then at last, in a hollow voice, Sol said, "Yeah, I do."

But that wasn't the end of it. Having elicited the answer she wanted from him, Joy in a few minutes asked the question again. And again. Until at last Sol again gave her an affirmative answer.

Sheresky felt sorry for Sol. There was something about the scene that reminded him of *The Blue Angel*.

He was also annoyed at Joy. He hated the way she kept complaining to him about her husband screwing some dame, when all along she was having an affair with Sol. He hated the way she talked as if she were holier than thou. A victim.

There was someone else who knew—and yet didn't know—about the relationship between Sol and Joy. It was Lauren Wachtler.

Lauren and Joy had been seeing a great deal of each other
during the past year or two and, separated in age by only seven
years, had become close friends.

Lauren's grandmother, Joan's mother, Elsie, didn't like the
idea. "Joy's a viper," she grumbled when Lauren talked about
her new friend. But Lauren enjoyed the company of the glamorous stepcousin her mother had never permitted her to know during her teenage years. Joy, she felt, was very simpatico. She had
a way of paying compliments and of listening attentively and
even raptly that made Lauren feel, as she all too rarely felt,
beautiful and smart and altogether special. And as if that weren't
enough, Joy was incomparably generous. Whenever they went
walking together, Joy was sure to notice something amazing in
a shop window and just as sure to say, "Wouldn't you love to
have that?" and if Lauren allowed that she would, Joy generally
went out and bought it for her.

One day, in a burst of intimacy, Joy hinted to Lauren that she
was having an affair with her father.

The idea upset Lauren. She knew her father liked Joy. He
always seemed very happy when he was around her. And she
knew that Joy liked her father. She'd seen her flirting with him,
adjusting his tie, touching his hair. But an affair? Soon after Joy
intimated that she was having a sexual relationship with Sol,
Lauren asked her father to take her to lunch and demanded point-
blank to know.

Sol looked her in the eyes, swallowed, and said, "No."

Lauren didn't know what to believe.

If Joy had worked at developing a relationship with Lauren,
Sol had been working at developing one with Jessica. He wrote
her notes on his creamy, embossed court of appeals stationery,
he bought her games and played them with her, he sang her
songs and plucked out old tunes on a guitar, and he talked to
her about right and wrong, good and bad. One day he invited
Joy to bring her to a session at the court of appeals. "The cases
on Tuesday were pretty good," the twelve-year-old wrote to Sol
appraisingly afterward. "I mean, I thought they were fine. Maybe

it's because it was my first and I don't know the difference between a good lawyer and a bad lawyer.''

Sol was fond of her and used her remarks to augment an article he wrote for the *New York Law Journal* on the subject of overzealous attorneys.

She was an easy child to be fond of. She had turned into a beauty, fair-complexioned, lithe, and blond. In addition, she had a temperament as attractive as her looks. The rest of her family—Joy, Jeffrey, even Evan—were combustible, volatile, but twelve-year-old Jessica was as tranquil as a summer's day.

Sol sometimes daydreamed about being married to Joy and being the little girl's stepfather. But the idea of marrying Joy never conquered his reluctance to leave Joan. Throughout the spring of 1990, he kept telling Joy that he would do so soon, and some nights when he would have ordinarily gone home to Manhasset, he stayed away, sleeping in his mother's Manhattan apartment or a little pied-à-terre he and Joan maintained on East 75th Street. But then he would go back to Manhasset, back to Joan. And although he'd told Joy it was okay for them to be seen in public together, after a while he changed his mind and said it wasn't.

His waffling made Joy angry. So did the fact that he wavered about their summer plans. First he told her he'd spend the summer with her. Then he said he wouldn't.

She couldn't count on him for anything, and she told a friend that fears of ending up husbandless would sweep over her, threatening her self-esteem and stirring up ancient anxieties. Her mother, she said, had taught her that being without a husband was practically a crime.

Sol was aware of Joy's fears, and as the summer wore on, he finally promised her that he would leave Joan on Labor Day weekend. In the meantime, he said, he'd move out of the marital bedroom and sleep, when he was at home, in an upstairs room. But Labor Day came and went, and at the end of the holiday weekend, he was still living with Joan.

Joy's brother, Bruce, got married that September, and Joan Wachtler went to the wedding, which was held at a loft in lower

Manhattan. She arrived early, in the company of Sol, who was going to be performing the ceremony, and as soon as she got there, he went to talk to the bride and groom, and she was left alone. No one she knew was there yet. At a loss about how to kill the time, she went outside, and there she ran into Joy, who had also come early.

Joan hadn't seen her stepcousin in several years, not since the unpleasant encounter they'd had at the Long Island University dinner, but although she'd taken a strong dislike to Joy on that occasion, today she was ready to let bygones be bygones. Joy was looking very nice, she thought, not as ostentatious as usual. In fact, she was wearing a very tasteful black enamel pin with a modest sprinkling of diamonds, the kind of thing Joan herself liked. She went over to Joy and complimented her on the pin.

"What are you doing with yourself these days?" Joy asked her.

Joan told her about the geriatric center she was running at the Y. But as she talked, she saw a look of repugnance come over Joy's face. Then, "How can you stand to be around those sick old people all the time?" Joy said.

"Somebody has to do it," Joan told her. "And anyway, I don't look at it that way. It's very rewarding, what I do. If we didn't have the center, many of the people who come would have to be institutionalized."

Joy wasn't persuaded. "I think it would be really terrible. That kind of work."

Joan was relieved when other people started arriving. But since many of them were members of the family, she remained at Joy's side to greet them.

A mistake, she realized in a few minutes. As the guests filed past, Joy kept turning to her to comment cruelly on their appearance or characteristics, spicing her observations with vulgarities. She spoke so roughly that Joan got the feeling that, for some reason, Joy was trying to shock her. Joan hadn't heard such language since she'd gone to graduate school and taken a course in counseling drug addicts, where the teacher had used the roughest language he could in order to train the students not to be shocked by street talk. Joan, remembering her class, felt angry with Joy. What did Joy think? That she didn't *know* words like that? Or was she trying to embarrass her? Make her feel old and old-fashioned because she didn't use those words? Whatever her motives, Joan didn't want anything more to do with her step-cousin. She moved away from her and avoided her throughout the rest of the wedding. And that was that, except that on the way home, she couldn't help telling Sol what she thought of his precious "ward," this hurtful woman on whose financial affairs he'd been lavishing so many hours and so much energy these past few years. "I don't know how you spend any time with that woman," she said. "I think she's crass. And classless. And besides, she isn't even pretty. Not nearly as pretty as she used to be."

During the next few weeks, Sol, who had been unable to leave Joan, yet unwilling to part from Joy, unable to give himself wholly to Joan, yet unwilling to deprive himself of Joy, continued to vacillate and to put off choosing between the two women. And then he came to a decision—or at least arrived at a course of action. He told Joy he had a brain tumor. He seems to have believed that if she thought he had a brain tumor, she wouldn't want him for a husband, wouldn't want to spoil her young life by saddling herself to a sick and possibly doomed man.

His choice of a disease with which to extricate himself from the relationship—his choice of a brain tumor rather than, say, cancer—was not entirely haphazard. For a number of months he'd had symptoms that could, he had learned after doing some research, be the result of a brain tumor. His left leg pulled and felt numb; his left foot dropped. The symptoms were so marked that he later said he truly believed that he had a brain tumor. But he did nothing to verify that belief, underwent neither of the diagnostic tests, the CAT scan and MRI, that might have proven or disproven the existence of a tumor. He hadn't wanted to, he would later explain, because the diagnostic tests entailed lying under apparatuses that created a feeling of entombment, and he was claustrophobic.

Nevertheless, he informed Joy that he'd gone to Long Island Jewish Hospital and had a brain scan, that it had shown a shadow on his cortex, and that he was making arrangements to go to the Mayo Clinic for further testing.

Joy seems to have been unsure at first about whether to believe him. Or at least, she wanted a reading on whether he had a brain tumor from her favorite astrologist, Elizabeth Racine. She swore by Racine, who'd been doing horoscopes for twenty-five years and had a big following among celebrities. Going to Racine's nearby apartment on East 82nd Street, she entered the inner sanctum, a small smoky room where the bookcases were lined with astrological tomes, and she revealed to the astrologist what Sol had told her.

Racine confirmed that Sol had a brain tumor and even had a theory about what might have caused it. "Ask him," she directed, "if he ever had a head injury when he was young."

Joy did, and to her astonishment learned that once, when he was around five years old, he'd been hit in the side of the head by a heavy chain he'd been playing with at a garage.

Joy was amazed at Racine's perspicacity. And so, Sol told her, was he.

Sol's reports to Joy about his brain tumor became ever more dire—and more elaborate. He was back from the Mayo Clinic, he told her one day. They'd said his tumor was inoperable. He was attending physical therapy sessions, he told her another day. Their purpose was to teach him how to cope with the loss of motor skills that he would face as a result of the tumor. Then at last, he told her that he didn't want to burden her with his medical condition, and that therefore they should stop seeing each other.

Joy, predictably, got upset—and seemed truly concerned. She wasn't the kind of woman who would abandon a man just because he was sick, she told him. No, she would stick by him, so he wouldn't have to face his medical problems alone.

A short time later, Sol told her he had fallen and gone to a hospital. He also told her that the hospital had called Joan, who'd come to the emergency room and been informed about his brain tumor. He was indicating to Joy that he wouldn't have to face his medical problems alone anymore.

He continued to see Joy after that, but only occasionally. When they got together, the sex between them was still intense. But most of the time they just stayed in touch through the telephone, and by the start of the new year, 1991, a mood of melancholy began to sweep through Sol's life. "I cannot escape the feeling that I could enjoy life a bit more if I didn't care quite as much about what others thought of me," he wrote in January to a Yale student who had inquired about his philosophy of life. "Unfortunately, the strictures of a civilized and easily scandalized society have kept me from the ultimate happiness of saying or doing whatever I wanted at any given time."

He also felt tired a lot of the time, so tired that at times he could hardly keep up with his work, which increasingly entailed lobbying the legislature for enough money to keep the courts running at full capacity. Last year, after his dispute with Cuomo, he had failed to get the judicial raises he'd wanted, and this year, Cuomo and the legislature were indicating that they would be slashing his budget drastically. It was a terrible mistake, Sol believed, because New York's courts were more overloaded than they had ever been and needed all the money they could get in order to keep running. To prevent the cuts, he began to present his arguments to state legislators, sometimes making as many as twenty-five presentations a week.

The task was grueling. There were days he felt he could barely muster the energy for it, let alone perform his regular court duties of holding conferences and hearing arguments. And one day he sought out a doctor in Nassau—he was careful to choose a physician who was not his regular practitioner—and asked for something that would pep him up.

The doctor, an elderly man, prescribed Tenuate. It was an amphetaminelike drug that acted on the central nervous system and was most often used for dieting. Tenuate was not a dangerous drug if used for a short duration. But its manufacturer discouraged chronic use, because Tenuate could produce "overstimulation, nervousness, restlessness, dizziness, jitteriness, insomnia, anxiety, euphoria, depression," among other things, and if used in combination with other drugs that acted on the central nervous system, it could cause a "psychosis, often clinically indistinguishable from schizophrenia."

"You gotta find me a woman," a lawyer named David Samson said over dinner one night, in April 1991, to his buddy and sometime client Larry Bathgate, finance chairman of the Republican National Committee. "All I do is go to work and come home and go to sleep."

Samson had been married for twenty-five years to his college sweetheart, a woman Bathgate had known even longer, having gone to high school with her. But the pair had broken up a few months ago, and Samson had moved from his home in Short Hills, New Jersey, to an apartment on East 81st Street in Manhattan.

"You don't know what it's like," Samson went on. "I was at a cocktail party the other night, and all these people went out to dinner together, but no one asked me along. So I went by myself to a little place over on Eighty-second Street. And then, I'm sitting there, eating alone, and Georgette and Bob Mossbacher come in. And they see me there. Eating *alone*. It's embarrassing. You gotta find me a lady."

"Sure," Bathgate said. "I'll look around."

Sol was not altogether himself that spring. The amphetaminelike drug he was taking was not only energizing him but making him speed through his obligations like a hurtling train. A woman who attended a political dinner with him in May noticed that he seemed present but not present. "He's *wired*," she said to her husband. "His attention span is about twenty seconds. And it's as if he's off by himself, as if there's a plastic box around him. He isn't *with* the rest of us."

Joan noticed it too. But she didn't *know* she was noticing, or rather, she didn't know *what* she was noticing. On a trip to California, where Sol was to receive an honorary degree from the Claremont University Center and Graduate School, she complained to John Maguire, the president of the institution and an old friend, that Sol was exceedingly wound up and restless. "It's not so much fun to travel with him these days," she told Maguire, "because as soon as we get to our hotel, he's on the phone for hours and hours. And I can't get him to stop talking."

As she spoke, Joan herself seemed unusually taut and tense. Indeed, Maguire had never seen her look so frayed. "Is anything wrong?" he asked her.

She shook her head. "I guess I'm just killing myself at work."

Sol, in his vanity, thought Joy was still in love with him and that he could have their relationship back any time he chose. She still called him constantly, asking his advice about financial and political matters, and she still seemed to be hoping that her therapist, Eleanor Sloan, whom Sol was continuing to see, would eventually find the key to unlock him from his marriage.

But in fact, Joy was getting tired of her aging and reluctant married lover. One thing particularly bothered her. Now that she was separated from Jeffrey, she didn't have a suitable partner to accompany her to the White House when she was invited there for dinner.

She took her son Evan, once. And another time, she took a casual friend, a theatrical agent.

The agent found her beautiful that night. She wore a short dress and more modest jewelry than she generally wore, and to him she looked like the epitome of Park Avenue chic. He also noticed that the President and the Vice President were exceedingly cordial to her. They really like her, he thought. They're not just being political.

He liked her too. He'd heard some bad things about her. That she was tough. That she was aggressive. But as far as he was concerned, what she was was strong. Strong women don't have it easy, he thought. People call them names. They call them bitches. Not him. He liked strong women.

But unfortunately for the agent, Joy wasn't interested in him.

She knew what she wanted. Someone handsome, powerful, rich. Someone who could replace both Sol and Jeffrey in her life. And someone who would be not just a man she could be seen with, but someone she could marry.

To find him, she enlisted the aid of many people she knew. One of the acquaintances she asked was no help at all. He was William Koeppel, the Republican party leader who had scoffed at her Harmonie Club speech. He still didn't like Joy, though he'd seen her around more and more often in recent years. He'd even begun hearing around town the unsettling rumor that she was the girlfriend of his idol, George Bush. She must have started the rumor herself, Koeppel thought. To add to her luster. Because she always wanted center stage. Like that time when he'd been to a dinner party at Dan Quayle's house with her, and just when he and the Vice President had been deep in conversation, Joy had come over and edged him out of the way. "*Pushed* me out of the way," he remembered. "No, *shoved* me out of the way." So when she questioned him about a widower who was a member of the same exclusive Florida country club to which he belonged, asking, "Is he as rich as they say?" he snapped, "I'm not his accountant." And when she persisted, asking if he could introduce her to him, he barked, "I'm not his social secretary."

But some people were genuinely helpful to Joy in her quest. Larry Bathgate was one of them.

She ran into him at a luncheon for Barbara Bush at the Plaza Hotel, and leading him to a quiet corner of the room, she said, "You've got to find me a man."

Bathgate immediately thought of his old friend David Samson. But because he loved to horse around—he had a comic style that was four-fifths Jackie Mason, one-fifth Woody Allen—he asked Joy just what she was looking for in a guy. "Tell me what you want," he said. "You want short? Tall? Thin? Fat? A basketball player? What?"

"I want a guy who's between forty-five and sixty," Joy said.

"You want Jewish?"

"He doesn't have to be Jewish, but Jewish would be nice. And he's got to be presentable."

"I got the guy," Bathgate said. "Fifty-two. One of only two named partners at a law firm with eighty partners. Six feet two inches. A hundred and eighty pounds. And blond, with blue eyes."

Joy's eyes lit up. "There *is* such a guy?" she asked.

When Bathgate nodded yes, she took out her card and said, "Great. Give him my card."

Right after lunch, Bathgate called David Samson. "I've got a woman for you," he said. "She's terrific. A ten."

Samson was pleased, but he announced that he had a dilemma, because he'd just been told about another terrific woman. "Another ten," he allowed. She'd just broken up with her husband, a proctologist. "Which one should I call first?" he wanted to know.

"Where does the proctologist's wife live?"

"Ninety-second and East End."

Joy lived at 83rd and Park, just two blocks from Samson. "Start with the one closest to you," Bathgate advised. "You can take her out in the neighborhood and walk her home. The other one, you gotta take a cab to get her home. And whaddya do? See her up? Have the cab wait? It's your first night. Who needs all that pressure?"

Samson said, "Yeah, you're right. I'll call Joy first."

But he didn't call right away. He was busy with other things, and he put her number aside.

After her conversation with Bathgate, Joy may have begun sending out signals to Sol that she was no longer willing to tolerate his waffling. Or perhaps Sol himself was sick of his indecision, and sick of himself. He told Lauren, who by now knew for certain about his affair, that he was thinking of "breaking up" with Joy. "I can't leave your mother," he said. "We have forty years of history together. And you. And the other kids. And now, the grandchildren."

Lauren wanted to help him. But she didn't see how she could. It was a terrible burden to have to counsel a father in a matter of the heart. "You have to make your own decision," she said.

Not long afterward, he made one. Or thought he'd made one. It was the same one he'd been making time after time. He would tell Joy he wanted to cool their relationship. But he wanted to tell it to her in person. He called her, and made a date to meet her at Eleanor Sloan's.

In Philadelphia, he had a therapy session with Sloan, and then

150

checked into a hotel with Joy. He was feeling resigned. It was clear to him that, for all Eleanor's therapy, he was no closer than he'd ever been to leaving Joan or giving Joy what she wanted—an open relationship. He told her so, and she wasn't surprised. "I had the feeling you were going to dump me," she said.

For a moment he had the idea that Joy hated him. That she loathed him for not having left Joan. But that was the way it was. He *couldn't*. Or at least, he hadn't. So he tried to make an end to it and even tried to anticipate what would surely come next. "Maybe you ought to start seeing other men," he said.

Joy didn't let on that she'd already been putting out feelers for other men. "I will never," Sol remembered her saying, "love anyone the way I love you."

David Samson had not forgotten about Joy, and one Tuesday afternoon in July, presumably a few days after Joy's night in Philadelphia with Sol, he telephoned her. Apologizing for calling at the last minute, he said, "You're probably already busy, but if you're not, can you go to dinner tonight?"

Joy, despite being asked at the last moment, said yes with alacrity.

At eight o'clock, her doorman announced Samson, and she opened the door to her apartment. But as she opened the door, her little dog, Coco, scampered out and began barking fiercely. She tried to restrain him, and she was bending down to scoop the dog into her arms when she saw a pair of men's shoes in front of her. And above them, trousers. And then, she looked up, and saw David for the first time. "She looked up and there he was," Larry Bathgate would say later. "A fuckin' Jewish Adonis."

Bathgate, who was privy to the details of their first date, was impressed by how quickly they took to each other. "David took her to Nicola's, bought her a bottle of wine, and four hours later, they were in love."

David had rented a vacation house in Bridgehampton, not far from Joy's place in Southampton, and over the rest of the summer Joy saw him regularly. She also continued to see Barbara and George Bush, once spending the weekend as their guest at Camp David.

In the fall, she invited her new boyfriend to accompany her to one of the Bushes' White House dinners. David more than lived up to her dreams of the ideal escort. When she introduced him to the President, he said he was here just to squire her around, and Bush eyed her appraisingly and joked, ''Tough duty!'' Then David said, ''You don't know the half of it!'' which made the President guffaw. David was perfect. A man she could take anywhere. And a man who was available for marriage. Or who would be, once he got his divorce.

She didn't tell Sol, whom she still spoke to frequently on the telephone, that she had a new boyfriend. She just told him she was seeing other people, implying that there was no one for whom she had any special feelings. But after a while, she felt she had to tell him.

They met for dinner; as always, he'd been worried about being seen with her, and he'd chosen an obscure restaurant in Queens where no one they knew was likely to dine. She told him she'd met a man with whom she'd become seriously involved. She couldn't help being a little taunting. Sol had put her through hell. So she confessed that her new man was younger and richer than he was. And when Sol complained at her disloyalty—he must have thought that even though he'd suggested she go out with others, nothing would come of it and she'd stay faithful to him forever—she reminded him that it was his idea. ''You said I should find another man to date,'' she told him.

He kept asking her who the man was. But she refused to identify him.

Afterward, Sol was bitter. One day she can't turn around without me, he thought, and the next she's gone on to someone else. It stopped on a dime. It's good-bye, Charlie.

Calling Joy, he badgered her to tell him who her boyfriend was and whether she was sleeping with him, but she wouldn't answer either question.

Soon, he started crying whenever he thought about her. And sometimes he cried even when he wasn't thinking about her. And the more he cried, the more his loss seemed immeasurable.

He was about to suffer another, different kind of loss too. All year, he'd been lobbying Cuomo and the state legislature in an effort to get more money for the courts. But instead of granting him more money, the governor and the legislators had reduced his allotment, giving him not only millions of dollars less than he'd asked for but millions less than they'd given him the previous year. The cuts were so severe that, he felt certain, he would have to close down civil-trial courtrooms all over the state and lay off five hundred employees. He dreaded having to do that. Just thinking about having to tell people they'd be out of work brought tears to his eyes—but then, he was always weepy these days.

He'd tried leaning on his old friendship with Cuomo to get him to give him more money. But Cuomo had stopped taking his telephone calls. And the last time he'd tried to reach him, Cuomo had directed his counsel, Elizabeth Moore, to deliver a message from him. The message was that he wasn't going to give the courts "one cent more." And, Moore had added, Cuomo had told her to tell Sol not to lobby him personally anymore.

It was a slap in the face. Another slap in the face. But this one, he decided, he could do something about. He could sue the governor and the legislature, on the grounds that they had violated the state constitution by failing to finance the judiciary adequately. Courts in other states had filed such lawsuits, and a few had been successful. And at the least, Sol told a reporter from the New York *Daily News* on September 26, a lawsuit would "detail a decade of neglect where now in New York State we have come to accept excessive plea bargaining and lengthy delays."

That afternoon, he filed his lawsuit.

He was still taking Tenuate, and perhaps the medication played a role in his drastic decision to sue. Certainly, when he subsequently went on television to explain why he had filed suit, he seemed manic, fevered, a man whose words raced from his mouth in a pressured profusion. And certainly some reporters covering what quickly got termed a "feud" between the governor and the chief judge noticed that Sol's behavior was peculiar. "He could not stay seated at his desk and attend to his lunchtime turkey sandwich," wrote one, Robin Pogrebin in *The New York Observer*, "since he was constantly jumping up to pace the red carpet, point for emphasis, and pound law books." But most people, listening to his words and viewing his behavior, attributed his manifestation of manic symptoms to the stressful action he was taking—rather than the other way around.

Joan was one of the many people who assumed that Sol's hyperactivity was caused by the strains of the lawsuit against Cuomo. When he was home, which wasn't often, because he was busy conducting his battle up in Albany, she paid little attention to him. For one thing, he was so supercharged, he was hard to be around. For another, she was particularly busy. Not only was she holding down her job at the Y, but she was doing campaign work again. Her youngest child, Philip, had decided to follow in his father's footsteps and run for public office, and he was trying to win a seat on the North Hempstead Town Council, just the way Sol had done at the start of *his* political career. In a way, it was burdensome for Joan, whose job at the Y was increasingly demanding, to have to spend time campaigning. But in another way, it was pleasurable, a return to old times, a nostalgic activity that reminded her of the days when she and Sol had been young and whatever had come between them had not yet reared its head. So every morning she would rise at six, do her exercises and industriously swim laps, and then turn up at the Great Neck Republican party headquarters.

Randa Pittel, a young attorney who was also working on the campaign, was struck by how unpretentious Joan was, given the fact that her husband was someone Pittel thought of as royalty among judges. She'd once argued a case before him and found him noble, regal, imposing. Joan was different. She came to the headquarters wearing pants and a sweater or T-shirt. She didn't wear much makeup. And while she looked quite young, she made no bones about the fact that she was a grandmother. Indeed, she seemed enchanted by her grandchild, Philip Wachtler's little girl, who sometimes came down to the headquarters with her parents. Joan would stop whatever she was doing to cuddle the baby.

*   *   *

While Joan was working on their son's campaign, Sol was brooding on his injuries. "Where are you?" he demanded of Joy at the start of the Columbus Day weekend. She'd called him on his car phone after he'd left several messages for her.

"I'm in the Hamptons," she replied to his question.

"I'm on my way out there too. To see my daughter Marjorie." He thought she would invite him to come over and see her. He still hadn't comprehended that she was finished with him. But all she said was, "That's nice."

"When will you be back in the city?" he asked her next.

"Sunday night."

"I'll be up in Albany on Sunday," he said. "I'll give you a call."

On Sunday night, he began telephoning her. He called her apartment in the city. Then he called her house in Southampton. He got no answer at either number, and he called them again and again. Then, after a while, he got upset.

Was it jealousy that was plaguing him? Could this be the source of his discomfort? No, he was worried about her, he told himself. He was worried that something had happened to her. And to Jessica. Because Jessica wasn't at either of the numbers, either.

He began calling her friends, and at last he reached one of them. "She's probably with David Samson," her friend said.

The name meant nothing to him. But when he finally got Joy on the phone the following night, he said angrily, "I know about David Samson. You've been sleeping with him, haven't you? You've been spending weekends with him." Then he wanted to know if she'd taken Jessica with her, and when she said yes, he got moralistic. "You and Jessica were sharing a house with David?" he admonished her. "How could you?"

"I know what you're thinking," he recalled her saying defensively. "But let me just tell you something. After David and I were finished, I always went back to the bed next to Jessica's, and when she got up in the morning, I was always right there beside her."

"Yeah, but while you, before you were finished——" he said. And then, his old puritanical self surfacing, he scolded her.

"Don't you think that was— You know she's fourteen years old, and you've known this guy for only two weeks, three weeks."

Joy didn't tell him how long she'd known David. She just said, "Jessica is very mature. She understands these things."

Her casualness shocked him. When he and Joy had been seeing each other, they'd avoided making love when they were under the same roof as Jessica. What had been the point of all their care and self-denial, if now her mother was breaking all the rules? But the most important matter on his mind was being with Joy again. He told her he wanted to see her. And once again, she startled him.

"I would never see two men at the same time," she said.

"What about when you were with Jeffrey, and you were having an affair with me?" he argued.

"That was different," she said. "I was married."

He didn't understand her, didn't comprehend the crucial difference between deceiving a newly beloved partner and a no-longer-loved husband. If she had cheated on Jeffrey with him, why couldn't she cheat on David with him? But there was nothing he could say to make her change her mind. She didn't want to see him again.

She made that even plainer the next time he called her. And she also boasted about her new lover. "David's handsomer than you," she said. "He looks like a younger edition of Lloyd Bridges. He has a wonderful athletic build—he's a real athlete. And he's richer than you. He earns five times as much money as you."

Not long after that conversation, Sol stopped eating, and whenever he went to bed, he tossed and turned for hours.

PART 3

"This Judge Is Either Crazy or Criminal"

CHAPTER 9

"Something is terribly wrong [with Sol]," Joan wrote in her diary not long after Sol and Joy broke up. "He's acting strangely. Very depressed, irritable, emotional. . . . [He went to] Florida [to visit his mother]—came back, told me it was the worst three days of his life—death, old people—he feels he's dying. . . . Doesn't understand what's happening to him. Feels disassociated with himself. Feels a beautiful day is ugly. Hasn't slept in weeks even with pills—lost fifteen pounds. Doesn't eat at all—drug-related?"

He had told her by then that he thought maybe they ought to separate. He loved her, he said, but he couldn't live with her any longer—not until he got his head together. He'd even begun moving some of his clothes out of the house. But then he moved them back in. Joan hardly knew what to think.

But it seemed to her that whatever else might be going on with him, he was depressed. After all, she'd been head of a mental-health clinic for years. She begged him to see a psychiatrist.

Sol refused. He was afraid, he told her, that if he went to a psychiatrist, news that he had a mental problem might leak out. If it did, his career would be ruined. He'd have no more credibility as a judge, and he'd never be able to run for governor. He'd be stigmatized, like poor Tom Eagleton.

He didn't tell Joan that he was already seeing someone in the mental-health field—Eleanor Sloan.

In his sessions with Sloan that fall, Sol complained bitterly about David Samson and tried to get the therapist to tell him whatever she knew about Joy's relationship with her new lover. He also attempted to convince her that being intimate with Samson would be unwise for Joy. "He's done bad, bad things that will eventually come out," he told her, and suggested that if she really cared about Joy, she'd check into Samson's background.

He himself had already done so. He had asked one of his law clerks to conduct a computer search into Samson's past and one day, while going through his clerk's findings, had discovered that Joy's new lover was the lawyer for a refuse disposal company that was having a contractual dispute with Essex County in New Jersey. The dispute, he read with interest, "could mushroom into intense environmental litigation."

He had also obtained a copy of his rival's biennial New York bar registration form, on which Samson had scrawled his distinctive signature—a loopy scribble that looked more like the letters *i,l,e,u* than it did like the name "David Samson."

Not settled yet on what use he could make of these materials, Sol directed his secretary to start a special "David Samson" file in his Mineola chambers and keep the papers there.

Did she know Samson was married, Sol asked Joy over lunch soon after he'd started his David Samson file. Did she know that he owned a home in Short Hills, New Jersey, in which his wife was still living, and that the mortgage had recently been paid off?

He was trying to show her that he had special and intimate knowledge about the man she was going to bed with—knowledge that might lend weight to something else he told her that day, which was that Samson was a bad guy. He was so bad, Sol said, that he was afraid for her. But she wasn't to worry. If Samson didn't treat her well, he'd be there for her, he'd stand up and protect her.

Despite his effusiveness, the lunch did not have a happy outcome. Joy made light of his warnings and refused to entertain doubts about her new lover. Frustrated, he was reduced to trying to elicit from her a promise that if Samson ever broke off their relationship, she would return to him.

Though dismayed, after the lunch he took comfort in the fact that he could still talk to Joy. After all, he reminded himself, she hadn't said she never wanted to hear from him again. And one night not long after their lunch, when he was out of town on a speaking engagement, he used the pretext that he needed a restaurant recommendation and phoned her from his lonely hotel room. She talked to him. But she was brief, and afterward he felt strangely dissatisfied and dialed her again.

But this time when she answered, he just hung up.

Over the next few weeks, he did this again and again. Perhaps he was lovesick and longing for the sound of her voice. Perhaps he was furious and trying to provoke her, make her pick up the phone and hear it turn dead in her hand. Whatever his motive, time after time when she answered her phone, he put down his receiver with a soft click.

Joy would one day say that she hadn't suspected that Wachtler was responsible for the harassment she experienced. But she seems to have at least suspected that the hang-up calls she was suddenly receiving were being made by him. Norman Sheresky, her lawyer, would say later that one day not long after the calls started, she told him about the hang-ups and said, "Sol's harassing me."

Sheresky thought she was being ridiculous. Sol Wachtler harassing someone? Impossible.

But Joy was insistent. "I want it to stop," she said. "Tell him to stop."

Sheresky was embarrassed at the very notion of going to the chief judge of New York with the accusation Joy was leveling. But he did what Joy asked. He met with Sol and said, "She thinks you're calling and hanging up."

"She's crazy," Sol said.

He had, by then, begun making hang-up calls to other people too, to David Samson at his office—he didn't know the phone number in Samson's Manhattan apartment, which was unlisted—and to Samson's wife, Elaine, at her New Jersey home.

He had also, by then, conceived of a plan that might bring about the rift between Joy and Samson that he so desired. Suppose a private investigator began to investigate Samson and uncovered his relationship with Joy? Mightn't that worry the New Jersey lawyer, perhaps even scare him so much that he'd hurry back to the arms of his wife? Mightn't it frighten Joy too and send her back to *his* arms? Convinced that he might be able to bring about this outcome—perhaps he had faith that it could work because he himself was such a worrier about scandal—Sol decided to pretend to be a private investigator and, in that guise, to pass along word of the affair between Samson and Joy to some interested parties.

It would not be difficult for him to take on a role. Frequently in his life, he had played the trickster, and often he had trafficked—for purposes of amusing people—in impersonation. Now he would use his skills at masquerade for a different reason. For a reason close to his heart.

The first person to whom he pretended to be a private eye was Jeffrey Silverman, the husband from whom Joy was separated. Calling Silverman, he said his name was David Purdy, that he'd been hired to investigate Samson, and that inadvertently he'd stumbled onto Samson's affair with Joy.

After that, he sat back and waited. Silverman, he no doubt expected, would inform Joy about the call, and Joy would at once be on the phone about it to Samson. The two of them would be devastated! And soon he'd hear from Joy herself that her lover had left her or that she'd decided to leave him.

But by week's end, he had received no such word, and on Election Day, he once again played at being Purdy—but this time he directed his pitch toward Elaine Samson. Calling her up, he spoke as Purdy, said he had information about her husband and another woman, and told her he'd be willing to sell it to her.

Coolly, Elaine asked him who had hired him to investigate her husband.

Sol didn't answer.

A moment later, Elaine hung up on him.

Undaunted, he took another shot at calling her the next day. This time, he told her he'd give her his information for free, and he proceeded to tell her that the woman her husband was seeing was a very rich individual named Joy Silverman. They slept together in Silverman's house in Southampton, he said, and in Samson's house in Water Mill. Not only that, but they dined together in Manhattan twice a week, eating in expensive restaurants and talking about *her,* Elaine.

Then, giving Elaine Joy's unlisted home telephone number, Sol asked her to provide him with her husband's Manhattan address and phone number. But Elaine wouldn't do it.

Two days later, he tried to get this information from her again. And the next day, and the next, and the next. To no avail. But that didn't discourage him. It was true he was no closer than ever to knowing how to reach David, but every time he called Elaine, he gained some advantage. Every time he called her, he presumably made her anxious. So presumably she would want to communicate her concern to her recently departed husband. Then presumably, *he* would become concerned, and sooner or later, either he or Joy would get concerned enough to stop seeing each other. Or at the very least, Joy would call him and say that she was terrified, and that she needed him to come to her rescue the way he'd always done in the past.

Joan, unaware that her husband was impersonating a private investigator or making hang-up calls, knew only that Sol still seemed depressed. He had many of the classic symptoms of depression, among them weight loss, disturbed sleep, and an inability to concentrate. Each of these telling symptoms could, of course, have been caused by the Tenuate he was taking, for the drug, often used as a diet pill, can produce loss of appetite, insomnia, and jitteriness. But in addition, Sol was uncharacteristically pessimistic and blue. Worried, Joan persisted in her pleas that he see a psychiatrist. And at last, when he had repeatedly turned down her suggestion, she asked Dr. Geraldine Lanman, their family doctor, to stop by the house and have a look at him.

Dr. Lanman, when she examined Sol, agreed with Joan's hypothesis. Sol *was* suffering from depression, she said, and she prescribed Pamelor, a standard antidepressant, to elevate his mood, and Halcion, a controversial but still widely used hypnotic, to help him sleep. In addition, she directed him to stop taking the Tenuate and various other medications he was taking for headaches, among them Percogesic, Tylenol No. 3 with Codeine, and a steroid-based elixir of antihistamines.

Sol filled his new prescriptions on November 11 and that day again called Elaine Samson and again asked her for David's home number. She wouldn't give it to him, and he called her ten days later with the same request. Then, on the day after Thanksgiving, he called once more. But this time, perhaps because his initial attempts to scare Elaine and thereby frighten David and Joy had not resulted in the reunion he craved, he said something to her far more ominous than anything he'd ever said before. He had dirty pictures of David and Joy together, was what he said. He'd sell them to her, if she liked.

"Where did Jessica spend her Thanksgiving?" Sol asked Jeffrey Silverman, who knew nothing of the judge's longtime affair with his wife or his present efforts to woo her back, over lunch at the Harmonie Club early in December. Sol had called Jeffrey and set up their meeting.

"With Joy and this fellow Samson," Jeffrey informed him.

Though Sol had expected as much, it disturbed him to hear his suspicions confirmed. "Jeffrey, this is your *daughter*," he lectured the former husband of his former lover. "Doesn't it bother you that she would have her Thanksgiving dinner with a live-in?"

"No," Jeffrey said. "I had Thanksgiving with *my* girlfriend."

Sol was troubled by Jeffrey's nonchalance. But he couldn't seem to make Jeffrey see the wrongfulness of exposing the little girl to her mother's lover. He gave up, and spoke of other things. "How's he managing, this Samson?" he asked. "How well do you think he's putting up with Joy's mouth?"

Jeffrey shrugged. "I understand that Joy is walking on eggs with Samson right now."

Suggesting, as it did, that Joy was on her best behavior with her new lover, the answer gave Sol little comfort. But he didn't let Jeffrey know his disappointment. "I wonder how long *that* will last," he said cynically.

He missed Joy terribly that pre-Christmas season. He was still yearning for her and still feeling melancholy. He told his trusted chief administrator, Matthew Crosson, who had earlier noticed that he seemed deeply tired and unable to focus on administrative matters, that he'd been depressed and was taking an antidepressant. He told his fellow judges that this had been the worst year he had ever experienced. But to no one did he confide the feelings of loss and longing that still continued to sweep over him.

Shortly before the holiday, even though Joy had told him that not only didn't she want to see him but she didn't want him turning up at her apartment, his need to be in touch with her was so great that he went to her building anyway and left her a gift and a letter.

"Joy," the letter began, "five years ago a friend—she became my best friend—sent me a framed proverb. It read:

> Cherish yesterday
> Dream about tomorrow
> Live today

"I have been looking at it all these years, but never really understood it until this month.

"I couldn't resist getting you a holiday gift. A longtime habit—like a longtime love—takes a long time to die."

He signed it, "Always, Sol."

Afterward, he must have felt in bad need of a pick-me-up, because a little before Christmas, he disobeyed his doctor's orders. He once again renewed his old prescription for Tenuate.

Shortly after the court of appeals reconvened after the Christmas recess, Sol dropped his lawsuit against Mario Cuomo in return for the promise of an extra nineteen million dollars for the courts in the next state budget and the passage of cost-saving laws that would provide another fifteen million. His lawsuit against the governor, which had seemed to many to be foolish or ill-conceived, had proved to be politically wise. The pressure had worked.

Sol opened that 1992 session with a tribute to a former chief judge, Charles Breitel, who had recently died. Leaning engagingly forward in his high-backed chair, he praised his predecessor in fluid, silver-tongued sentences. If he was depressed that day— or on his way to that remarkable other pole of depression, mania—it was impossible to tell. And throughout 1992, whenever he took the bench—although his inner mood, he would eventually claim, swung from a disconsolate low to an extravagant high—his behavior would seem as reasonable, as thoughtful, as *gentle,* as it did on that first day of the new session.

When he was off the bench, it was another story. Fed by Tenuate, which reduces inhibitions and produces arousal, as well as by Pamelor, which can also promote arousal and agitation, and Halcion, which can cause irritability and extreme excitation, his brain swirled feverishly with thoughts of Joy, and increasingly he continued to focus on one thing and one thing only: getting her to come back to him. And soon, the trickster in him seems to have concluded that this could be accomplished by making Elaine Samson think that her husband wanted to reunite with her. So on Valentine's Day, he sent Elaine a mash note, signed with a forgery of David Samson's distinctive signature. It showed a big lovable bear pointing to his heart and saying, "Even though we're far apart, I know exactly where you are every second of every day—right here." In March, he sent her another such card. It showed a little teddy bear saying, "I can go through life without a lot of things, but I can't last a day without you!" It too was signed with a forgery of David Samson's signature.

Perhaps Sol expected that Elaine, receiving such sentimental greetings from her husband, would become energized to woo him back from Joy. Or perhaps he expected that she would communicate the sentiments of the cards to Joy, thereby raising doubts in Joy's mind as to the loyalty of her lover. Whatever his hopes, he went on plying Elaine with love cards supposedly from her husband. One, with a picture of a spring flower, said,

"Like the wonder of the first fragile blossom and the promise of Easter morning, thoughts of you bring me joy." Another, with a cartoon of a man sitting alone with his puppy, said, "Hi! I was just sittin' around doin' nothin', like I so often do when I don't have anything to do, and I got to thinkin' about YOU and Me and Us, and I got sorta all misty-like." Still another showed two little pigs, and said, "Thinking of you. Let's get reconnected."

But by the time he mailed the last love note to Elaine, something had happened that sparked a new and more noxious plan in his mind. Late in March, he had read in *The New York Times* that the residents of Linden, New Jersey, were fighting the building of a hazardous-waste incinerator. The lawyer for G.A.F., the company that wanted to build the incinerator, was David Samson. Samson was quoted in the article, as was a woman named Beatrice Bernzott, the leader of a citizens' group opposing the incinerator. Two days after the article appeared, Sol attempted to make it appear that Samson was up to no good, that he wanted to bribe or even threaten Bernzott. Claiming to be an associate of Samson's, he called the civic leader and told her ominously that Samson wanted to discuss the incinerator project with her. The following day, he thickened his plot. He called Samson, claimed to be Bernzott's husband, and left a message saying that his wife had been receiving threatening phone calls. His plan seems to have been to make Bernzott tell the police or the press that Samson was harassing her, and to make Samson deny the allegation—he knew enough from his years in politics to realize that many people, hearing a denial, would conclude that where there was smoke, there had probably been fire.

By this time it was early April and Joy's birthday was coming up. She'd be forty-five on April 8. Sol had been asked to make a speech in Florida, and he'd accepted the engagement, doubtless hoping that if he were away from his familiar haunts, he could banish his obsessive thoughts of how to win Joy back. But his weekend in Florida proved disastrous. He couldn't stop thinking of her, couldn't stop remembering how important her birthdays always were to her. He felt so blue that he didn't want to be with anyone, and he drove alone to Disney World, where he tried to amuse himself by going on rides, just the way he used to do when his kids were little and he'd take them to Kiddie City.

But as he drifted through underground grottoes and hurtled dizzily up and down tracks in the sky, he kept seeing all around him hordes of smiling parents, laughing children, lovers with arms entwined. Their happiness highlighted his own lack of it, producing in him acute feelings of loneliness and misery.

Desperate, when he returned to New York, he stepped up his efforts to frighten Joy back into his arms. He called Beatrice Bernzott collect, saying he was David Samson, and tried to get her to accept his call. She refused. He called her again. And again. But when his calls to Bernzott didn't result in any apparent police or press attention to Samson, he abandoned that line of tactics and turned at last to yet a new plan.

He would frighten Joy, he decided, Joy herself. He would make her think that Samson—or someone pretending to be Samson—was haunting her, sending her and her beloved Jessica dirty and scary messages through the mail.

In mid-April, he began seeking out cards that would do the trick.

Joy was at home when, one morning in late April, she opened her mail to find a belated birthday greeting. It was a card whose front panel bore a picture of a bear and the words "On your birthday, CUCUMBERS are better than men."

When she turned to the inside of the card, she saw a long commercially printed message, all in capital letters:

THE AVERAGE CUCUMBER IS AT LEAST
SIX INCHES LONG.—CUCUMBERS STAY
HARD FOR A WEEK.—A CUCUMBER WON'T
TELL YOU SIZE DOESN'T COUNT.
—CUCUMBERS DON'T GET *TOO* EXCITED.
—A CUCUMBER NEVER SUFFERS
PERFORMANCE ANXIETY.—CUCUMBERS
ARE EASY TO PICK UP.—YOU CAN EAT
A CUCUMBER WHEN *YOU* FEEL LIKE.
—A CUCUMBER DOESN'T CARE IF YOU'RE A
VIRGIN.—A CUCUMBER WON'T ASK, AM

I THE BEST? HOW WAS IT?—NO MATTER
HOW OLD YOU ARE, YOU CAN ALWAYS GET
A FRESH CUCUMBER.—A CUCUMBER
WON'T POUT IF YOU HAVE A HEADACHE.
—WITH A CUCUMBER YOU NEVER HAVE TO
SAY YOU'RE SORRY.—A CUCUMBER
WILL NEVER LEAVE YOU FOR ANOTHER
WOMAN.—YOU ALWAYS KNOW WHERE
YOUR CUCUMBER'S BEEN.—CUCUMBERS
DON'T LEAVE YOU WONDERING FOR A
MONTH.
—IT'S EASY TO DROP A CUCUMBER.
—NO MATTER HOW YOU SLICE IT, YOU CAN
HAVE YOUR CUKE AND EAT IT TOO!!!

HAPPY BIRTHDAY!

The card was signed with a forgery of David Samson's loopy signature and three big *X*s, for kisses.

Joy was annoyed by the cucumber card. But her irritation must have been nothing compared to that which came over her when she opened another envelope that had come in the mail that same morning. This one was addressed to "Ms. Jesse Silverman"— her daughter Jessica?—and showed a buxom woman reaching into her refrigerator for a soda can. Inside were the words:

1. A DIET COLA IS SATISFYING ALL THE TIME.
2. YOU CAN DUMP A DIET COLA WHEN
   YOU'VE HAD ENOUGH.
3. IT GENERALLY LASTS LONGER.
4. IT'S AVAILABLE IN A VARIETY OF SIZES.
5. YOU ONLY NEED ONE.
6. DIET COLA COMES IN A CAN, NOT IN YOUR
   MOUTH.
7. WHEN YOU SWALLOW A DIET COLA, YOU
   ONLY GET 1 CALORIE.
8. A DIET COLA DOESN'T DIRTY YOUR SHEETS
   OR DISHES.
9. A DIET COLA WILL SILENTLY AND
   PATIENTLY WAIT FOR YOU.

10. YOU CAN IGNORE A DIET COLA FOR DAYS
    AND IT WILL STILL BE THERE WHEN YOU
    WANT IT.
11. A DIET COLA RESPECTS YOU AS MUCH AT
    NIGHT AS IT DOES IN THE MORNING.
12. WHEN YOU SWALLOW A DIET COLA, IT
    DOESN'T LEAVE AN AFTERTASTE IN YOUR
    MOUTH.
13. PEOPLE DON'T TALK IF YOU'VE HAD 3 OR 4
    OF THEM.
14. NO PRIVACY IS NEEDED TO ENJOY ONE.
15. EVEN IF YOU SPILL ONE IN BED, IT WON'T
    MAKE YOU SLEEP IN A WET SPOT.
16. YOU CAN HAVE A HEADACHE AND ENJOY IT.

This card, too, was signed with a replica of David Samson's signature. But Joy was sure the cards weren't from him. They were clearly from someone who had reason to want to annoy her, harass her.

Soon after he mailed the dirty cards, Sol went through Joy's financial records and made a startling discovery. He learned that despite his always having viewed Joy as a spendthrift, she'd managed to save $150,000 out of the $300,000 a year she was receiving from Jeffrey and her trust. Maybe he ought to cut off her trust payments, he began thinking. Maybe he'd suggest as much to Norman Sheresky.

Early in May, he called the lawyer. Joy, he told him, would probably receive a greater maintenance award from the judge presiding over her divorce if she didn't get any income from her trust.

The lawyer said he'd speak to Joy about the idea.

Joy turned it down. It smacked of harassment to her. Meanwhile, the harassment by mail was getting worse. Only last week, she'd received two even more disgusting cards. One showed a woman who appeared to have drunk something that had caused her eyes to roll and her head to expand hideously. "Under the

circumstances, you seem to be handling things fairly well!!!"
said the card's printed message, and beneath it was a handwritten
message, "But soon I'm going to fuck you over!!!"

Another card showed a bear falling down a mountain and said
on its front panel, "Life is peaks and valleys," and on its inside
panel, "And the peaks are greased!"

Beneath that, the sender had penned in another of his own
messages. "Especially for you, Bitch!" he had written.

Still, the most worrisome card had been addressed not to Joy but,
once again, to her daughter, or at least to "Ms. Jesse Silverman."

On the outside was the picture of a fluffy kitten sniffing a
flower. On the inside was a wrapped condom.

The card also contained a typewritten message. "I look forward to visiting you this summer," the message said. "School
should be great fun for you.

"BUT YOU MUST BE CAREFUL. The enclosed should be
used by your boy friend before you do 'IT.' "

It was signed with another replica of David Samson's signature, and beneath the signature was an additional line. "P.S.,"
the line read, "I have a picture of your mother doing 'IT' which
I will send you soon."

Though Joy had intercepted this perversion that seemed intended for her daughter, and didn't let the girl see it, she was
frightened by the new threatening cards. She made up her mind
that the next time she spoke to Sol on the telephone, she would
tape their conversation. And she also told Sheresky that under
no circumstances would she follow Sol's suggestions concerning
her money. They couldn't be trusted.

Sol didn't let up on his plan to cut off Joy's income from the
trust. In mid-May, he again discussed it with Sheresky, and after
their conversation, which had apparently left him dissatisfied, he
wrote a preening letter to the lawyer that warned that under the
terms of Bibbs's will, he himself was the deciding voice in how
the trust money was distributed. "You will note that I," he said,
"have the discretion to withhold income which, year after year,
would become part of the principal. I also have the power to
distribute principal whenever I wish."

A week later, he wrote Sheresky another letter, this time telling him that he had presented Joy's case as a hypothetical one to six other judges and that all the judges had agreed that his notion was a sound one:

> The six judges said that they would award maintenance, based on the established standard of living enjoyed by the wife at the time the action was commenced, less the amount of income which she received from her trust.
> The same six judges said that if the income from the trust was suspended, prior to the commencement of the action, and for whatever reason, the trust income would not be a factor in computing the amount of maintenance to be awarded.
> Six to nothing, Norman. Think about it.

Joy, when she heard about the letter, was pretty sure Sol was using his role as trustee of her trust fund to intimidate her. It was a goal not so different from that of the dirty letter writer.

When he wasn't involved in activities that concerned Joy, Sol behaved in his usual pleasant, considerate, and entertaining fashion. One evening early in June, he captivated an audience of seasoned politicians and hard-nosed reporters at a dinner of the Legislative Correspondents Association in Albany by poking merciless fun at Governor Cuomo. Cuomo was so indecisive, he joked, that at his wedding ceremony he'd said to his bride, not "I do," but "I might." Cuomo was so obsessive that he was only now getting ready to toss his hat in the ring for the 1988 presidential nomination.

At each of his one-liners, his audience roared, but they laughed the hardest when he said that if he ran against Cuomo in 1994, his campaign slogan would be "Anyone who would appoint me as chief judge is not fit to be governor."

He also told jokes about Vice President Quayle, and two days after the dinner, when Joy called him, her tape recorder on, he repeated one of them to her. "I said that when Dan Quayle was a little boy, he worked very very hard because someday he wanted to go to the electoral college.''

Joy got angry. "Why would you do that to him? You're on the same ticket as he is, or you will be.''

Sol said he'd never have to run at the same time as Quayle, and then he launched into an attack on Bush. "Let's be honest here,'' he said. "The President has done some bad things. He's alienated a lot of people, he's alienated a lot of Jews, he's alienated anyone that thinks about or is concerned about women's rights, he's devastated the legal profession by his last two appointments to the Supreme Court, and he seems to be determined to give away the presidency to the conservatives. One of his bad choices—and I apologize for saying this, because I know you're close to him—is Dan Quayle. A bad mistake.''

Joy leaped to Quayle's defense. "Dan Quayle's gotten a terrible rap from the media. I think he's much better than people give him credit for. I'll tell you something. I was at his home for dinner, and he really impressed me.''

"But what right does he have to pass judgment on the way people lead their lives?'' Sol objected.

"You mean the Murphy Brown incident?'' she said, alluding to Quayle's attack on the TV character for having a child out of wedlock. "It's absurd.''

"Excuse me!'' Sol expostulated. "You think he'd approve of your lifestyle? Of my lifestyle?''

Joy defended Quayle. "He knows my lifestyle. He doesn't show any disappointment in me. I'm invited to his home. He considers me his friend. They just called to tell me when he's going to be in town.''

Sol continued to criticize Quayle, and soon Joy was telling him that she was sick of politics. "I think politics has got to be the all-time sleaze, with the all-time sleaze buckets. I am so turned off with government and politics. I am not turned off with the President, because of his loyalty and decency to me—''

Sol interrupted to tell her that he, too, had been loyal and decent to her.

Joy brushed past his remark and asked why he wanted to run for governor.

"You know, honest to God," Sol said, "I feel I can make a difference. I think there are things—"

"Oh, yeah, yeah," Joy mocked him. "Make a difference."

Despite her taunting, Sol continued to talk about his goals. "Well, you know, maybe, maybe I just think this state is so hungry for some change, it's so anxious not to keep descending the way it has been—I think there are programs and initiatives that I would love to take. Sometimes I get so enthused about this thing and then I pull myself back because I don't want to get too enthused."

Joy ran out of patience. "It's something you always wanted to do anyway," she snapped. "You're basically a politician at heart. You are. And you had the opportunity to become a politician with Cuomo, and you took it and enjoyed it."

"I didn't enjoy it," Sol protested.

"You enjoyed it."

Everything they talked about that afternoon turned into a quarrel. And the quarreling got more and more intense, especially after Sol mentioned that he was going to attend a fund-raising party for Long Island University that Jeffrey had organized. "You screwed his wife, for crying out loud," Joy said harshly, "and you're going to go to a party that he's giving?"

He reminded her that Jeffrey had once come to a similar party that had been given for him—it was while he and Joy were still lovers, and she'd come too—and he said that he felt obligated to return the favor.

But Joy got ticked off. "I find it ironic," she said, "that you, who never let anybody tell him what to do, and you who oftentimes don't give a shit what people say or think, because you find a way of getting yourself in and out of situations, would feel obligated to go to this because he did that for you."

"Wait," Sol tried to stop her.

"But you weren't obligated to be having an affair with his wife," Joy went on.

"Oh, stop that business, will you please?" Sol begged.

But she wouldn't stop, she laughed derisively at him, and her tone got strident, and at last he promised docilely that he wouldn't go to Jeffrey's party.

He'd given in, but soon after he did so, his docility turned to aggression, and he not only once again brought up his idea of withholding her trust income, but said of his idea, "If you don't like it, sue me. I'm going to withhold from you. That I can do anyhow. I can do that arbitrarily."

Yet once those challenging words had surged to the surface, he repressed his anger and once again became gentle and placating, and tried to persuade her that his idea was a sound one. Then he became boastful, as if to impress her with how powerful he was, and suggested that he could manipulate her divorce proceedings for her because no one would ever dare question him, the chief judge. "Let them ask me," he said, "let the judge"— and at the very thought, he laughed sardonically—"let the presiding judge over the trial say to me, 'Are you doing this collusively in order to prevent her from getting money, so she gets more by this, is it collusively?' " He'd tell them, he assured Joy, " 'Absolutely not, Your Honor.' " And that would be that. "You think they're going to believe me? You're damn well right they are going to believe me."

He had said something unwise, something he may have long believed but which most likely he would not have said had he known he was being taped. He had said he was above the law.

Joy filed the tape away for future use.

Who was David Purdy? Like a novelist, to whom the name of a character often occurs before the character's lineaments and personal history become clear, Sol had invented a private eye named David Purdy, but he had not yet fully imagined him. What did he look like? Where did he come from? What sort of man was he? One day, it struck him that the private eye ought to come from Texas. Maybe from Houston. Yes, he'd be a Houston guy, down on his luck, just like the characters in the novels of Raymond Chandler. He'd be in need of money, would be so broke he'd have to live in a YMCA. But how much would that cost him? Again like a novelist—writers of fiction generally feel they need to know everything about their characters, even when they don't plan to utilize all that they know—Sol called a Y in Houston and inquired about the cost of a room. He also asked how large the rooms were. And after that, he could *picture* David Purdy. Could see his body—fat and slovenly. His face—toothless and ugly. He could hear his voice too. His southern accent—a drawl just like the one he used when he told Bubba jokes. His language—vulgar and smutty. And he could imagine him pacing up and down in his tiny cage of a room, longing to break out and make people—Joy—take notice of him.

One night, when he was in Sedona, Arizona, to which he'd traveled in order to give a speech at a meeting of the Nevada Bar Association, he gave life to David Purdy. It was the night before he was due to deliver his speech. He'd taken some Halcion, but it hadn't made him sleepy—if anything, it had charged him up—and so he told the sponsors of the conference that he had an important opinion to write and asked them for a typewriter. They brought one to his room, and he began typing. But what he typed was not a judicial opinion. It was a letter to Joy. And although the fingers that pressed the keys were his, the voice that emerged from the page was Purdy's.

He had dirty pictures of Joy taken in David's house in Water Mill, "Purdy" wrote. "I also have some terrific audio tapes of you talking to some friends at your Southampton house. Some interesting chit chat about your personal life and some big shots. I can send them some pictures too.

"But everything I have is for sale. I'll give you a chance before I send my material to your husband Jeffery [*sic*] (At PLY-GEM) and to Jessica at school and to others. Samson's wife was not interested in buying what I have to sell. But she's an innocent bystander—you are the home breaker—yours and her's [*sic*]."

As Sol wrote, he became more and more exhilarated. Joy would be scared out of her wits by this letter, he thought. And she'd never know it was from him. Because Purdy wasn't anything like Sol Wachtler. Purdy was a lowlife. Purdy was a creep. Clattering away at the keys, he typed another paragraph, letting Purdy's voice emerge at its most vile.

"Just think," he wrote, "if that fucker had not decided to dump his toxic waste in Linden, I would not have discovered your cheating. He's screwing you like he has screwed us—the only difference is that you're enjoying it. I promise I'll not charge you as much as he paid off those commissioners. You will be hearing from me soon.''

When he was done, he signed the letter with the peculiar signature he had been using for Purdy all along—an imitation of David Samson's signature. And he added, in words that the upright, clean-speaking judge, Sol Wachtler, had never been known to use: "P.S. You know what GAF stands for? Godamned Ass Fuckers.''

He had been at the typewriter for hours, he thought when he stood up. The letter had taken forever to compose. But much later, long after he mailed it, he realized that he had written just a few short paragraphs.

Joy was horrified by the letter from ''Purdy.'' She talked to Sheresky and consulted private investigators about tracking down the person who had written it. But although she informed the investigators that she was pretty certain she knew who it was, they told her it would be difficult to prove. She had nothing but instinct to go on.

The discrepancy between who Sol knew himself to be and the image he liked to project to the world began to show—but ever so glancingly—that late spring of 1992. A colleague mentioned to him that his mother was seriously ill with cancer. The usually compassionate chief judge gave no response. A female law clerk handed him a one-page memo on an issue pivotal to a case he was about to hear. The usually polite chief judge railed that the memo was too long, that he'd wanted just one line. And one day in his chambers, he scoffed aloud at a videotape showing a cerebral palsy victim against whom he had ruled in her suit with a pharmaceutical manufacturer.

But for the most part, Sol conducted himself as he customarily did—affably hearing cases, responsibly attending administrative meetings, energetically making speeches. Then, one day late in June, he took a trip to Virginia, where he spoke at his alma mater, Washington and Lee, and at the Brookings Institution, and while there he once again took to a typewriter and compounded his trickery. This time, however, he didn't write as Purdy, but in the voice of a new character, a woman, someone who could add to Purdy's credibility by saying she knew him. Someone who could add to Purdy's fearsomeness by suggesting he had links to an infamous pair of kidnappers, Arthur and Irene Seale, who had recently been arrested and charged in the tragic abduction and killing of Sidney Reso, an executive with the Exxon Corporation.

Pretending to be this new character, he wrote first to the U.S. attorney for the District of New Jersey, whose office was handling the Seale case. "Arthur and Irene Seale were in the process of a blackmail scheme effecting [*sic*] Mr. David Samson of 7 Robbins La., Short Hills, N.J.," he wrote, "and Mrs. Joy Silverman of 983 Park Avenue, New York City."

It all started when I tried to stop G.A.F. from building a hazardous waste incinerator in Linden. I hired the Seales to get a line on all the principles [*sic*] of G.A.F. with the hope of finding if there were any payoffs or anything else to help defeat the proposal.

During their surveillance and after some digging, they found out that the attorney for G.A.F., David Samson from the firm of Wolff and Samson in Roseland, was having an affair with a woman named Joy Silverman. Mrs. Silverman is a very wealthy woman in charge of the Bush campaign in New York. Her husband is a billionaire.

The Seales have pictures of the two of them making love in a house on Long Island and some audio tapes. They have been threatening Mrs. Silverman and her daughter to extort a payoff. I had absolutely nothing to do with the blackmail and am sorry for this whole thing.

When he was finished with that letter, he copied it and sent the same missive to the office of the prosecutor for Morris County, New Jersey. Then he wrote a letter introducing his new character—he hadn't yet given her a name, but eventually he would dub her Theresa O'Connor—to Joy. "By now you probably know," he wrote to her,

that you don't have to worry about the Seales anymore.
For the part I played in their blackmail scheme, I am

truly sorry. They were retained only to assist me in getting information on the G.A.F. "Bigs." I never intended that they should pursue their own scheme.

Now that they have been put away, I'm sure you won't have to worry anymore. God Bless you and your daughter.

On his way home from Virginia, Sol stopped in Elizabeth, New Jersey, and mailed the letters from there.

Joy was getting frantic. She wanted the letters to stop.

Eleanor Sloan, who was still giving Sol psychotherapy, tried to intercede. On the day after Sol returned from Virginia, she telephoned him at his Albany chambers.

Did he know that Joy had been receiving threatening and obscene communications? she asked him. Was it possible that someone in his office was involved?

Sol flew off the handle. How could anyone think a thing like that, he reproved her. Then he demanded that the letters and cards be turned over to him. He'd get to the bottom of what was going on. He'd take them, he said, to the New York State Police for investigation.

There was no way Joy was going to turn over to Sol Wachtler the letters and cards she'd been receiving. Or to the New York State Police, for that matter. It was hard to imagine them undertaking an investigation of the state's chief judicial officer. No, she'd go to the FBI, she decided. She'd go to the *head* of the FBI. William Sessions. She knew him. She'd met him in Washington on a couple of occasions.

Soon after Sloan had been rebuffed by Sol, Joy prevailed on Norman Sheresky to let Sol know what she had in mind. "Tell him," the lawyer recalled her saying, "I'm going to go to the FBI."

Sheresky wasn't happy about the assignment. He knew Sol had been obsessed with Joy. Sheresky had even tried, recently, to cure him of his preoccupation by introducing him to another woman—Mary Anne Stephens, the ex-wife of Jackson Stephens, a billionaire investment banker from Little Rock, Arkansas. Mary Anne, who was active in Republican politics and fund-raising, just like Joy, was a slender beauty with dark hair, dark eyes, and a wide, engaging smile, just like Joy, and she had a delightful, bubbly personality. But Sol hadn't gone for her. He'd still been hung up on Joy. However, that didn't mean he'd done the things Joy was accusing him of, Sheresky thought. Sol, he was certain, wasn't capable of such things.

But Sheresky was a good soldier. He'd do what Joy wanted, he promised. And he made an appointment to meet Sol for drinks at the Algonquin.

In the hotel's cool and comfortable lounge, they chatted about this and that for a while, and then Sheresky came to the point. "Those letters Joy's been getting," he said to Sol, "she knows they're from you."

"She's crazy," Sol said, just as he'd said months ago when Sheresky had said Joy suspected him of making hang-up calls to her.

Still, Sheresky persisted. "She's going to go to the FBI," he warned.

"Good. I think she should," Sol said solemnly. "In fact, I'll help her."

"She doesn't need your *fuckin' help!*" Sheresky exploded. "She knows the fuckin' President of the United States!"

Sol's expression didn't change. He seemed as genial as ever.

After his meeting with Sheresky, Sol was cautious for a while. He didn't stop sending Joy letters, but the letters he sent were reassuring rather than threatening. He wrote them in the voice of his good character, Theresa O'Connor, not his bad one, Purdy.

To flesh O'Connor out, to *know* her in the way an author knows his characters, he had gone to extraordinary lengths. He had called the information operator in Linden, New Jersey, the town in which the scenario he was developing for her required her to live, and asked for the names of Catholic churches there. He'd liked the first name he'd been given the most. It was the Church of the Holy Family. Yes, Theresa O'Connor would worship in a church like that, he'd thought. And once he'd known at just what church O'Connor would worship, he'd called the church and gotten the name of its priest—a Father German. Then he'd called Father German and asked him when masses were held.

One day, he drove to Linden and tried to get into the church. He wanted to see it, smell it, hear the sounds O'Connor would have heard.

But despite his research, he'd come at the wrong time. The church was locked. He tried one door, then another, but none would open, not even the back door, where they put out the garbage. At last, he contented himself with just walking around the neighborhood, trying to see it with Theresa O'Connor's eyes.

That night, according to Sol, he remained in Linden, sitting in his car for hours. With him was a letter he'd written in Theresa O'Connor's voice. But he didn't want to mail it until dawn. "There were several post boxes there, and I wanted to find the *right* one," he would one day explain. "So I had to wait there until the sun came up. See it reflect off the post box. The first box the sun hit would be the right one to mail the letter in. The one that would give the letter all the right meaning."

The letter he finally mailed that morning alluded to the compromising photographs and audiotapes that "Purdy" had once offered to Elaine Samson, and continued, "I will not send you the pictures because I've been told that sending them would be a crime. I will tear them up and the tapes too. You will not hear from me again."

Then "O'Connor" begged for Joy's patience while "she" explained herself.

Please listen to my story. Linden has spent over $300,000 to save our children from the G.A.F. hazardous waste. We're not going to give up.

My try was stupid. I hired a private eye to get something on a G.A.F. big. He fell on Samson and by tracking him back and forth from Short Hills found you and where you lived. He took some pictures and decided *on his own* that he was going to get money from them. First he tried Mrs. Samson—that was last year. At first she said she would be interested, but after several conversations she said she didn't care. I thought he was going to give it up but then he decided to get more on you. He followed you to Long Island on a few of your trips there.

When Reso was found, he took off, but first he left me

the pictures and tapes which I just found. I don't think he had anything to do with the Reso thing, but I have written to the authorities in Morristown and Newark about him.

I am sincerely sorry about this and I wanted you to know the facts. Before you blame me too much, think about your daughter and try to imagine haw [*sic*] you would feel if a hazardous waste plant was to be put in your backyard. I know—you would probably just move away, but there are some of us who can't afford to.

I ask for your forgiveness but *please please* tell Mr. Samson that he should think of another place where many people do not live.

Sol mailed Joy letters from ''O'Connor'' throughout July. And by the seventeenth of that month, his imagination had spurred him to give his new character an elaborate history and a more distinct way of expressing herself. ''Dear Mrs. Silverman,'' he wrote as if he were O'Connor,

I know I promised not to write again, but I had to write this one last letter. Not for you, but for myself and my salvation. At Mass this morning, Father German said that all sins can be forgiven except for despair. It seemed as though his homily was directed right at me.

I have been a parishioner of the Holy Family Roman Catholic Church all my life. I have not been able to sleep for three weeks because of my part in the matter concerning you. At confessional Father told me that part of my penance was to tell you all I know and that I should do it before depression becomes despair. As God is my judge, and as his son and the fruit of the Blessed Mother's womb Jesus is the guardian of immortal soul, this is the truth.

Sol had given O'Connor what might best be called a stereotypical Irish Catholic style. She was a cliché, just as David Purdy was a cliché, the prototype of the down-at-heels private eye. But both characters were far more realized and inventive than any Sol had created during his brief stint as a writer, back at Washington and Lee. "I have lived here in Linden my whole life," O'Connor's July 17 letter went on, displaying the love of home and family that a religious woman presumably would feel.

> I know you must think of it as an ugly smoke stack town, but it's my home and where I am bringing up my children. My children are as precious to me as your daughter is to you.
>
> When G.A.F. bought the land and planned a hazardous waste incinerator, all I could think of was how my children would be poisoned. I know of the promises—but there are hundreds of stories of "promises" which have left children with cancer and brain and other damage. I was determined to keep this from happening to my children.

Then, Sol launched O'Connor into her complex confession. "The beginning of this year when things looked unstoppable a man named David Purdy called," he had her reveal, as if following her priest's instructions to tell all she knew.

> He said he was a private investigator from Houston, Texas (he said he was living at the YMCA there and gave me his telephone number: 713-659-8501.) He told me that he had some information about a David Samson who was the lawyer representing G.A.F. and that knowing of my efforts to stop the incinerator he thought I might be interested. He said he might be able to get Samson to back off by threatening to go public with the intimate story of your relationship. Purdy said we could hire him for $10,000— $5,000 right away, and $5,000 if Samson laid down on the G.A.F. application. Considering what was at stake, the price did not seem too much to pay. I borrowed the money and hired Purdy. He moved to a hotel in Linden.

"O'Connor" then claimed that Purdy had originally been hired by Elaine Samson, who had wanted compromising pictures of her husband and Joy to use in getting a divorce.

Purdy took pictures. He told me they were of the two of you eating together, walking together, and going into your or his apartment house together. Mrs. Samson said that these were not the kind of pictures she meant. She wanted pictures—as Purdy put it—of the two of you "doing it."

It took Purdy a long time, but he got the pictures. But when he called Mrs. Samson to tell her, she said she changed her mind. She said there wasn't going to be a divorce and she was no longer interested.

It was after that, O'Connor continued, that Purdy came to her, and offered to sell *her* his pictures and tapes. But, she protested,

he never told me of his blackmail plan. I would not have been part of that. But he did tell me of the pictures and tapes. God help me, I was foolish enough to think that this could help us in getting Samson to back down. I now realize how stupid I was—but I was also desperate. . . . then the commission ruled against Linden and it looked as though we were lost. I told Purdy that he was not going to get any more money.

That's when he told me he could get all the money he wanted from you. I swore to him that if he blackmailed you, I would go to the police.

The next day the Seals [*sic*] were arrested for kidnapping Resa [*sic*] from Exxon. The police said they were looking for an accomplice and I thought that Purdy was just the kind of misery who would do such a thing. I told Purdy I was going to turn him over if he didn't get out of town. He really got scared, gave me the pictures and tapes, and said he was leaving town. I haven't heard from him since.

That's when I wrote you the first time—to tell you not to worry. I also wrote the Morristown Police and the U.S. Attorney telling them of my suspicions about Purdy. I also destroyed the pictures, which were shameful, and destroyed the audio tape, which I never listened to.

I know you must hate me for my role in this thing. I am self educated and never thought of myself as a stupid woman. I have always tried to be a good person and except for this one foolish thing, I have succeeded.

I have been told that with this act of contrition, God will forgive me. I hope that you will find room in your heart to do likewise.

Sol was playing with Joy the way a cat plays with a mouse. He was giving her respite before tormenting her again; he was encouraging her to think that her troubles were over now that the good-spirited "O'Connor" had destroyed the blackmail pictures and tapes and sent the evil-spirited "Purdy" out of town.

Joan Wachtler, who knew nothing about her husband's elaborately orchestrated plot or his clever invented characters, was beginning to dread being in Sol's company. He was tense, irritable, faultfinding. He fought with her about the tiniest things. Like the garbage. If he came home and there was garbage in the trash can, he would insist it be taken out right away. She'd say it could wait until after they ate—but he'd say no, and he'd grab it and take it out before she even sat down to her meal.

He was even worse when they had guests. One night, shortly after he sent the reassuring Theresa O'Connor missive to Joy, they had friends to dinner, and the whole evening he kept talking and talking, not letting anyone get a word in edgewise. And what he was talking about was himself. Just himself. He was so self-absorbed and he so monopolized the conversation that Joan was embarrassed and the next day felt compelled to call the guests and apologize.

Toward the end of July, Joy received another note from "Theresa O'Connor"—a religious card with the biblical inscription "Let us therefore cast off the works of darkness. And let us put on the armour of light." But if for a moment this card lulled Joy, made her feel—like the mouse temporarily released from the cat's paws—that her harassment was coming to an end, she soon had a rude awakening. She learned that Elaine Samson had

had a letter saying, "I'm sure your husband's girlfriend would love to hear [the tape] where you tell me that you weren't interested in the pictures I had and then told me to get one's [*sic*] of them having sex. Blow the whistle on me and I promise you will be sorry."

Whatever "O'Connor" had said, "Purdy" was clearly back.

In his therapy sessions with Sloan, whom he was continuing to see, Sol never talked about writing threatening letters. Instead, he told the therapist that he was distressed to think that Joy thought him capable of such a thing. And one day, toward the end of July, he said to Sloan, "I've *got* to dispel this notion Joy has that the person who sent her those terrible letters was me. I've got to see her, talk to her about this."

Sloan told him, Wachtler said, that she'd try to get Joy to meet with him, and if she succeeded, she'd call him to set up an appointment. But she didn't call, and when he tried to call her, he kept getting messages that she'd just stepped out. She's dodging my calls, he thought. Joy's probably told her not to speak to me anymore. Because she thinks *I'm* Purdy.

It upset him. He longed to have Joy believe Purdy was real. He longed to have her fear David Purdy and lose sleep over him. And shortly after his failure to reach Sloan, he decided to make Purdy more real by giving him not just a voice, but a *presence*. He'd *impersonate* the detective, he decided, dress up the way he always saw Purdy in his mind's eye—wearing a Stetson hat, a string tie, and cowboy boots. Then he'd turn up somewhere, go someplace where Joy would be sure to hear about him. That ought to convince her that Purdy was real. And that he wasn't him.

He chose David Samson's apartment building as his destination. After months of trying, he had finally learned where David lived, and on a Friday afternoon, having first established that his rival was out on Long Island, he went to his address on East 81st Street and engaged the doorman there in conversation. "Tell Mr. Samson," he drawled, "that David Purdy from Houston, Texas, stopped by to see him."

Throughout the rest of that hot and humid August, Sol spent

186

more and more time in the character of Purdy. He had refined his vision of him, had decided that the private investigator wouldn't just dress in Texas style but be toothless and obese, which would make him totally different from dentally perfect and elegantly slim Sol Wachtler. His years of doing impersonations for his children and for friends, his years of stepping into the stance and gait of various characters when he told jokes at parties and political dinners, served him well. He practiced at being Purdy, shuffling when he walked, puffing out his abdomen and pulling his shirt from his waistband to make himself look fat, drawing his lips over his teeth to make himself appear toothless. And in Purdy's guise and getup, he began walking around the city. One day, he rode a crowded elevator while trying to be Purdy and abruptly stopped playing the role when he noticed that people on the elevator were staring at him.

By the end of August, Sol was ready for an acid test of his ability to impersonate Purdy—a trip as the shabby private eye to Joy's apartment building, where the doorman knew him personally. Before he ventured forth, he called Joy in Southampton to make sure she was out of the city. When she picked up the phone at her summer place, he said nothing, and he was just hanging it up when he heard her speak. "Poor boy," she said, and clicked her tongue against her palate, making a *tsk-tsk* sound, the kind of sound one makes to a baby or a pet. "Poor boy."

She was on to him, he knew. On to the fact that he had called her and hung up. Maybe even on to the fact that he had sent her obscene cards. But she *couldn't* think he was Purdy. She couldn't think a man like him would go to the lengths of impersonating a private eye. Sure that he was right, he donned his cowboy outfit, stuffed cloth beneath his shirt to increase his girth, and set out for her building. There, he shuffled into her lobby and handed the doorman a letter. And because he wanted to be certain he'd be remembered, he chatted awhile with the doorman, telling him to be sure to tell Mrs. Silverman that he was going to be getting his teeth fixed soon.

The letter he left was filled with veiled threats. "After making some calls," it said,

I found out that you and the boyfriend were on Long Island—(like you said to me on the phone—tsk, tsk, tsk). I had stopped by 145 East 81st [David Samson's residence] and they had let me in long enough to install some of my new equipment in 4A (of course, 1st I had to identify myself, but they were very cooperative). Nice digs— and I was pleased to see that you have already moved some of your stuff in. My bugs are smaller than a gnat's ass so they won't get in your way.

I'm sorry I wasn't in town last week to help you greet Jessica. I had some work to do in Houston (I thought for sure you would be there [for the Republican convention], but I guess your place was up here).

I'm on my way back, but I should be back in the fall. I'll tell you then how much it will cost you to get me out of your life.

Just how crazy *was* Sol Wachtler? Joy must have wondered when she received this last communication from Purdy. Could he possibly have in mind doing some harm to her daughter? She hadn't, despite her threats earlier in the summer, gone to the FBI. No doubt she'd been advised by various of her wired and politically savvy friends to wait before calling in the bureau until Sol made a specific threat, because it would be easier to nail him, to stop him once and for all, once he did. But now the situation was different. "Purdy" was saying he was coming back. Should she call the FBI? Or go on waiting for a specific threat? She decided to wait. But she advised all her friends not to speak to Sol under any circumstances. She no longer wanted him scared off. She wanted him caught.

It didn't take Sol long to realize that Joy had told her friends to cut him off. One day soon after he'd dressed as Purdy and gone to Joy's building, he tried to reach Paola, and she, just like Eleanor Sloan, didn't return his calls. But he was so hell-bent on scaring Joy that Paola's distancing herself from him did not make him rethink his plan, did not cause him to consider that Joy *did* think he was Purdy. In fact, on September 12, he once again dressed as the private eye and once again delivered a letter to her doorman.

"I was back in town this weekend," this new letter said,

> and visited the apartment where you and your boyfriend shack up (more difficult to get in this time—did you tell them about me?). I replaced one of the bugs. Either it wasn't working or you people screw very quietly.
>
> I left your nightgown on the blue bedspread just to let you know I was there. I also took a small suveneer [*sic*] which you will hardly miss (consider it a down payment for all my trouble).
>
> I'll pick Jessica up at school in a month or so when I'm back in town. Don't worry, by that time—like I told your doorman—I'll have my new teeth in. I wouldn't think about embarrassing her—not nearly as much as the 4 pictures of you getting it in Water Mill would embarrass you (although some of your friends—and I know who they are, would love to see them). I have the negatives and can make an unlimited amount of prints.
>
> If you are ready to talk business—and you better be— put a notice in the Oct. 1 out of state edition of the NEW York Times. It should read:
>
> LOST Texas Bulldog, answers to name David.
>
> The ad should be plased [*sic*] in the LOST AND FOUND Section. I will contact you at the listed number and we can talk terms. Don't disappoint me or you'll be very sorry.

"LOST Texas Bulldog, answers to name David." When Joy read the letter directing her to take an ad in the *Times,* she knew it was what she'd been waiting for. A true blackmail letter. She consulted with her various advisers, and a week after receiving the letter, she traveled down to Washington and saw William Sessions at the FBI.

"I heard from a fellow," Sol would one day say, "that Sessions got the call [to see her] from Bush."

CHAPTER 10

Carrie Brzezinski, special agent of the FBI's Newark, New Jersey, office, didn't think she was going to like Joy Silverman the day she and her partner, Bill Fleming, were assigned to meet her and look over those ominous letters and cards she'd been receiving. It was a Friday, the day after Joy went to Washington to speak with William Sessions, who had sent the case to Brzezinski's office because many of the letters Joy had received had been postmarked from New Jersey. "My expectation," Brzezinski remembered, "was someone—well, all I knew was she lived on Park Avenue, and you have your expectations, and mine was, she's going to be someone hard to deal with, or who'll demand a lot." So Brzezinski, who hailed from Milwaukee, Wisconsin, and hadn't lived long in the metropolitan area, wasn't all that eager when she went down to the lobby of the FBI building to get Joy and bring her upstairs to the office. Then, the first thing that happened was that she forgot Joy's last name. "I felt like an idiot! But I remembered her first name, so I said, 'Joy?' like I knew her, and she goes, 'Yeah.' She was very nice. She wasn't turned off by it. She wasn't, you know, uppity about it."

They went up to the office, and Brzezinski introduced Joy to her partner. Joy brought out the documents and the three of them looked them over and talked. "Joy was very scared," Brzezinski noticed. "And that showed. She broke down and she was crying."

"Who do you think is doing this?" her partner Fleming asked. "Is there anybody who might be angry with you for any reason?"

Joy told them about Sol, but Brzezinski and Fleming were reluctant to focus solely on him.

It could be Wachtler, Brzezinski thought. Or it could be someone trying to set him up. Or then again, it could be someone else. She's going through a divorce. It could be the husband. She's got a boyfriend. It could be the ex-wife. She's got doormen at her building. You never know what doormen might be involved in. Plus she's a wealthy woman. She's got a staff of people who aren't so wealthy. Did any of them have a grudge against her?

Getting Joy to tell her and Fleming about anyone and everyone who might have reason to harass her, she drew up what the FBI calls a "universe" of suspects. Then, she and Fleming sent the cards and letters Joy had brought in with her down to the FBI's Washington headquarters so that the handwriting could be analyzed, the paper examined for fingerprints, and the typing compared with that on other typewritten threats and extortion notes in the bureau's capacious files. They also asked the FBI's Houston office to check on whether there was a private investigator anywhere in Texas with the name David Purdy.

On Monday, the two agents met with Michael Chertoff, the United States attorney for the District of New Jersey. Chertoff, a gaunt and balding man who looked far older than his thirty-nine years, was known for his brilliance, tenacity, and fierce intensity. He could get so focused on a case that, as he himself once admitted, "You could set a bomb off in the courtroom and I might not know it."

Chertoff already had a glancing familiarity with the fact that Joy was receiving extortion threats. He had been supposed to try Arthur Seale, who had just pled guilty to kidnapping and killing Sidney Reso, and back in the summer, when his office had received Sol's anonymous letter warning that the Seales were scheming to blackmail David Samson and Joy Silverman, Chertoff had questioned Seale's wife, Irene, about the allegation. But she had said she knew nothing about it, and the matter had been put on a back burner.

Today, looking over the cards and letters Joy had received, Chertoff once again thought about Seale. Joy's cards and letters weren't so different from the kinds of notes Seale had written. Those, just like these, were intricate and protracted. And Seale, just like this Purdy character who was claiming to be a security expert, had boasted of his surveillance ability. More, Seale had demanded that Exxon get a special telephone number and put it in a newspaper ad headlined "Florida Cattle Ranch." And here was Purdy demanding Joy get a special telephone number and place an ad under the not altogether dissimilar heading "LOST Texas Bulldog." Was it possible, Chertoff wondered, that Seale was running the operation against Joy from jail, and that he'd never told his wife about it? Or was it a better bet to guess that Joy's extortionist wasn't Seale, but someone with a great familiarity with Seale's methods?

Well, they'd know soon enough, Chertoff decided. Turning to his deputy, Victor Ashrafi, he said, "Let's take the ad."

"Right," Ashrafi said. "We'll get a dedicated phone line, and we'll trap and trace the calls."

Brzezinski and Fleming had already begun following up on some of the leads they'd gotten from the cards and letters. They'd spoken briefly on the telephone to David Samson and learned that his wife, Elaine, had received cards and phone calls from a man purporting to be David Purdy. They'd driven out to Short Hills, interviewed Elaine, and taken away with them the cards she'd received. They'd gone to Linden to the Church of the Holy Family and spoken with Father German. Now they drove into Manhattan and talked to Joy's doorman and the doorman at David Samson's apartment building to see if they could get a description of David Purdy. Both doormen remembered him well. He was a fat man, they said. An older guy, wearing western regalia. And there was something funny about his mouth or his teeth.

When they got back to their office, there was word from Houston. Yes, there was a licensed private investigator named Purdy.

Fleming was excited, sure they'd be able to crack the case right away. He got on the phone with Houston at once. "What does Purdy look like?" he asked his counterpart there.

"He's a young guy," the Houston agent said.

"How young?"

"In his twenties."

So the Texas Purdy wasn't their man. But who was?

"LOST Texas Bulldog. Answers to name David. Please call 212-555-2169," said the ad that the Newark FBI placed in the Lost and Found section of the out-of-state edition of *The New York Times* on September 30. From that day on, Brzezinski and Fleming began "sitting on the location," spending their time almost solely in Joy's apartment. Their job was to watch over her and to coach her about what to say if someone called the number listed in the ad. They wanted certain things from that conversation. They wanted her to keep the caller on the phone as long as possible. They wanted her to tell the caller she didn't understand him, so that he'd repeat himself. And they wanted her to get him to say exactly what was going to happen to her if she didn't pay him the money. Was he going to hurt her? Take her daughter? "We wanted to get his threats very specifically on the tape," Fleming remembered, "so that there wouldn't be any room for interpretation later on."

Joy listened to the instructions carefully and promised to stay cool, so that she wouldn't frighten off the caller by becoming tearful or angry.

The first call came on Saturday, October 3. The caller hung up, but the court-ordered trap-and-trace device that the FBI had installed in Joy's apartment tracked the number instantly. It was a number assigned to Sol Wachtler's car phone.

Still, Brzezinski and Fleming, even after learning the results of the trace, weren't sure the caller was Sol. It could be someone who had access to his car, they speculated. It could be a driver. An employee.

They continued to tutor Joy. "You gotta get him to talk to you," they said. "And keep him on the line."

Sol called again on Sunday, October 4. This time, he dialed Joy from a pay phone in a Laundromat in Glen Oaks, New York, not far from his Manhasset home, and, using a voice-disguising device he'd bought at a spying-equipment shop, said he was calling on behalf of David Purdy, who'd be phoning himself from out of town next week.

Joy had learned her lessons well. "Pardon me?" she asked politely, as if she hadn't heard him.

"Purdy'll be calling you collect from out of town next week," Sol reiterated.

Joy tried her luck again. "You'll have to repeat that," she said. "I can't understand you."

Sol seemed to grasp that the call was being taped. "I know you're recording this," he said. But he continued to repeat that Purdy would be calling next week, and then he brazened ahead, "The price is twenty thousand dollars."

Sol used the voice disguiser again on Monday, October 5; Wednesday, October 7; and Friday, October 9. That was the day he called Joy while attending a judicial conference in Reno, made the bizarre claim "I'm wearing a diaper," and responded to Joy's question about what he was threatening to do to her daughter with, "Why don't you fucking find out, lady? Why don't you just fucking find out? Why don't you just not pay me, and see what goddamn happens?"

In New York, a few days after that call had been traced, Chertoff sat down with Ashrafi and the FBI people to discuss what to do next. "This chief judge is either crazy or criminal," he said. "We can't have him running the court system of New York."

"We could go to him privately," someone suggested. "Confront him with the evidence. Make him resign."

Chertoff was skeptical. "We don't have a locked case," he said. "What do we do if we go to Wachtler and he says, 'This is bullshit. This is ridiculous. A setup.' I can see it now. He kicks us out of his office, and we're left sitting around with our knowledge. That's not an acceptable way to leave things."

"Let's arrest him," someone else suggested. Chertoff didn't want that, either. The evidence so far was all circumstantial. If they went to court, they'd probably lose. "We need more," he said. "We need an overwhelming case. Not just calls, but proof that it's him making the calls. Solid observation or, better yet, a fingerprint."

Esposito agreed. He'd have his agents tail Wachtler, he said. "But in a loose way," he cautioned. "We don't want to scare him off."

Chertoff nodded. "But we don't arrest him right when we see him making a call," he warned. "Because you never know until later if the recording is working properly. Or if maybe he's just saying something innocuous. We have to have gotten the recording and listened to it. And we have to have a fingerprint. Only after we've got all that, would I agree to arrest him."

Sol was up in Albany, where increasingly he was behaving in a grandiose and scattered fashion. His clerks noticed that he barely listened to them when they tried to talk to him about complex issues, that he refused to make changes in documents once they'd written a draft, and that he no longer called them together for the traditional evening briefings at which they customarily prepared him for the next day's arguments. One day, his clerks insisted on a briefing. Sol said he couldn't be bothered, because he had to have a haircut. Then he thought better of what he'd said and backtracked. "Okay," he told them, "if you want to brief me, come with me." The clerks piled into his car, and talked to him as he sped through traffic and then raced on foot through a mall to reach his barbershop.

He was hasty and distracted with family members too, so much so that his daughters found themselves competing for an iota of his attention.

"How long were you on the phone with Daddy?" Lauren asked one of her sisters one day.

"Twenty seconds," her sister answered. "How about you?"

"Twenty-one!"

I won this little bout of sibling rivalry, Lauren comforted herself. But it's little consolation, considering all the things I wanted to discuss with Daddy.

After that, she began writing down the matters she wanted to talk to her father about, so that she'd be sure to get them all in before he said, "Okay, gotta go."

Sol wasn't frenzied when he was on the bench. On October 22, he heard his last case of the early autumn session of the court of appeals, a case involving environmental issues. "The legislature wants something done, but you say that, because there's no single municipality or agency or group to do it, it shouldn't be done?" he said to a lawyer opposing environmental restrictions. "Why doesn't the county itself undertake [setting policy]?" he said to a lawyer in favor of the restrictions. "That would be a magnificent gesture."

Mike Trainor, one of Sol's clerks, was present in the courtroom. Sol's asking good questions, he noticed. Running things smoothly. Just like he always does.

Brzezinski and Fleming were still spending most of their time in Joy's apartment. There had been no further communications from "Purdy," no opportunity to trace a call and send agents to try to get a fingerprint from the phone, or to actually observe who was making the call. But on October 27, Sol decided to call Joy again.

He was at the Harmonie Club that night, where he and Matt Crosson had called a meeting of prominent civic leaders to catch them up on developments in the state's judicial system over the past year. Sol filled the assembled guests in about the court system in general and about his now-resolved lawsuit against Cuomo. But he kept scrambling dates and statistical information.

"You screwed it up to a fare-thee-well," Crosson said to him when the meeting was over and the two of them had settled down in the club's sedate dining room to have a drink and dinner together.

"I did?"

"Yeah," Crosson said. But the chief seemed distracted and

restless, so Crosson didn't dwell on his mistakes. He talked to him instead about the upcoming presidential election, and when he had finished eating, said good-bye and left the club.

As soon as he was gone, Sol went into a lobby phone booth and dialed Joy's number.

"Is Mrs. Silverman there, please?" he said to a maid who answered the phone.

"Who's calling, please?" she inquired.

"This is David. Is she there?"

"What David?"

"David," was all he'd tell her. "Is she there? Where is she?"

"Let me see," the maid said. "David Baker?"

"Where is she?" he demanded.

"She went out."

"When will she be back?"

"I don't know."

Frustrated, he said good-bye and hung up. But he wanted to find Joy badly, and early the next morning he called David Samson, looking for her.

"Is Joy Silverman there?" he asked, speaking to Samson from a phone booth at the Long Island Jewish Hospital.

Samson said nothing.

"Put Joy Silverman on the phone!"

Again, Samson said nothing.

"Can you hear me?" Sol asked.

But when Samson again made no reply, he said, "That's all," and hung up.

For a few hours, he put Joy out of his mind. He drove into the city, where he was scheduled to be the moderator for a lunchtime seminar on mediation at the headquarters of the New York County Lawyers Association. When he walked in, he spotted his old friend and onetime competitor for the chief judgeship, Milton Mollen. "Do you think I should take the mike and go down into the audience, Phil Donahue style?" he asked Mollen.

"By all means, do it," Mollen said. "The audience will love it."

Sol did, handling the discussion in what was, Mollen would later recall, "his usual warm and witty way."

But that night, he again tried to reach Joy, dialing her from a pay phone outside a Boy Scout camp in a countrified area of Roslyn, New York, eight-tenths of a mile from his home. This time, she was home.

"Are we all set for November seventh?" he asked as soon as she answered.

"I can't hear you," she said.

"Are we all set for November seventh?"

"Well, I don't understand one thing," she challenged him, attempting to stretch out their conversation so that he'd stay on the phone. "How do I know that this is all going to be over on November seventh. You haven't left me any package. You expect me to just leave twenty thousand dollars without getting something back?"

"I'll tell you what you're getting back, lady," he said. "If you don't do it, if you fuck me up at all, I promise you it will cost you two hundred thousand dollars to get your daughter back. How does that suit ya?"

Joy tried to keep him on the phone, but he had hung up.

Joy was jumpy after this call. Brzezinski and Fleming had already gone home to New Jersey for the night, but she wanted to speak to them, wanted to let them know about this latest, more substantial threat. She dialed Brzezinski at her apartment. "I got another call," she said.

"What'd he say?"

Joy summarized the conversation, and as soon as she was done, Brzezinski leaped into activity. She called the FBI's contact person at the telephone company to find out where the call had come from, learned it was Roslyn, New York, and telephoned Fleming.

He wanted to go out there. "Let's take the phone," he said. "Let's get out as fast as we can and take it."

"What if we do and he comes by and notices it's missing?" Brzezinski asked. "What if it tips him off?"

"He won't come back. He's never used the same phone twice."

"There's always a first time."

"Yeah, but if we hit a home run, if we get his prints, we'll put this thing over the top."

They decided to go. And a few minutes later, Brzezinski picked up Fleming in her white Mustang. It was late, around eleven P.M., but there was still a lot of traffic on the roads. "Damn," Fleming said. "By the time we get there, who knows if the prints will be recoverable."

"Yeah," Brzezinski said. "Dozens of people could have used that phone booth after our guy did."

They worried about it the whole time they were driving, but when, after nearly two hours, they reached Roslyn and arrived at the location of the phone booth, they relaxed. The booth was alongside a road, but it was on a dark corner, with nothing but trees and bushes around it. "Not many people would want to make a call from a spot like this," Fleming said.

"Not at night," Brzezinski said.

Unless they're nuts, Fleming thought. Or up to no good.

He slipped out of the car and into the phone booth. Brzezinski stood guard. "It's okay. It's okay now," she whispered when a stream of cars had sped by and the road was dark once again. He pulled out his crime-scene kit, slipped on a pair of latex gloves, grabbed a pair of bolt cutters, and snipped the telephone cord.

The handset swung free.

Stuffing it into a plastic evidence bag, Fleming hurried back to the car, and he and Brzezinski drove to FBI headquarters in Newark.

"I'd like to make an appointment," Sol said over a different phone a few days later—it was just before Halloween—to the receptionist at a beauty salon. The salon was a few doors away from the laundry shop at which he'd directed Joy to leave him twenty thousand dollars on November 7. "My name is Samson. David Samson," he went on. "But I can't make the appointment now." Then he asked the woman with whom he was speaking what her name was.

"Yesim Oklu," she said.

He promised her he'd call back soon for his appointment.

* * *

199

"Wachtler used that phone outside the Boy Scout camp," an expert from the latent-fingerprint section of the FBI's Washington headquarters notified the Newark office several days after Sol called the beauty salon. "His print was on it." The handset Fleming and Brzezinski had retrieved had been sent from Newark to Washington, where the identification division had used laser equipment to lift off every fingerprint and then matched them against a set of Sol's prints that had been taken years before, when he had joined the Army.

The FBI had the two things Chertoff had said he wanted—a clear recording of a specific extortion threat from Wachtler, and proof that he'd been in the phone booth from which the threat had been issued.

But now, Chertoff changed his mind about arresting Wachtler and decided to wait a few more days. It was nearly November 7. Why not see if he was really going to go through with his plan to extort money from Joy, and if he was, catch him in the act? Why not watch him closely and find out if he was in this alone or had some coconspirators. Convinced this was the best plan, on November 3, Chertoff requested the FBI to put Wachtler under close, not loose, surveillance. From now on, there'd be agents following his every move.

The day Chertoff decided to ask the FBI to start closer surveillance, Sol attended a high-powered political luncheon in Mineola. It was the annual luncheon of The Has Beens, a group of influential Republicans all of whom had once held political office. One of them was Sol's old friend Joe Carlino.

For some time now, Carlino had been touting Sol for governor in 1994. "With this guy's family," he'd been saying to various and sundry rainmakers, "if we can get him to take this thing, this will be one of the best-funded elections the Republicans have ever had. Plus, we got a product with him. A good product."

Today, Carlino's buttonholing seemed to have paid off. Throughout the luncheon, many of the still-powerful Has Beens came over to Sol and told him he ought to run. Carlino, sitting alongside Sol, joined in with them. "You have no obligation to Cuomo," he said to Sol. "He's done some bad things."

Sol nodded.

"You've been on the court a good long time," Carlino went on. "Whadda ya going to do? Sit there till retirement? There's more to life than that."

Carlino was pretty certain Sol was in agreement. So, "Ya oughta announce now," he told him. "You're king of the walk today."

"We've got time," Sol replied. "I want to wait a year or so. Because if I announce now, I'll have to step down as chief judge. I'm going to wait, and when it's closer, I may do it."

Carlino was pleased with the answer. It seemed to him that at long last, Sol was ready to make the run they'd been talking about for years.

At about two-thirty or three o'clock, Sol got up to go. He was flying to Louisville, Kentucky, he explained. He was going to be making a speech there.

He said a fond good-bye to Carlino and drove to the airport. There, he called Joy again, and once more pretended to be Purdy. He told her he was in an airport, but said he was on his *way* to New York. And then he asked, "Are we in business?"

Joy, thinking fast, parried. "I said to you when you called me before that I want to know what I'm getting back, and when I'm getting it back, and I'm not just going to leave money there, just leave it and not have anything back in return."

"Now listen here! I'm trusting you. I'm trusting you not to put me on to the police, right?"

"I didn't call the police. But I'm not gonna just leave twenty thousand dollars for you as a present."

"I'm trusting you," Sol repeated. "But look. Listen to me. If I don't come back with that twenty thousand dollars, I'm gonna stay in New York and snatch your kid. Now, I mean that."

Joy had decided to be as tough as her tormentor. "Well, let me tell you something," she said, and began challenging him with the bravado of a detective-novel moll. "I'm not dropping off twenty thousand dollars only to have you come back to me two weeks from now and ask for another twenty thousand dollars."

"I'm not gonna do that," Sol said.

"No? You want to make a deal with me? Look, I want this over with, okay? I don't like what's going on. I want my life back, but I'm not about to have you come up on my behind two weeks from now—"

"If you want your life back, leave the goddamn money."

They continued to argue, each of them playing a role, until Sol hung up and caught his plane to Kentucky. When he arrived there, he called Joy from the Louisville airport, and this time claimed to be in New York. "Now listen carefully, girl," he said. "Listen good. You get twenty thousand dollars to [your doorman] Ramón. He will drop it off at ten-fifteen. At one o'clock in the afternoon, I'm gonna give you all the papers you want. Also, I'll give you the name of the fat pig who brought me into your life. You understand that?"

"Where are you going to put it?" Joy asked.

"They're going to be dropped off," Sol said. "They will be given to your doorman." Then he made a stronger threat than any he had made before. "If you don't do it," he said, "I'm gonna spend the rest of this year making your life a nightmare, and you'll end up spending ten times the twenty thousand to get your girl back. Now, do you understand what I'm saying? I'm gonna give you thirty seconds to tell me what you're gonna do."

Joy said she just didn't get it and began demanding that "Purdy" drop off the pictures and tapes he had for her at the same time he picked up the money.

Sol laughed. "You think I'm some kind of fool, girl? They would arrest me on the spot. Okay, now are you gonna do it?"

"Wait, wait, wait," Joy begged him. "Wait."

"No, I'm not gonna wait. You're gonna get everything you want at one o'clock in the afternoon, and then I'm taking the evening plane back to San Antonio. Okay, is that a deal? Are we on? I'll give you ten more seconds."

Joy continued to ask for guarantees, and Sol got uneasy. "You're tracing this goddamn call," he said. "I'm getting off!"

"I'm not tracing anything," Joy lied. "I just want this over with, and I want some kind of guarantee that you're going to be out of my life. What guarantee do I have that I'll never hear your voice again?"

"You'll never hear my voice again," Sol said. "You'll never hear from me again."

"How do I know that?"

But Sol was tired of Joy's temporizing. "You just give the twenty thousand dollars to Ramón," he said. "I'm gonna be there ten-fifteen at the Shanley." Then he hung up and took a taxi to his Louisville hotel.

The morning after Sol arrived in Louisville, a surveillance team of five FBI agents in five separate cars was assigned to follow him as closely as possible. They were part of what was increasingly becoming a major FBI operation—eventually there would be some eighty agents working on Sol's case.

The Louisville agents saw nothing untoward at first. Sol was picked up at his hotel by Donald Burnett, the dean of the University of Louisville's law school, driven to the campus, and given a short tour. Then he gave a lecture to the dean's constitutional law class. Afterward, he attended a luncheon at the University Club, gave an interview about himself and the New York court system to the campus radio station, and talked about the law with a group of select students. By then it was five o'clock, and he repaired to his hotel room to dress for the trip's main event, a banquet at which he would be addressing a group of eminent Kentucky lawyers and judges.

At the banquet, which was held in his hotel, Sol spoke as eloquently as ever. The chief justice of the Kentucky Supreme Court found his speech insightful. Dean Burnett thought it intelligent and knowledgeable.

But afterward, Sol didn't linger in the banquet hall—he was catching an early plane to New York the next morning, he explained, and he retired to his room, where he remained through the night.

At dawn he checked out of the hotel. He took a cab to the airport. But he directed the cabdriver to take him, first, to a shop at which he might buy some pornographic items. The driver stopped outside a shop called the Blue Movie Adult Bookstore.

Sol went in, made a purchase, then got back into his cab and headed for the airport.

The FBI surveillance team had been tailing him. Conferring by radio, the agents decided some of them ought to go into the shop and see what he'd bought. Was it something he planned to use in his plot to extort money from Joy? Three agents followed Sol to the airport, while two went into the adult bookstore, where, identifying themselves, they asked the salesman what his previous customer had purchased.

"Two porn flicks," he said.

"Which ones?" one of the agents asked.

The salesman shook his head. "I don't remember. We got so many of 'em."

"He buy anything else?"

"Yeah. Cards." He gestured toward a display of pornographic playing cards. "Two decks of Raunch-O-Rama."

"You got any more of those?"

"Sure."

The salesman showed them the cards, and the agents said they'd take two decks too.

While they were making their purchase, Sol reached the airport.

That night, back in New York, Sol attended a dinner being held in the Bronx by the Tribune Society, an organization of nonjudicial court workers. The society was giving an award to Matt Crosson, and they'd asked Sol to present it. He rose from the dais in the chandeliered banquet hall, strode to the podium, and began telling jokes. His timing was perfect, and his deadpan impeccable. He delivered a stream of punchy one-liners and amusing anecdotes, and then, saying Crosson was "a man of unexpected abilities," he used that bit of praise to tell one of his favorite jokes.

It was the story about the variety show emcee who auditions potential contestants only to find yet another one who says he does bird imitations. "So the emcee says, *'Bird* imitations? We're not interested,' " Sol bantered. "Whereupon"—and here he raised his arms and flapped them—"the contestant turned around and flew away."

It brought the house down. Sol's in top form, the novelist and judge Edwin Torres thought. Ebullient. Hilarious. *Beautiful.*

The next day, November 6, Sol worked in his Mineola chambers in the morning. He went over papers, did some reading, made some telephone calls. One of the people he spoke to was Milton Williams, the deputy chief administrative judge of New York City. Sol had proposed to Long Island University that they give Williams an honorary degree, and he'd just gotten word that the arrangements were underway. "I'm delighted," he told Williams.

"Me too," Williams said, and came away thinking, Sol Wachtler's a super person. Always going out of his way for other people.

In the afternoon, Sol drove up to Albany. He went to his house, the house where he had first made love to Joy and where, that first day, he'd wondered guiltily if she'd ruin his life by pursuing him, "fatal attraction" style. There, he dialed Elaine Samson and, pretending to be David Purdy, offered again to sell her pictures of Joy and her husband.

Elaine declined, and shortly thereafter, Sol drove to the New York State Bar Association, where he was scheduled to attend a dinner.

His colleagues were pleased to see him, and some of them prevailed on him to address the gathering. He did, making a forty-five-minute impromptu speech. It was a lively speech. "Vintage Sol Wachtler," John Bracken, the president of the association, thought.

After dinner, Sol asked his driver to take him to his chambers at the court of appeals. En route, he gave an interview over his car phone to Fred Dicker, a reporter for the *New York Post*. What did he think of Senator Al D'Amato's surprising victory in last Tuesday's election? Dicker wanted to know. What did he think were Cuomo's chances of getting appointed to the Supreme Court? And what was happening with his own political career?

He answered Dicker's questions so cooperatively and at such length, commenting as he talked on New York's many problems, that the interview wasn't finished when he arrived at the court of appeals, so he promised the reporter he'd continue talking to him once he was upstairs in his chambers. Dicker called him there, and they talked some more. He sounded, the reporter would later say, "happy, decidedly upbeat, and politically engaged," albeit "slightly manic—overly excited."

When he was finished speaking to Dicker, Sol leaned forward on his leather-topped desk that had once belonged to Benjamin Cardozo and began writing letters, scribbling his thoughts onto scraps of paper, then copying them out both in bold black handprinting and on his typewriter. Tomorrow it would be exactly twenty years since he had first sat at that desk. No matter. Concentrating on the future rather than the past, he wrote a letter to the New York tax authorities in which he made anonymous allegations against David Samson. And then he wrote a letter to Joy, a letter he could deliver to her tomorrow if she left him the twenty thousand dollars that "Purdy" had been demanding.

It was a long letter, and he sat late into the night in the nearly deserted building composing it. "You expected me to give you everything I've collected and learned for $20,000?" he wrote. "Are you stupid or do you think I'm stupid? I may be a shit-kicker but I'm not a dumb shitkicker."

The letter continued:

> It took me a year and over 1,000 miles in a rented car going between the Big Apple and New Jersey. I spent days in flea bag motels, and a hundred hours parked in New York City watching your comings and goings. I made over 100 phone calls to track you and make a record of your habits.
>
> I got into Val's house on Rosewood Lane, and spent over three days parked in front of the Sutter house waiting for the two of you to be there alone during the day because you didn't leave on enough lights at night when you were screwing. And then I had to rig up a remote camera in the house because I couldn't take pictures from the outside because you kept the fucking blinds drawn. And I had to wait until you came back without the kids.

DOUBLE LIFE

Did Purdy sound sorry for himself? Well, why shouldn't he? He was supposed to be dying. His creative imagination afire, Sol continued with the litany of the detective's efforts.

I had to buy expensive recording equipment. And climb through backyards to tape you at your house (When I was at Rosewood a jogger questioned me—when I was in your backyard one of your gardeners spoke to me—I had to con my way out of both situations). I spent over ten days on Long Island living like a hobo. I think that's what got my diabetes kicked up (I was out of commission for most of June and July. I guess you thought I was out of business.)

I had to buy expensive bug transmitters and bribe my way into your boyfriend's apartment. I was there twice (once the cleaning lady Maria caught me coming out but I conned her too). I got great audio. Your boyfriend has a good sense of humor but he also has a lot of gas. (You saw me once when you were waiting in the lobby, but you were too busy looking in the mirror).

I went to your hotel twice (I couldn't get into your room but one of your doormans [sic] brought me into your lobby and was going to let me talk to your young lady—as he called her). I left notes for you on both my visits and tipped your doormans [sic] pretty good. I told Ramón that I was going to be walking Jessica home from school afternoons when she got back and when he noticed I had no teeth and a big gut (water from the diabetes), I promised I'd have false teeth and would lose the gut so as not to embarrass her.

Do you think I went through all of this for a shitty $20,000? I saw how and where you shopped. $20,000 is loose change to you. When I need more, I'll be back, if I don't croak. At least your $20,000 bought you some quiet. If I hadn't got it, everyone you know and everyone your husband knows and every member of every board you belong to would have received wonderful material like this. And I would be going back on some future date with $200,000 or Jessica. You were smart to pay the $20,000.

He'd written so much, but the letter wasn't done. It needed a picture, the kind of picture he'd been telling Joy all along that he had of her. Something shocking and pornographic. Taking out his pack of Raunch-O-Rama cards, he chose one that showed a woman masturbating a man, photocopied it, and attached it to the letter. Then he added:

I know you don't think this picture is of you. But it is. His hand is on your head and you are holding his wad. (He's definitely not from Texas.) The next picture in the series, you're putting his wad in your gobbler.

I've got two others where he's mounting you. You look pretty good in all except one. I took a lot of pictures but only four are recognizable. Next time I'll give you the stuff, but it will cost you more than another $20,000. You see, I was paid a little by someone else, but like this letter tells you, I put in a lot of work and I'm very sick.

The photostat is lousy—you look better in the picture.

Now he was done. He signed the letter with the loopy signature he had once copied from David Samson's bar application.

But what if she didn't leave him the money tomorrow? What should he say to her then? Remaining in his chambers, he composed yet another letter to cover that possibility.

This one was shorter and more brutal than the first. "You stupid lousy cunt,"-he wrote. "I'm going back to Texas now. You better hope I die soon because if I don't you'll wish you were dead. You better kiss your daughter good night every night."

Then, at last, he was finished.

Michael Chertoff drove from New Jersey to Manhattan early the next morning. He knew that Sol had instructed Joy to put twenty thousand dollars in used hundreds and fifties in the manila envelope he'd sent her from Reno, and that he'd insisted she have her doorman Ramón put the envelope in the cellar entrance to Shanley's laundry shop today at precisely ten-fifteen. He knew, too, that the FBI had arranged to have all of that take place this morning. So he was hopeful that sometime after ten-fifteen, Wachtler—or possibly an accomplice of his—would pick up the money. If and when that happened, they would have Wachtler. They would have him not just making threats but actually completing an act of extortion.

In Manhattan, Chertoff reported to the New York FBI's command center. The FBI had launched a massive operation to track Wachtler that day. Forty agents would be keeping him under surveillance out in the field, some of them in cars stationed near Wachtler's home in Albany or Joy's home in Manhattan, others on foot—there was a fellow in jeans and a casual jacket who was standing near Shanley's laundry, and another biding his time at a table in a nearby pizzeria. In addition, numerous FBI officials would be monitoring and directing the field from their headquarters, the command center, a tiered room equipped with the latest in expensive technology.

Chertoff, when he entered, saw glittering and futuristic technology—communications-control panels, TV monitors, walkie-talkies, two-way FM radios that would encode every word transmitted from the field agents to the command center, giant screens on which the progress of today's manhunt would be projected, and banks and banks of telephones. He had never seen so many phones in one room. But only two of them seemed to be in use, he noticed. At least, virtually everyone in sight was crowding around only two phones, the ones with open lines to the field agents. At one of them, Ronald Mahaffey, the New York FBI's coordinator for violent crimes, was calling out the most important reports coming in from the agents.

Chertoff joined the tight cluster of men listening to Mahaffey and greeted those he knew, among them James Esposito, New Jersey's top FBI man; Jim Fox, the head of New York's FBI; and Manhattan's U.S. attorney, Otto Obermeier.

One of the first reports Chertoff heard as he joined the group threw him for a loop. The agent stationed near Shanley's was radioing that there was someone dressed in western regalia parked nearby. "A cowboy!" he was shouting. "There's a cow-boy out here in a disabled car!"

Chertoff did a double take. Was there really a David Purdy after all? But the cowboy, a man in a Stetson hat, proved to be merely a tourist, an unfortunate fellow whose car had broken down. A tow-truck operator soon towed him and his car away.

About a half hour later, Wachtler was spotted coming out of his house in Albany. "He's in his car," an agent parked on the roadway just outside his property radioed. "He's driving himself. He's heading south."

There was a long downtime after that, as Wachtler drove toward the city. Chertoff, trying to relax, shot the breeze with the FBI men, drank coffee, chewed a bagel.

Joy was hearing the radioed reports too. She was sitting in her living room with Brzezinski and Fleming, and they were ex-plaining to her what the agents were doing and what some of their lingo meant.

Fleming thought she seemed wonderfully calm. In part it was because things were coming to an end, he figured, so soon she'd be getting some relief from the anxiety that had plagued her for months. But in part it was because there was no more for her to do. Everything was out of her hands. It was as if she was an outsider now, a spectator watching events play out.

At ten o'clock, her doorman, Ramón, set out for the cellar entrance to Shanley's, two blocks away.

Ramón reached Shanley's in just a few minutes. He looked around him, then nervously set down on the cellar stairway the manila envelope with its twenty thousand dollars in used bills. The agent on the street radioed Mahaffey that the envelope was in place, and Mahaffey tersely relayed the message to Chertoff and the others. Just then, an agent who had been following Wach-tler down the New York State Thruway from Albany called in. Wachtler, he reported, had pulled over to a rest stop in Ramapo, New York, about a fifty-minute drive from Manhattan.

"He's sitting in his car," Mahaffey relayed. "He's getting out of the car. He's going to a pay phone. He's dialing a number."

Suddenly, there was a call from an agent monitoring the beauty salon near the spot where the money had been dropped. "The receptionist at the hair salon is coming out," he radioed. "She's picking up the envelope. She's going back into the shop."

Up in Ramapo, at the rest station, the agent who was watching Wachtler provided a counterpoint. "Wachtler's pacing up and down next to his car," he radioed. Then, "He's going back to the phone."

The agent outside the beauty salon saw the receptionist reenter the shop. Then he saw her walk to a wall phone. "She's talking on the phone," he called in. Then, "She's disappearing into the back of the shop with the envelope."

Was she an accomplice? Chertoff wondered. He wanted the FBI to let the receptionist go about her business, to see if she and Wachtler were going to meet somewhere. But Esposito had a different view. "Maybe the woman's just a dupe," he suggested. "But anyway, we'd better follow the money. It could get split up back there. It could disappear. Let's have an agent go in and get the package."

"It'll blow the set," Chertoff argued. "If anyone was going to come in and get the money, they won't do it if there's an agent inside."

But Esposito's view prevailed, and shortly an agent went into the shop, retrieved the money, and interviewed the woman who had gone out to get it. Soon, he was radioing in her story. The receptionist hadn't known the caller, he radioed. But the caller knew her. "Is this Yesim Oklu?" he'd asked when she'd first picked up the phone. Then, he'd told her he was Mr. Samson and that his car had broken down on the highway, just when he was due into the city to pick up a package. He'd asked if she could get it for him and promised that if she did, he'd give her a big tip when next he came in. That's why she'd gone out and gotten the package. Then when she brought it back, he'd asked her to open it. That's when she'd gone to the back of the shop to ask the shop's owner whether she should follow the caller's instructions. But he'd said she shouldn't, and she'd told the caller this, and he'd said okay, he'd send someone else, a "Miss Heather," to pick up the envelope shortly.

Chertoff, hearing her tale, realized that she hadn't been in league with Wachtler. She'd been an innocent—a helpful—by-stander. But he was still worried that Wachtler might have an accomplice.

Now an agent following Wachtler on the thruway saw him stop at an A&P in Scarsdale, not far from his daughter Lauren's house. "He's tearing up some paper," the agent radioed. "He's throwing it in a trash can."

"Get it!" "Get it!" several people in the headquarters shouted, and Mahaffey directed the on-site agent to do so. A moment later Mahaffey was reporting that the pieced-together scraps of paper said, "You stupid lousy cunt. I'm going back to Texas now. You better hope I die soon because if I don't you'll wish you were dead. You better kiss your daughter good night every night."

Chertoff breathed a sigh of relief. The evidence that Wachtler had been writing the notes to Joy was now overwhelming.

"What's bothering you? You seem very blue," Lauren Wachtler said to Sol only a few minutes after the agent at the A&P read the contents of the torn letter to Mahaffey. Sol had driven from the supermarket to Lauren's house.

"It's nothing," he said.

"Something's bothering you," Lauren said. "Do you have a headache?"

"No."

But Lauren was sure there was something wrong with her father. He'd arrived with presents for her daughter, and he'd sat down with a children's book to read the little girl a story, but no sooner had he gotten a few sentences out than he'd jumped up and begun walking around the room. And then he'd sat down and started reading again. And then jumped up again. She'd never seen him so distracted. Though, if she stopped to think about it, he'd been distracted and scattered for some time now. Always going from one thing to another, with no real continuity.

Lauren didn't spend the whole time of her father's visit in his company. A friend of hers, a decorator, was over at the house too, and at one point she and the decorator left the room. "Your father's so good-looking,'' her friend said when they were alone. ''And so wonderful with your daughter. He's terrific!''

Lauren shook her head. ''There's something bothering him. I don't know what it is.''

Sol didn't stay at her house long. After three-quarters of an hour, he said he had to go into the city. And by twelve-fifteen, he was in his car again.

Lauren, who had an errand to do, got into her car too and drove as far as the highway, with him following her, and then he headed down the road to New York.

Was Lauren ''Miss Heather''? Chertoff wondered for a moment. But no, he decided. She'd driven off in a different direction.

At one o'clock, he heard that Wachtler, who had reached the city, was parking at Second Avenue and 88th Street. Then, ''He's getting out of his car,'' an agent radioed Mahaffey. ''He's putting on a cowboy hat.''

''Are you sure?'' Chertoff heard Mahaffey ask the agent who was radioing in his observations.

''Yes,'' the agent said.

''What's he doing now?'' Chertoff heard Mahaffey ask.

''Putting on an overcoat,'' the agent radioed. ''And a string tie.''

''He's putting on a *what?*'' Fleming said to Brzezinski. ''A string tie?'' He and Brzezinski had been ordered to leave Joy and go downstairs once Wachtler had started heading for the city, and they were sitting with two other agents in a car parked a block from Joy's house, avidly listening to the radioed reports. ''He's dressing up as Purdy!'' Brzezinski cheered. Fleming began to whoop and give the other agents high fives. ''He's gonna do something now, for sure,'' he said. ''Maybe he's gonna come for the money!''

Eager to know what was going to happen next, the carful of agents kept their ears glued to the blow-by-blow radio bulletins coming from uptown. Wachtler was taking an envelope out of his car, they heard. Wachtler was flagging down a taxi. Wachtler was leaning into the cab and engaging the driver in conversation.

"What's that all about?" Fleming said.

"Beats me," Brzezinski said.

A moment later, they heard, "Wachtler's giving the cabdriver the envelope and a ten-dollar bill. Hey, the taxi's taking off."

As soon as he heard that, Fleming knew what Wachtler was up to. "That envelope's going to Joy!" he exclaimed.

Brzezinski knew too. "I'm going for it," she said, and was out the door of the car before Fleming heard from uptown that Wachtler had gotten back into *his* car and removed the cowboy hat and tie.

Brzezinski, dodging pedestrians now, raced to Joy's building. She arrived seconds after the cabdriver dropped off the envelope with the doorman. "I'll take that," she said in her most authoritative tone, and flashed her identification. But the doorman was new. Someone she hadn't met before. He refused to hand it over.

They didn't have doormen back home in Milwaukee, but Brzezinski hadn't been spending her days on Park Avenue for nothing. She'd learned a few things about dealing with doormen, and she said in a commanding tone, "This isn't a matter for discussion!"

He gave her the envelope.

Back at the command post, attention had momentarily coalesced around the cabdriver. After dropping off the envelope, he'd pulled away from Joy's building and picked up a passenger.

"Let's pull him down," one agent said.

"No," Chertoff said. "Let's wait and see what he does. He could be an accomplice." He was almost positive Wachtler had an accomplice. For one thing, during one of the phone calls Wachtler had made as Purdy, the FBI had thought they'd heard a woman's voice in the background. For another, his letters had come from places he hadn't been. Like that letter from San Antonio. Chertoff, not knowing about the helpful stewardess in the Denver airport, pleaded with the agents to hold off on stopping the cabdriver.

But a moment later, the cabdriver dropped off his passenger

and picked up another one. Chertoff realized it was unlikely he was an accomplice. Not if he was just going about his business.

Fox directed an agent to stop the driver.

But now the tension in the room increased, grew virtually palpable. Word had just come in that Wachtler, who had stopped for a while at a gas station, was heading out on the FDR Drive and onto the Triborough Bridge toward Long Island.

So he isn't going to pick up the money now, Chertoff thought. Maybe he's planning to come back later. Or send someone else. Or maybe he's not going to get the money at all. If he doesn't, do we have enough to prosecute him?

All around him, the FBI men were saying they did, and that it was time to arrest Wachtler. But although a part of Chertoff thought they might be right and knew that if they arrested Wachtler now, they'd have a strong case, a practically unbeatable case, another part of him wanted to keep the surveillance going. Wanted to see what Wachtler was going to do next. Wanted to know for certain whether he had accomplices.

Unsure, he withdrew into a small conference room with Fox and Esposito and some of the other top men to confer. What to do next?

"This is the strongest case I've seen in twenty-four years with the bureau," Mahaffey assured him.

Fox agreed. "Let's arrest him now," he said. "While he's on the expressway."

"Yeah, he may be heading home," Esposito said. "And you never know what's gonna happen if you wait to arrest a guy till he's home. There could be weapons around. Or people. Someone could get hurt."

But Chertoff wasn't ready. I'm the one who has to make the decision, he thought. I'm the one who has to move this thing along once we get to court. "I need to know what's in that last letter," he said. "If it says thanks for the money, have a nice life, I'm inclined to sit on things, so we can do more surveillance. If he's left the threat open—then okay. But I need to hear that last note."

Esposito raced out of the conference room, grabbed a phone, and telephoned Fleming and Brzezinski, who had gone back upstairs to Joy's apartment. Fleming answered the call, and as soon as he did, Esposito thrust the receiver at Chertoff and switched on the speaker box. "What's in the letter?" Chertoff said. "Read us the letter."

Fleming opened the envelope and began glancing at the densely packed paragraphs.

"Quickly!" Chertoff demanded.

Fleming's eyes raced down the page, and he summarized what he saw. Purdy's efforts. His self-pity. Then, "He says, 'Do you think I went through all of this for a shitty twenty thousand dollars?' " he read. "He says, 'Next time it'll cost you more than another twenty thousand dollars.' "

Chertoff's eyes hardened. The threat was still open. The scheme was still on.

Slamming down the phone, he gave up on the idea of waiting for an accomplice—though he never gave up wondering if there was one. "Unless anyone has any objections," he said, "let's take him down!"

Sol was nearly home. He had just called Joan to ask if she wanted bagels. And he was planning to stop for them in a shop near his house when suddenly, just as he was leaving the Long Island Expressway, three cars sped up out of nowhere and surrounded him. They forced him to the side of the road.

He pulled over and five men jumped out of the three cars and forced him out of his. They were rough. They were terrifying. They slammed him against a fender.

What was happening, he wondered, scared, and who were these men? Terrorists, he decided. Yes, terrorists, come to kidnap him because they knew he was an important personage.

But within seconds the men, saying they were from the FBI, were cuffing his hands behind his back.

"What did I do?" he asked. "What is this all about?"

"Extortion," one of them said.

For a moment Sol Wachtler relaxed. It must have to do with one of the cases I've heard, he thought. Probably someone who didn't like the way a decision went has accused me of taking a bribe. Well, I've never done anything like that. I don't have a thing to worry about.

He didn't even think about Joy Silverman, or so he would eventually say, until much later.

To the agents who arrested him, however, he seemed aware of the charges against him right from the beginning. He had made a tragic mistake, he told them several times after they'd put him in a bureau car and started driving him back toward New York and federal court.

"Do you know what the worst part is?" he asked. "The judges! What will all the judges think? They looked up to me." Then he told the agents that it had recently been decided he was going to be the Republican candidate for governor in 1994, and that because of his mistake, his great political career would come to an end.

"Oh, my God," he said several times. Then, "Oh, my God. I could have been governor."

CHAPTER 11

The news of Sol Wachtler's arrest was on radio and television within hours. There was almost no one who heard it who wasn't stunned, shocked. Wachtler? That embodiment of propriety and judicial rectitude? Wachtler! The people who knew him and had spent time with him recently were the most startled. Matt Crosson, who took on the chore of notifying the state's administrative judges about what had happened, kept thinking, "It can't be! It's bizarre." Judge Edwin Torres, who had been with Sol at the Tribune Society banquet two nights before, mused, "It's beyond bizarre. It's in the realm of the fantastic." Judge Milton Williams, who had spoken to Sol on Friday morning, reckoned, "It's an aberration. Maybe he's got a brain tumor." Judge Judith Kaye, who had sat on the bench with Sol daily and who would eventually be named chief judge in his stead, speculated, "It's as if somebody else invaded his body." And Joe Carlino, who had known Sol ever since he'd gotten out of the Army, surmised, "If ever there was a case of Dr. Jekyll and Mr. Hyde, this is it."

Additionally, many of those who knew him thought Joy Silverman and the FBI had overreacted, cried fire when there was only smoke—but they weren't acquainted with the devastating details of Sol's calls and letters.

* * *

Sol was arraigned in federal district court in Manhattan at about seven-thirty that night. He had asked Paul Montclare, his daughter Lauren's husband, to represent him, and Montclare requested that the judge release him on his own recognizance.

Michael Chertoff wanted him detained. Sol was potentially dangerous, he thought. He might try to hurt Joy or Jessica. He might try to kill himself. "Send him to a hospital," he agreed at last. "But there's gotta be tight security. Federal marshals guarding him."

Joan was waiting at the hospital that had been chosen—Long Island Jewish, where for years Sol had been a board member—when her husband arrived. It was around midnight by then, but her son Philip was there, too. And Lauren; she already knew from her husband Montclare some of the details of what Sol had done, and she'd been saying ever since she heard about them, "It's like one of Daddy's Bad-Boy George Raft stories. A *major* George Raft story!"

Joan entered her husband's room, a windowless nine-by-ten-foot compartment, and immediately Sol began to cry. "I'm sorry," he wept. "I've disgraced you. Disgraced the family. I'm sorry. So sorry."

Joan began to cry too. Then she put her arms around Sol and hugged him. "I love you," she said as her arms enfolded him. "I love you very much." And after that, for the next half hour—that was all the time she could have with him, the marshals had explained—the two of them sat there, crying and hugging, while Sol tried to explain what he'd done to bring him to this spot.

When he told her he'd been in love with Joy, it was like a knife in the heart. But she and Sol had been through a lot. You don't stay married for forty years without going through a lot. She refused to let his confession crush her. She rallied her ego—she'd always had a strong ego—and said to herself, Joy! How could he have fallen for Joy? I'm prettier than she is, I'm thinner than she is, I'm smarter than she is—and I have more money.

Thinking that way made her feel better. Tougher. And although the marshals were just outside the door and she *hated* not having privacy, she hugged Sol again.

She was going to stick by him, she'd decided by then. He must have been mentally ill. That had to be the explanation.

When her half hour was up, she said good-bye to Sol without further ado and went outside to assume, resume, her role as matriarch of their now-wounded family. She told the children to take turns going in to see their father, and while they were deciding who should go first, she conferred with Sol's internist, Dr. Lanman, who had admitted him to the hospital, and with Robert Match, the hospital's director, about finding a psychiatrist for her husband.

By two A.M., she had chosen one—Dr. Sanford Solomon.

Dr. Solomon was in bed and asleep when he received a call from Dr. Lanman. He didn't know Sol, and he hadn't watched TV that night, so he knew nothing about the chief judge's arrest. Dr. Lanman filled him in. Then she asked if he'd see the famous patient. He said yes, and that he'd be over in the morning.

"Can't you come sooner?"

"Wait a minute," he said. "You mean you want me to come over now?"

"If you can," Lanman urged.

Solomon got dressed and into his car, and he was at the hospital by two-thirty A.M. Joan and the children were still there, but they left once he went into Sol's room to interview his new patient. So did the marshals, who agreed to let him conduct the interview in private.

Sol was dressed—he was wearing a charcoal gray suit—and he was sitting in a chair. But even so, it was difficult for Solomon to imagine the man facing him as the chief of anything, let alone of the state's judiciary system. The man seemed rolled in a ball, curled up inside himself. And he looked dreadfully sad.

"I've done some terrible things," he said. "I've ruined my family."

Solomon, a genial, compassionate man, a tennis player and an expert in psychosomatic medicine, immediately struck up a rapport with him and soon got him talking about what he'd done. Sol explained that he'd been in love with Joy, who'd jilted him, and that he'd grown depressed and written her threatening letters.

But when he talked about the letters he didn't seem to see—or at least to explain—the logical pattern underlying the threats, nor their slow inexorable escalation over the months. Rather, he spoke confusingly, and confusedly, told things out of sequence, and sounded unsure about when various things had occurred. He's bewildered, Solomon thought. Completely bewildered.

"What bothers you most?" he asked.

"What I've done to my family," Sol said. "I always told my children that when I died, I wouldn't be leaving them much money, but that I would be leaving them the Wachtler name. Now they're going to be ashamed of that name."

"Did you have any thoughts about what the consequences of your behavior might be?"

"No. I never even thought about it."

While they were talking, a nurse came in and told Sol to get into his pajamas and go to bed. He did, and they went on with their interview.

"How did you feel when you made the phone calls? Mailed the letters?" Dr. Solomon asked.

"I felt I had to do the things I did," Sol said. "Like something was driving me to do them. And then afterward, after I did them, I'd feel this great relief."

"*Why* did you threaten Joy?"

"I thought that she'd get scared and call on me to help her. Call me back into her life."

They talked for over an hour, and then a marshal entered the room, grasped Sol's leg, and chained it to the bed's metal frame.

Dr. Solomon looked down in discomfort. Was this any way to treat a man who was sick?

He took his leave soon afterward, leaving orders that Sol should be given no medications except Valium, to calm him.

Three days after his interview with the psychiatrist, Sol was released from the hospital and went back to Manhattan's federal district court for a hearing. He had by then hired an older lawyer with more years of experience than his son-in-law—Charles Stillman, of Stillman, Friedman, and Show. Stillman had been working frantically to cut a deal with Chertoff that would allow Sol to be placed under house arrest.

Sol was dressed, that morning, in his expensive-looking gray suit, the one he'd worn at the hospital, the one he'd been wearing when he was arrested, but he seemed only a shadow of his former self: someone thinner, shorter, less substantial in every way. He walked to the defense table with his eyes cast down and took his seat silently, hands folded.

Stillman tried to distract him. He joked with him, made small talk. Sol smiled and nodded. But his responses seemed automatic. When he was not being spoken to, he kept his eyes fixed motionlessly on the front of the courtroom.

Then, "All rise," bellowed the court clerk, *"The United States versus Sol Wachtler,"* and the judge, a woman named Sharon Grubin who had been an admirer of Sol's when he sat on the other side of justice at his high court of appeals bench, entered the courtroom.

She wanted to know, before she agreed to release Sol to home arrest, whether he was dangerous. Chertoff took the position that he was. "The evidence developed in this case suggests a pretty strong threat," he said. "We're obliged to take it seriously, whoever the defendant is." Nevertheless, he was willing to let Sol stay out of jail, provided that at home he was monitored by security guards—paid for at his own expense—and an electronic bracelet, which would report his movements to the police.

Did he need *both* these constraints, the judge asked.

"They certainly are not as foolproof as the Metropolitan Corrections Center," Chertoff said wryly. He was hinting that the judge would be justified if she chose to send the celebrated defendant to jail, and Sol pressed his lips together, as if restraining a cry.

Judge Grubin ended the hearing. She was granting the home arrest, she said. Then she directed a remark to Sol. It was an admiring, even a fawning, remark. "Chief Judge Wachtler," she said, "if my decision in releasing you reflects even a small amount of the wisdom you have shown on the bench, we will have done right."

Sol had held himself together until then, but hearing her words of praise, the kind of praise he had heard day in, day out for much of his life, tears flooded his eyes.

He was still, officially, chief judge of New York's highest court. His fellow judges on the court of appeals had held a meeting and declined to suspend him, and although he himself, shortly after his arrest, had asked his family to issue a statement saying he was temporarily withdrawing from his position, he had subsequently revoked the statement. Now, leaving Judge Grubin's courtroom, he realized reluctantly that he had no choice but to resign, and as soon as he arrived at his Manhasset home, he telephoned the acting chief of the court of appeals and informed him he was stepping down.

Charles Stillman was known for his skills at working out deals, and over the next few weeks, he began the process of seeking a deal for Sol, one that would keep him out of jail. The scuttlebutt among the press corps was that he would be successful. "When the deal is done," predicted *Newsday*'s Jim Dwyer cynically, "[Wachtler] will plead guilty to something that carries the approximate weight of having mailed a letter with an incomplete zipcode."

Psychiatry was at the core of Stillman's endeavor. If Wachtler could be shown to have a serious mental condition, perhaps the prosecution would go easy on him.

Two weeks after he was released from Long Island Jewish Hospital, Sol was sent to New York Hospital–Cornell Medical Center's Payne Whitney Psychiatric Clinic for further psychiatric evaluation.

Dr. Frank Miller examined him there. He found Sol's behavior inappropriate. "For approximately forty-five minutes," he would later explain, "Mr. Wachtler imitated the David Purdy character. He was so enamored by his creation that he insisted upon demonstrating Purdy's walk, talk, mannerisms, and gestures. Since Purdy was toothless, Mr. Wachtler instructed me to pay particular attention to the way he positioned his jaw and lips to conceal his teeth. When I realized that I was not able to interrupt this monologue, I asked two other physicians to join us in the hope that their presence in the room would calm him. To my dismay, their presence only served to intensify his display, and I asked them to leave. Although the situation of the interview was sobering and grim, he was not able to appreciate or grasp it.''

In short, Miller saw in Sol many of the characteristics of mania, among them poor judgment and an expansive and grandiose mood, the same characteristics that had marked Sol's behavior toward Joy.

New York's former chief judge, Dr. Miller would eventually conclude, had been manic during the period he tormented his ex-lover, and he had been so because he suffered from bipolar, or manic-depressive, illness, precipitated and exacerbated by the many drugs he had been taking.

This was a different diagnosis from the one toward which Dr. Solomon was leaning. He, too, believed Sol to have been manic when he threatened Joy. But he was convinced that his mania had resulted not from an underlying manic-depressive illness, but solely from the drugs he had been taking. Sol's was a "toxic mania," Dr. Solomon theorized. The difference might seem slight to a lay person, but it was very significant, for if Sol were a true manic-depressive, his mania was likely to return unless he was treated with lifelong doses of lithium. But if his mania had been caused by drugs alone, he would be all right in the future, provided he avoided medications that made him toxic.

While he was at New York Hospital, Sol was exceedingly depressed, even despairing. "I feel," he said to one of his nurses, "as though I'm already dead." But he wasn't suicidal, he assured her. "I wouldn't visit that on the good people I've already hurt."

He still thought about Joy a lot, sometimes with an odd, lingering affection. He *missed* her. Missed her still. Or missed what she had come to represent to him: a Helen, a Beatrice. A fantasy.

But at other times, he thought about her angrily, especially around New Year's, when he learned that Charles Stillman had received a letter from one of her lawyers demanding that Sol give up his position as trustee of her trust and the trusts of Bruce, Van, and Honey Wolosoff as well, and that he return all commissions paid to him during 1992. "I'd rather go to jail than let her have the money," he fumed to one of his nurses, "because she would blow it all in one day."

*   *   *

Joy was on St. Barts. She'd flown down with David Samson, and with Jessica and Evan. She swam and sunned and feasted, and after a while she began to relax, to put aside, however slightly, the ordeal she had endured all year.

A woman editor who met Joy at a party that week found her cheerful and friendly. She'd heard that in New York, Joy had been hiding out, avoiding the glare of publicity, and was pleased to see that, now that she was on St. Barts, she didn't have to be reclusive.

The two women were on the same flight back to New York, and before the plane took off, they talked some more and their children chatted, clicked. But the two families didn't have an opportunity to say good-bye. When the plane landed, Joy and her party were whisked through customs by two customs officers.

"Who is she?" the editor overheard one of them say to the other.

"Someone big in the Republican party," the other man said. "I think Bush wanted her to get special treatment."

Sol's immersion in psychiatry was just beginning. Charles Stillman, wanting as much expert opinion as he could get, hired two other psychiatrists—internationally known authorities—to have a look at his client, and Sol, who had once claimed to fear the stigma of the probing profession, saw the doctors willingly, hopefully. Both men, Dr. Donald Klein, one of the country's leading authorities on psychiatric medications, and Dr. Robert Spitzer, who had written the standard diagnostic manual utilized by virtually all psychiatrists, agreed after examining Sol that most likely he had been suffering from mania—probably a drug-induced mania—when he undertook to frighten Joy.

Next, Sol was examined by the prosecution's mental-health experts. The first to see him was psychologist Louis B. Schlesinger, who gave him a battery of psychological tests. Early in their first session, which lasted four and a half hours, he was struck by Sol's extraordinary social skills. This fellow's got a way of making you feel that you're the most important person in the world, he thought. But when the session was over and he had had time to reflect, he came to the conclusion that Sol's interest in others was actually a pose, a mask. He *acts* as if he cares about you, Schlesinger decided, but at the bottom, his feelings toward others are shallow, manipulative.

By the time he had spent another five hours with Sol, the psychologist had noted many other things about the former chief judge, among them that he was very naive about women and that he had an unusually strong need for attention and admiration. Wachtler, Schlesinger became convinced, was the type of man who is highly vulnerable to rejection, the kind who, when turned down by a woman, feels as if he's been *injured,* given in some essential core of himself a veritable wound.

Using these clinical insights and the results of the tests he'd administered, Schlesinger was ultimately to add an astute new diagnosis to those that had already been made of Sol—he felt the former chief judge might have a narcissistic personality disorder. It is a condition marked by feelings of grandiosity, a lack of empathy for others, and a profound sense of entitlement. "It's not unrelated to psychopathy," Dr. Schlesinger would one day explain, "and indeed, there's a clear psychopathic streak to Wachtler."

Prosecution psychiatrist Dr. Steven S. Simring, who was the next to see Sol, found the famous patient's only sickness to be "lovesickness." That was a sickness not listed in the psychiatric diagnostic manual, he would later point out in a report filed with the court, yet it was

> no small matter, because individuals who have been spurned by the objects of their love can develop any number of symptoms which look like depression, including loss of appetite, crying, and loss of interest in the outside world. It is certainly not uncommon for people to commit suicide after the failure of an important relationship. [But] the point is that Sol Wachtler's symptoms were not caused by some mysterious mental illness that was visited upon him, or by the injudicious use of psychotropic medication. . . .
>
> I do not think that anyone can be unmoved by the misfortune that befell Sol Wachtler. . . . he had been a good

man who led a life of dedication to work and public service. Perhaps the problem was that Sol Wachtler was too dedicated, too much involved in taking care of his responsibilities toward others, while neglecting his own emotional needs.... [He] spent many years in a loveless marriage, accepting it for what it was, essentially denying that he had any emotional needs of his own. When Joy Silverman came along, he was starved for her affection and the passion that she stirred in him.

But, Simring concluded, when Joy broke off the affair, Sol became angry—"perhaps he genuinely did not appreciate how angry he had become"—and sought revenge.

Stalking is a vengeful deed, not an act of love. The letters that Judge Wachtler wrote to Ms. Silverman and the others leave little doubt how enraged he really was.... I can only conclude that he must have found some satisfaction in directly observing the effect on Joy Silverman of his threats and coarse language.

At the time Drs. Schlesinger and Simring interviewed Sol, the former chief judge had not yet been indicted. Chertoff had agreed to wait before indicting him until the results of the medical evaluations were in. If Wachtler had an organic problem severe enough to excuse his conduct, he told Stillman, he might be willing to forgo pressing criminal charges.

But it better be something serious, he told his staff. The defense better show Wachtler has something in his brain that's pressing right on the part that does right and wrong.

In the middle of January, Chertoff learned the results of the doctors' examinations and was informed by Stillman that the defense wanted a deal based on the theory that at the time Sol threatened Joy, he'd been suffering from an attack of mania caused by bipolar, or manic-depressive, disease or a toxic reaction to drugs. The former chief judge would plead guilty, Stillman indicated, provided he was indicted on charges that didn't automatically require jail time.

Chertoff was unimpressed by the offer. He didn't think Sol was a true manic-depressive. "We know enough about the disease," he said to Ashrafi one day, "to know that a true manic-depressive can't control his mania. So if Wachtler was one, he'd have been manic on the bench. He'd have been rattling on, and the people around him would have been talking about it. About him."

"Which certainly wasn't the case here," Ashrafi agreed.

"Yeah," Chertoff said. "The FBI interviewed scores of people who interacted with him while he was conducting his campaign against Joy, and no one noticed anything unusual about his behavior. Nothing."

Chertoff had, in general, little patience with psychiatric arguments. By profession and philosophy, he believed there was good and evil in the world—good and evil and right and wrong—and that not every evil act needed to be explained as an illness, something to be treated. Which was how, he sometimes mused, a whole lot of people who put great store by psychiatry viewed things. Besides which, psychiatrists were always stretching. Take those symptoms of mania Wachtler's doctors had come up with. Like Sol's having feelings of grandiosity. Yeah, well, if you're chief judge, you're going to feel grandiosity, aren't you?

There was something else Chertoff believed. It was that many crimes got committed by people who were depressed. Or manic. Or under stress. "They've lost their jobs," he explained to a journalist one day. "They're disappointed in love. But, hey, that's the human condition. Okay, so life isn't hunky-dory. But you're supposed to be able to control yourself. And if you can't—well, that's what we've got the criminal law for."

On February 1, Chertoff indicted Sol on five felony counts: one count of making a false statement to the government, namely when Sol had accused the Seales of trying to blackmail Joy; three counts of using the U.S. mail to promote blackmail, namely in the letters Sol had written to Joy, Jessica, and Elaine Samson in which he'd threatened to injure Joy's reputation; and one count of extortion, based on the many letters and calls in which Sol had posed as Purdy and demanded money in exchange for compromising photographs and audiotapes of Joy and David Samson.

The indictment also pointed out that as part of Sol's "extortion scheme," he used his power, influence, and resources as chief judge of the New York State Court of Appeals to obtain information and promote his plan.

If Sol went to trial and was convicted of all the counts, he could be sentenced to five to sixteen years in prison. If he pled guilty to the charges, he could be sentenced to a year to eighteen months.

Sol was devastated. And he was still upset when, sixteen days later, he appeared at the court to which his case had been assigned, the U.S. District Court in Trenton, New Jersey, to lodge a plea to the indictment. Dr. Solomon, who had been seeing him two times a week ever since he got out of Payne Whitney, had put him on a regimen of lithium, the standard drug for the control of mania, and Prozac, the country's most widely used antidepressant. He was, presumably, in emotional balance, chemically speaking. But when he entered the courtroom, a paneled hall adorned with gilt-framed portraits of famed, long-dead judges, he looked drawn and shaken, his body hunched, his hands dangling limply in front of him.

Joan was with him. When he parted from her at the velvet rope that led to the defendants' dock, she kissed him boldly and possessively.

The Honorable Anne Thompson, the judge who would be taking his plea, arrived a moment later. She was a tall, reserved woman, a former prosecutor—the first black woman to serve as a prosecutor in New Jersey—and the state's first female and first African-American federal judge. She had been a judge for fourteen years, but this was the most high-profile case over which she had presided.

She kept the proceedings brief. She ordered the indictment read, then asked Charles Stillman how his client intended to plead.

"Not guilty," Stillman said. "Not guilty by virtue of insanity."

Judge Thompson, never a woman to dawdle, nodded, and set a trial date several months in the future.

But neither she nor Chertoff nor Stillman expected the once-eminent judge looking up at her from the well of the courtroom to go to trial. A trial would be costly. Messy. An embarrassment. Rather, the point of setting a trial date was that now plea negotiations could begin in earnest.

Why should his client plead guilty to extortion? Charles Stillman demanded of Chertoff soon after the indictment. Sol hadn't extorted money—just *threatened* to extort it. He'd never picked up the twenty thousand dollars Joy had left for him in the manila envelope, the day of his arrest. Couldn't the government drop the extortion charge?

"Maybe," Chertoff said. "But even if we do, Wachtler's going to have to do jail time."

"What about letting him serve half the time at home?" Stillman asked. "Or in a halfway house? A work-release program?"

"I don't know," Chertoff said.

But in the next few weeks, his position hardened. He examined the federal sentencing guidelines and concluded that he would have to insist that Sol spend the bulk of his sentence in jail.

His feelings toward Sol had also hardened. He had learned that Sol, who was still the trustee of Joy's trust as well as of other Wolosoff family trusts, had, on the day before entering his not-guilty plea, authorized a payment to himself of $38,665 in trustee commissions and another payment of $20,000 for a lawyer representing him in a suit over the trusts. He was entitled to the money, he'd said. It was due him for work he'd done on the trusts in 1992.

This guy's unbelievably nervy, Chertoff thought. How can he claim he was insane all that year, and yet that he was doing sound work handling the trust money?

Money—Bibbs's money—had brought Sol and Joy together, but now it drove a final wedge between them. She wanted him out of her financial affairs—wanted him to return not only the payments he'd just withdrawn but all the money he'd taken in 1992, and she wanted him to resign his trusteeships and let her and her family appoint whomever they wanted to replace him. He wanted to keep the money and to appoint his daughter Lauren as his successor.

Joy felt that no Wachtler, neither Sol nor his daughter, had the right to handle her stepfather's money. Not after what Sol Wachtler had put her through.

Sol felt he most certainly had the right to handle the money—Bibbs had given that right to him, and to Lauren after him, should he ever have to resign. Bibbs had even said it was their legacy. It had always irritated Sol that Bibbs, for whom he'd done so much, Bibbs, who had made a second fortune on the Florida land Sol's own father had sold to him, had left him no outright inheritance—but the old man had left him this indirect one, and he didn't intend to give it up.

In March, the fight over Bibbs's money intensified, and both Joy and Sol began to sound as if they were convinced that all that lay at the core of the other's heart was greed. Joy pointed out that Sol had, over the years, collected more than $800,000 as executor of Bibbs's will and from commissions on the family trusts, and told people that Sol, whose judicial salary was $120,000, had always resented people with real money. Sol pointed out that Bibbs had always accused Joy of being a spendthrift, and told people that he was beginning to think that Joy might have started her relationship with him *because* he was in charge of her trust. "I wonder whether she ever really cared for me," he mused one day. "I wonder whether she just said, 'Look, he controls my money.'"

He had stopped being as tearful as he'd been in the days immediately following his arrest or as shaky as he'd been at the time of his plea. And he had begun to accept that he was going to have to go to prison—he still hoped it would be for only a brief part of his sentence. But he was frightened about being put behind bars. And he was worried about the humiliation that pleading guilty to Chertoff's charges would bring him. He had spent his life concealing, perhaps even from himself, that his nature contained a dark as well as a bright side, had invested all his energies in being the model son, the overachieving adolescent, the perfect parent, the flawless friend, the principled politician, the peerless deliverer of justice. He had spent his life, more than most people do, in pursuit of reputation, renown, dignity. And now he was going to be humbled, forced to admit to acts that would make everyone who heard his admissions despise and revile him.

Dreading that public shaming, he passed his days seeking concessions from Chertoff—tried to get him to agree to drop the extortion charge as well as the charge that said he'd misused his office, and tried to get him to agree to let him enter into the record a psychiatric diagnosis, something that might soften public opinion about him.

Joy, on the other hand, was freer now than she had been in months, free to move about the city at will, free to stroll her neighborhood without perpetually looking over her shoulder. Moreover, her relationship with David Samson was going well. One day, she ran into the woman who had once criticized her for being overdressed and overjeweled. They met in a Madison Avenue coffee shop early on a Sunday morning. Joy was with David, she was dressed in a sweatsuit, and she was wearing almost no makeup, but her face was aglow with happiness. "Isn't David wonderful?" she said to the woman. "Isn't he the sexiest? Isn't he divine?"

"Do you promise to tell the truth, the whole truth, and nothing but the truth, so help you God?" a clerk in Trenton said to Sol on an unseasonably warm Wednesday at the end of March 1993.

"I do," he replied, his voice loud and firm. He had at last agreed to plead guilty, and while he had won no concessions concerning the amount of time he would probably have to spend in prison, he had won several of the things that were important to him. He wasn't going to have to plead to extortion or misusing his judicial office—the five counts of the indictment had been boiled down to one: that he had utilized interstate facilities to send kidnap and blackmail threats. And he was going to be allowed to include in his plea an affidavit from Dr. Miller that said that he had been suffering from a major mental illness during the time he had made his threats.

"Have you taken any medication within the last twenty-four hours?" Judge Thompson asked him.

"Yes, Your Honor. Prozac and lithium."

"What are those drugs?"

"They are for the control of a manic or depressive state."

"Would that affect in any way your present ability to understand what's going on, to comprehend and appreciate the circumstances in which you find yourself?"

"No, Your Honor. I have been assured by my physician that I am in balance at the present time and capable of understanding and doing that which has to be done."

Judge Thompson nodded, but she wanted to be sure that Sol himself thought he was mentally competent. "You are mentally ill but not mentally incompetent?" she asked. "Is that the distinction you make?"

Sol said yes.

A few moments later, Judge Thompson turned to the matter of Sol's mental health at the time of the crime to which he intended to plead guilty. "I cannot accept your guilty plea," she said to him, "unless you are prepared to acknowledge here in open court that you committed the crime when you were competent, sane, not disabled by reason of mental illness."

It was an essential question, one that Sol would have preferred not having to answer in the affirmative. But he had no choice. It was part, a major part, of the plea deal. So assuring the judge that despite the psychiatric report, he would shortly make a statement asserting he'd been mentally competent at the time of his crimes, he began reading from a prepared speech. "I at no time intended to kidnap or harm in the slightest way Ms. Silverman's daughter," he read, "and I never wanted to nor did I take any money from Ms. Silverman. The extreme nature of my threats were meant to cause Ms. Silverman to believe that, in fact, there was someone named Purdy, and to be in fear so she would have reason to seek Sol Wachtler's reassurance."

As he spoke, his voice grew even stronger, so that he could be heard throughout the courtroom. "At the time I made the threats, I was conscious and aware of my actions and understood the making of such threats was wrong and illegal. I have been told by several psychiatrists that I suffered from a mental illness during that year, but I do not believe this would or should excuse what I did. I was able to appreciate the nature and quality of my acts.''

It was done. He had pled guilty. But there was one more thing he wanted to say. ''I know, Your Honor,'' he began, and suddenly his voice weakened, became almost inaudible, ''that my behavior from late 1991 to late 1992 was foreign to my sixty-two years on earth. I am deeply ashamed and sorry for what I have done to others, to Ms. Silverman, to my wife and children, and to those who entrusted New York State's court system to my care. I know that I can never make up for these acts, but I want to express my profound sorrow and regret.''

When he was finished, he sat down at the defense table, rubbed at his eyes, and folded his hands together in a prayerlike position.

Chertoff was satisfied. Outside the courtroom, he told the press that the case had been one of the most important of his entire career because it had challenged the very integrity of the court system. ''People identified with Wachtler,'' he said. ''That is, prominent people did. Judges. Lawyers. They went around saying what a terrible thing this was for the defendant, as if we should give him special treatment, take him out of the category of everyone else.''

''Why do you think Wachtler snapped?'' a reporter called out.

''There was no snap,'' Chertoff said. ''That's the position the government takes, and it's the one we'll be taking when it comes to the sentencing. Wachtler's acts weren't the product of a severe mental illness. They were the product of anger. Here was a man who, by God's grace, had the things everybody dreams about, position, honor, an intellectually challenging job—and yet when he was scorned in one area, he simply couldn't let go. A snap? Mental illness? This was a man capable of going up on the bench and conducting lucid, erudite oral arguments—he wasn't a man who was staying home in a bathrobe, or going around like a screaming banshee.''

* * *

Going around like a screaming banshee? Joan Wachtler, when she read Chertoff's remarks in *The New York Times* the next day, was enraged, and for the first time since Sol's arrest, she stepped forward to defend her husband publicly. "I am a licensed certified social worker who has been practicing in mental health for sixteen years," she wrote in a letter to the editor of the *Times.* She continued:

> Michael Chertoff's characterization of a manic-depressive as someone "staying home in a bathrobe or going around like a screaming banshee" destroys the progress made by the medical-psychiatric community and the entire mental health profession in educating the public about mental illness.
>
> Mr. Chertoff with this stereotyped negative bias has made a retrograde contribution to the mental health movement, setting it back many decades to a time before the advent of clinical assessment, diagnosis, and treatment with psychotherapy and medication. He has redrawn the archaic picture of any person with a mental illness as an unproductive citizen—an out-of-control raving maniac.

"Whatsa matter, David? You didn't like my taste?" Larry Bathgate said to David Samson one day later that spring. Bathgate had just read in the *New York Post* that David had broken up with Joy. He'd read it in Cindy Adams's column. "Joy Silverman, the Judge Sol Wachtler fatal attraction," the gossip columnist had written, "is 0-for-5. Three marriages went poop. The extramarital affair with New York's former Chief Judge went poop . . . and now, her subsequently well-publicized romance with Jersey lawyer David Samson pooped. It broke up months ago. He's hunting for a replacement."

"Aw, Larry," David said. "You still believe everything you read in print?"

He insisted that he and Joy were still a couple.

So were Sol and Joan. But it was not easy to pick up the shards of their relationship. As for Joy, Sol was no longer in love with her. Indeed, he had come to feel that he had never really loved her, that he had loved, instead, the fantasy of love. Yet as late as the middle of July, more than nine months after she had effectuated his downfall, he wondered if he would always have a lingering sense of loss about Joy. She had been, for so long, the center around which his whole life had orbited.

Their long-term affair still aroused anger and resentment in Joan—perhaps it always would. One day, when Sol talked about Joy's having a different, more casual attitude toward sex than did the members of their generation, Joan snapped at him, "Joy's not that young!" and when he said she had been willing to cheat on Jeffrey, but not on David Samson, because she'd been *married* to Jeffrey, Joan sniffed, "Quite a standard! She wrote a new book!"

If she ever ran into Joy, she sometimes thought, she'd murder her.

But she was angry at Sol too. When he talked about Joy's astrologist, she blurted out, "How could someone as intelligent as you fall for that crap?" and when he said Joy's psychotherapist, Eleanor Sloan, had been a bright woman, she exploded, "Oh, God!"

Sol, placating her, told her he'd never loved Joy as much as he'd loved her, and that the thing he loved most about her was her empathy. "The way you can't even stand to see a movie where an innocent person gets beaten up. Joy's exactly the opposite."

But why, then, had he fallen in love with her? Why had he enjoyed seeing her?

Sol himself sometimes thought that maybe he'd enjoyed seeing someone who could be such a bitch.

Dr. Solomon was still seeing Sol twice a week. When the doctor sat in his small, book-lined office and reflected on his famous patient, he thought that a lot of what had happened to Sol could be traced to his childhood. To the way he'd been such a very good boy. He'd had tremendous needs for approval, so he'd always done everything he could to make the adults around him think well of him. And in a way, he still did. He was on the phone with his mother every day. "Hello, Ma. How are you?" *Every* day.

That was Sol. He worried about everyone. Took care of their needs. But not his own.

Take all that time when he and Joan weren't making love, all that time *before* the affair with Joy started. Other men would have acted a lot differently. But Sol didn't wander. He was still the good boy.

Of course, the end result was that he was very naive, sexually.

Joy had helped him with that. So in a way, she did good things for him, not just bad. She also told him how handsome he was, how smart. Which he needed. And wasn't getting from Joan. Joan's a very loving wife, but she isn't the type to fawn over a man.

Of course, now they would have to work on their marriage. Both of them. And Sol would have to work on becoming more aware of his feelings. Those headaches he always got? They had to do with his hiding his feelings from himself. Feelings like anger. Like his anger at Joy.

Dr. Solomon had talked to Sol about that. He'd told him that he believed he'd been poisoned by the drugs he'd been taking and that was what made him do the things he'd done to Joy. But was there anger behind it? You bet there was.

On June 29 the trust suit between Sol and Joy was settled. He agreed to give back the money he'd taken in commissions from the Wolosoff family trusts in 1993 and from Joy's trust in 1992 and to let Joy choose whomever she wanted to succeed him as trustee. She agreed not to challenge his administration of the estate. The last ties between him and Joy were over, severed. The last ties between him and Bibbs too.

Lots of his old ties were being severed. His old friend and chief administrator, Matthew Crosson, was stepping down from the position to which Sol had elevated him. There was going to be a farewell party for him this very night. Crosson had begged him to come, but he'd been reluctant. He hadn't been to a public event since his arrest, even though, now that he'd pled guilty, he no longer had to wear the electronic bracelet. But then Dr.

Solomon told him it would be a good idea for him to get out and about, and Sol decided to go.

He went to the party, which was being held in the glittering Tavern on the Green restaurant in New York's Central Park, accompanied by Lauren and his son-in-law Paul Montclare. Unsure of the reception he would receive, he stood for several minutes at the entrance to the party room, just feeling nervous and staring at the guests. They were mostly state judges—there must have been two hundred and fifty of them.

Then someone spotted him and, to his surprise, came over and grabbed his hand and said, "Hello, Chief!" And then some of the other judges saw him, and they began mobbing him, shaking his hand and kissing him and calling out, "Hey, Chief!" and, "How are ya, Chief."

And that wasn't the end of it. When Crosson got up to speak, he said such flattering things about him that all the judges began clapping and clapping for him. And some even began crying.

What's the *matter* with those guys? Chertoff thought when he read the account of Sol's trip to Tavern on the Green in a newspaper the next day. Don't they understand that what Wachtler did isn't simply a case of boys-will-be-boys?

It wasn't just this crew—judges!—who got it wrong. Ever since the case began, he'd been meeting people who shrugged their shoulders and said, "Well, man-woman stuff. What do you expect?" Didn't they know that this was a crime of violence? Well, there was no *act* of violence. But you had to be very inexperienced in the ways of the world not to understand that just by making threats, Sol had effectively done violence to a mother and a daughter.

Chertoff hoped Judge Thompson would understand it and would sentence Sol to the maximum prison time possible under the federal guidelines—eighteen months.

Hoping to influence her, he put together a thick packet of presentencing materials that contained every shred of evidence the government had collected against Sol.

*   *   *

DOUBLE LIFE

Charles Stillman was hoping Judge Thompson would give Sol only twelve months in prison—the minimum possible sentence—and would allow him to serve as much of that sentence as possible in a halfway house, and he, too, put together a thick packet of materials that might influence her decision.

His packet contained letters attesting to Sol's good works and character. There was one from New York's governor, Mario Cuomo. Another from New York City's mayor, David Dinkins. And there were scores of communications from other, less famous people.

The letters laid out a picture of Sol as a man who had spent his life dedicated to serving just causes. They pointed out that he had formed the New York State Judicial Commission for Minority Concerns to combat racial discrimination, established the Workforce Diversity Program to ensure fair hiring and promotion in the court system, and worked closely with New York's Task Force on Gender Bias to eliminate the unequal treatment of women.

The letters also reported Sol's numerous acts of kindness as a friend, and many spoke of him in glowing, admiring terms. "I always found Sol's great charm," wrote Vivian Berger, the vice dean of Columbia Law School, "to be backed up by the substance of character and genuine warmth as a human being."

"He represented for me," wrote the Reverend Frank N. Johnston, the former rector of the Christ Episcopal Parish in Manhasset, "the highest aspirations of our Judeo-Christian culture."

Sol was happy about the great outpouring of affection and support in the letters and hopeful that it would indeed influence Judge Thompson to give him a short sentence and a quick release to a halfway house. But he felt there was something more that could be done to make the judge look favorably upon him—and not just the judge but the public too. His story needed to be in the press. His story of mental illness. Told in his own words, and with his own spin on things.

Stillman wasn't sure it was a good idea. But Sol, like many politicians, had been in thrall to the press his entire life, and he believed in its power the way the ancients believed in the power of their gods. More, he was convinced he knew how to manipulate that power, make it work for him. So in the middle of the summer, feeling not unlike his old energetic and politically savvy self, he mounted an enormous publicity campaign, giving lengthy interviews to numerous local newspapers. In his interviews, he talked about his mental illness—the mania that had resulted from bipolar disease or a toxic reaction to medications, or both—and blamed the FBI, the U.S. Attorney's office in New Jersey, and Joy for not stopping his campaign of harassment.

It was, he seemed to be saying, *he* who was the victim. The state's victim. Joy's victim. In regard to Joy, his stance resembled the age-old one used by men who have abused women: What I did was her fault, not mine; it would never have happened if she hadn't gone walking there, if she hadn't dressed the way she did, if she'd said "No!" and meant it. Sure, he'd done bad things, went his message, but it wasn't his *fault*.

Not surprisingly, given the enlightened temper of the times, within a few days the campaign backfired. While several papers presented sympathetic or at least uncritical interviews with him, four days before September 9, the date that had finally been set for his sentencing, *The New York Times,* the forum that mattered most to him, pointed out in a front-page article that the former chief judge was "seeking leniency in the court of public opinion by impugning those who brought him down."

As the day of sentencing approached, Sol felt he couldn't get anything to come out right anymore.

On September 9, a dank and gloomy day, the press turned out in force to record the day's events, the closure they had been awaiting for nearly a year. Outside the limestone steps of Trenton's handsome WPA-constructed courthouse, there was a veritable trailer park of television vans, a battalion of cameramen, a phalanx of TV newscasters and newspaper reporters. Many of the journalists covering the story knew Sol Wachtler, had known him back in his palmier days, and felt pangs of pity for him, for he had always been immensely popular with them, a ready source of snappy sound bites and winning one-liners.

"Remember the ham sandwich?" one reporter reminded another. " 'A grand jury'll indict even a ham sandwich'?"

"Remember 'the death penalty is the chicken soup of politics'?" another reminisced. " 'A folk remedy that can't hurt, but hasn't been proved to do you any good'?"

Wachtler was being memorialized. He was dead—but the burial was yet to come.

Then he arrived and cameras whirred. But court officers swiftly whisked him indoors—him and his entourage, his children and their spouses, his psychiatrist, and three lawyers. There was Stillman, of course. And Theodore Wells, a highly regarded New Jersey lawyer who had been working with Stillman ever since the case began. And Paul Montclare, Lauren's husband, who had represented Sol when he was first arrested.

Only Joan wasn't there. Early in the morning, she and Sol had talked things over and decided that no matter what sentence Judge Thompson handed down, the day was bound to be traumatic. "Maybe you should stay home," Sol had said. And she had given him no argument.

"Mr. Stillman," Judge Thompson called out as soon as the court came to order. "Mr. Stillman, is there anything you would like to say in mitigation of sentence?"

"I would like to speak to you of Sol Wachtler, the public man," Stillman replied. "One must consider the nature of the man's life and the price he has already paid, and will pay, for what he did."

He then proceeded to spell out many of Sol's accomplishments and to urge Judge Thompson to consider the punishment he had already received—public disgrace, the loss of his judgeship, and the loss of his law license, which he'd voluntarily given up. "Sol Wachtler's sixty-two-year path through life," he asserted, "has been marked by extraordinary contributions and a commitment to the judicial system, which is a critical part of an ordered society. Along the way, he stumbled and fell. Quite simply, he will never fully recover from the injuries he has suffered from that fall. Surely, the dispensation of justice has room to credit Sol Wachtler for all the good he has done."

Chertoff, listening attentively, thought, I've got an answer for that! I'll turn it around, ask the judge to think about the guy who gets convicted and gives as the excuse for his crime, "I never had anything my entire life." The guy comes in, he says, "My entire life I was devoid of love, success, prosperity, and health. That's why I committed the crime. So don't punish me." But, hey, we don't accept that as an excuse for breaking the law—even though in some ways it's a more powerful argument than "I was rich, I was powerful, I had prestige, an unlimited vista—and I didn't get something I wanted, so I committed a crime, but don't punish me. I've been punished enough because I lost all my advantages."

Paul Montclare spoke next. "One should not equate insanity with mental illness," he declared, and then talked about Sol's mental troubles and the medications that had exacerbated them. "He was taking amphetamines," he reminded the judge, "he was taking antidepressants, he was taking steroids for chronic headaches, and he was taking Halcion, a drug that has been banned in England. The cumulative effects of these drugs on a vulnerable person like Mr. Wachtler cannot be underestimated. His judgment was impaired."

Mental illness? Chertoff thought. It's like they're trying to thread a needle with a camel! On the one hand, they're saying Wachtler had impaired judgment when it came to Joy Silverman and David Samson and all the other people he called while he was conducting his campaign. And on the other hand, they're saying that in all his capacities as a judge, he had unimpaired judgment. Well, you can't be a judge on autopilot. And anyway, if his judgment was unimpaired most of the time, how come in those unimpaired moments he didn't exercise his good judgment to prevent himself from doing what he did? It makes no sense.

By the time Sol's third lawyer, Theodore Wells, spoke, Chertoff was growing fidgety, his long, lean, Ichabod Crane figure shifting in its chair, his long, lean fingers riffling papers. He listened restlessly while Wells asked for twelve months' incarceration, to be served at a halfway house or community correction center, and if a halfway house was ruled out, imprisonment in the federal minimum-security prison in Pensacola, Florida. And then finally, Wells was done, and Judge Thompson was saying, "Mr. Chertoff?"

"Thank you, Your Honor," he began. "It is not a happy day to speak at a sentencing, at any sentencing, still less a sentencing in which a person who once occupied high judicial office confronts the court in the status of a criminal."

A few moments later, he was reciting the entire litany of Sol's crimes—the hang-up calls, the dirty cards, the card with the condom in it, the kidnap threats, the extortion letters, the use of court of appeals staff to obtain information about Samson, the attempt to implicate the Seales. "What Joy Silverman should have done, according to Mr. Wachtler," he flung out, "at least as he recounted to *The New York Times* last week, is she should have sought a protective order to prevent him from harming her, or she should have gone to the family members so they could seek help for him. Your Honor, it's the old theme . . . *She* should have stopped me."

When he finished with Sol and Joy, he turned to the question of whether antidepressant medication had caused Sol's crimes. "Pamelor and Halcion are the principal culprits in Sol's version of events," he said, leaving out any reference to Tenuate, the amphetaminelike drug whose use had predated them. "His lawyers say that all his truly aberrant conduct starts after he filled the prescription for these drugs on November 11, 1991. But the actual genesis of his scheme occurred well before he took those two medications. Two weeks before he took them, he called Jeffrey Silverman and, posing as a private investigator, asked Silverman if he was interested in retaining him to look into the activities of his wife. And five or six days before he filled his prescription, he called Elaine Samson and for the first time used the name and identity of David Purdy."

"Javert!" a famous television newscaster sitting on a front bench whispered loudly, referring to the heartless French detective in *Les Misérables* who mercilessly hounded poor Jean Valjean. But if Chertoff heard him, he gave no sign. He went on talking.

He talked about the poor man and the rich man, and about threading a needle with a camel, and finally, he said, "This was a crime of violence, even though there was no *act* of violence." Then he explained that harassment was a form of violence against women, and declared, "We don't deal with crimes against women very much in federal court, but the sentence ought to speak to that issue as well as to everything else."

When he was done, he asked for eighteen months of incarceration and opposed letting Sol serve his time in a halfway house.

Women's issues? Theodore Wells was on his feet as soon as Chertoff sat down. "Your Honor, could I please have a few minutes of response time? I will not be long."

Judge Thompson nodded, and he began to speak. "In terms of women's issues," he said, "there is another dimension to this case. It involves relationships not just between Joy Silverman and Judge Wachtler, but between Joy Silverman and Lauren Wachtler, her friend, and Joy Silverman and Joan Wachtler, the judge's wife." Yes, there *was* a whole women's issue surrounding the case, he tried to point out, and it wasn't the one Chertoff had been talking about. But he didn't call it by a name. Did he mean Joy's sexual betrayal of her cousin Joan? With the innuendo left hanging in the stale air of the courtroom, he moved quickly away from the matter, insisting, "There is no attempt to blame Joy Silverman for anything."

Sol had been listening to the arguments with his head hunched down between his shoulders. Now at last, it was his turn to speak. He rose from the defense table, laid some notes on a podium, and looked searchingly at Judge Thompson, sitting high on her elevated platform, as he used to sit high above the men and women who came before him for justice. Then he started talking. "The last time I appeared before Your Honor," he said, "I told you of my misdeeds. I told you then I was fully responsible for them. I don't blame anyone else for those misdeeds. They were my actions."

The words were coming out smoothly. Making speeches was an art he had been practicing since he was a boy. "I did this," he went on clearly. "And I apologized then and I apologize now to Mrs. Silverman, to Jessica, to my wife and children, to the court system, to the profession in which I served, to all those people who believed in me who I disappointed by my aberrant behavior—''

But then suddenly, he couldn't go on. His mouth was dry. His words were choking in his throat.

"Would you like some water?" Judge Thompson asked with concern.

He shook his head. Behind him, several of his children bit their lips. Above him, the painted eyes of New Jersey's long-dead famous judges stared sightless and impassive at his coughing figure. Then, he swallowed, and regained his composure. "I'm all right," he assured Judge Thompson, and although he wasn't, not really, and might never feel altogether all right again, he continued with his prepared speech. "In January of 1991, the New York State Bar Association presented me with its gold medal," he said. "The highest honor that can ever be given to a lawyer in my state. Yesterday, I received a letter from the president of the New York State Bar Association advising me that my name has been stricken from the membership rolls."

Several reporters, their heads up, their pens forming sentences as if directed by an autopilot device, sighed. The irony of Wachtler, the gold-medalist, and Wachtler, the outcast, had moved them, or at least arrested them, assured them they'd be leaving with that greatest of necessities, a good quote.

"Mr. Chertoff speaks of responsibility," Sol was continuing. "How do you manifest the acceptance of responsibility? First of all, by saying you are responsible, and then by showing a sense of responsibility. I have done this. After my arrest, my court convened and would not suspend me, but as soon as I could get to a phone, I called and told them I was resigning. I did not want to bring further or greater disgrace to the institution which I revered.

"More, because of the nature of my offense, I would not be automatically disbarred in the State of New York. Nevertheless, I have voluntarily filed my resignation from the bar. I didn't want to bring further disgrace to the profession which has nurtured me, and for which I have such high respect."

The courtroom was as quiet as a tomb. Only the scratching of pastels, as courtroom artists tried to capture his likeness, broke the remarkable stillness.

"My only hope now is to try to put my life back together again," Sol said into the silence. "To try to make amends for what I have done. And in my punishment, I would just hope that the Court would please consider my forty years of public service."

Then he sat down.

Judge Thompson had not tipped her hand, had not displayed, throughout the long morning of arguments, any reaction that might indicate what she was thinking, where she stood. Now she herself addressed the waiting defendant, lawyers, and spectators. She remarked that she was convinced that Judge Wachtler had lived an exemplary life—she had read about it in the papers the defense had submitted. She said, too, that she knew that there was a dispute among the psychiatrists who had examined Judge Wachtler, with the defense's doctors attributing his criminal episode to a major mental illness and the government's attributing it to no malady, just lovesickness.

But, "The Court cannot resolve the apparent conflict between the highly regarded doctors," she intoned. "Nor can the Court rationally explain the defendant's behavior.

"His bizarre acting out of make-believe characters, like David Purdy, the investigator from Houston, complete with cowboy hat and toothless diction, and Theresa O'Connor, the devout parishioner from Linden, New Jersey, seems beyond the norm for lovesickness. His simultaneous conduct as competent, responsible, professional chief judge of the Court of Appeals of the State of New York defies logical explanation."

Where was she going? Which side would she favor? She had given no clue. And then, it came. "In trying to perform the impossible task of understanding the defendant," she said, "we cannot lose sight of the fact that there were real victims here, people who endured protracted anguish and suffering as a consequence of the defendant's calculated actions. The defendant's behavior was not an expression of love. It was an expression of anger, intimidation, and grotesque control."

She paused, gazed down at Sol, and then delivered the sentence: fifteen months in prison—three more than the defense had wanted, three less than the prosecution had wanted. She had done the Solomonic thing.

She also levied fines against Sol, among them a fine of thirty-one thousand dollars to repay Joy for having had to hire security guards and tutors for Jessica. And while she refused to recommend to the Bureau of Prisons that Sol's sentence be served in a halfway house, she did agree to suggest to the bureau that he be placed in the minimum-security federal correctional institution in Pensacola, Florida.

He had lost, Sol knew. He had lost almost everything he had been fighting for. A short sentence. A halfway house. But there was still Pensacola to hope for. Standing in the courtroom, his three lawyers surrounding him, he tried to smile, and his lips curled up, but his eyes were misty. A few moments later, he retreated to a room down the corridor with the lawyers, his family, and Dr. Solomon. "It'll be all right," he said to his children. "It's going to be all right."

Dr. Solomon drew him into a corner of the room. "How's your head?" he asked.

"Oh, it's okay," Sol said. "I don't have any headache at all."

Dr. Solomon was astonished by his answer. "No," he said. "I mean, your emotions. Your *head.*"

Sol hadn't wanted to deal with feelings. Not here. Not now. But Dr. Solomon was standing alongside him saying, "It's good to cry. You've been through a great deal, you should let yourself cry." And at last, the tears that all morning had been lurking in the corners of his eyes and the back of his throat began to fall.

He grabbed a handkerchief.

In the afternoon, Joy, who had not attended the sentencing or any of the court sessions, came forward as a spokesperson for victims. "With Sol Wachtler's sentencing today," she asserted in a statement issued through her lawyers, "a message has been sent that society will not tolerate men who terrorize, stalk, abuse, and victimize women and children."

The next day, Joan Wachtler told Cindy Adams, "Joy's an avaricious person whose pathological greed destroyed a gentle and naive man. I've known Joy since she was a young girl. All her treasured possessions came from men. Two husbands. Two divorces, plus a third upcoming. And she wanted more, from *my* husband."

Sol didn't have to report to prison for another couple of weeks. Judge Thompson had granted him a grace period because September was the season of the most important Jewish holidays, Rosh Hashanah, the celebration of the New Year, and Yom Kippur, the Day of Atonement.

He used some of his last moments of freedom to try once again to tell his side of the story. He told it to Cindy Adams, saying, "Joy never knew her father. A psychiatrist told me that she's been taking it out on men ever since. That she destroys men. One by one."

He told it to Barbara Walters, adding, "The Talmud teaches us that a person who serves as a judge sits beside God, and I was given that privilege for twenty-five years, and it's lost to me now." He told it to newscaster Gabe Pressman. And when Pressman asked him what he might do when he got out of prison, he said he might teach law or become a spokesperson on the subject of mental illness—"educate the public with respect to the implications of it."

"Teach?" Dick Lavinthol, who worked in Chertoff's office, said when he heard about Sol's plans. "Educate the public about mental illness? I've got a better idea. Why doesn't he get out of jail and start a foundation devoted to stopping the harassment of women. The problem's endemic—but he could have a real impact. He could set up projects that would give men sensitivity training. And he could get grants to teach women how to handle harassment. He'd be a hero again!"

On Sunday, September 26, two days before he was due to report to prison, Sol was informed that the prison he was to report to wasn't the minimum-security facility in Pensacola, Florida, that he had requested, but the Butner Correctional Institution, a medium-security prison in Butner, North Carolina, that had a psychiatric hospital on its grounds.

He told his psychiatrist that he was exceedingly frightened. "It's dangerous," he said. "There'll be murderers there. There'll be people with grudges against judges."

But there was no recourse, and on the twenty-eighth, Sol traveled back to North Carolina, one of the states he had lived in as a boy, before he had gone north to prep school, before he had married Joan, before he had gotten to know Bibbs Wolosoff, before he had gone into politics and become a judge. Before he had met Joy.

As he was surrendering himself, photographers caught his picture. He looked young, boyish, his unlined face a Picture-of-Dorian-Gray mask.

Then, he was behind bars.

What had brought him to that pass? What had made him a perfect embodiment of what the ancient Greeks considered the only truly tragic figure—a man like ourselves who falls from a high place as a result not of vice or depravity but of some great error or frailty. There was *hubris*, of course. He had lived so long in the corridors of power, had opened so many of its doors, and had found himself a room with a seat that, thronelike, put him in command of the lives and fates of millions. He was not just above the law. He *was* the law. And that had made him vain, overbearingly proud.

Such a man takes it hard when a woman rejects him—especially if he has not often offered himself to a woman. To such a man, rejection is an affront, not a blow to the soul but a slap at dignity. It brings out the urge to punish.

Perhaps, in Sol's case, that urge might have stayed under control were it not for the inflaming effects of the amphetaminelike drug he began taking some months before he started his campaign against Joy. The drug Tenuate often promotes restlessness, feelings of invulnerability and of grandiosity. The drug did not cause his actions, but it enabled him to take the actions. It disinhibited him. It loosed or let him loose the dogs of wounded pride that gnawed at him.

One thing is certain. He became—there is no other word—demonic. And yet, even as he rode his demons, or they rode him, he never ceased being a fair judge, a fond family man, a loyal friend.

History tells us that from time to time there have been other men like this. Men—and women too. Invariably, they fascinate—but it is difficult to say whether that is because they are different from the rest of humankind or because they are Everybody writ large.

EPILOGUE

At the time this book went to press, Joy Silverman was, as far as her acquaintances knew, still seeing David Samson, and Sol Wachtler was still in prison—but not at the Butner Correctional Institution in Butner, North Carolina, the prison to which he had been assigned. Something had happened at Butner, something startling and enigmatic. Sol had been stabbed. He had received two wounds in his back, just above the right shoulder blade, wounds that penetrated his flesh to the depth of an inch, and were so close together, they could have been made by a fork with its middle tine removed.

The incident occurred on a Sunday evening late in November. According to Sol, he had been lying in his room—an unlocked private chamber in Butner's mental-health wing—and listening through earphones to a radio, when someone crept into the area, put a pillow over his face, and attacked him.

According to the FBI, which quickly undertook an investigation of the incident, the injury appeared to be self-inflicted. They based this hypothesis on the location and shallowness of the wounds, and on the fact that at the time of the stabbing there had been only one other prisoner in the area, a delusional inmate whom they apparently judged incapable of the crime.

Sol's family and his psychiatrist were enraged by the FBI's supposition. "Why would he have wanted to hurt himself?" said Dr. Solomon. "I'd been down to see him just before this happened, and he was doing great. Sure, in the beginning they had him cleaning the grounds, picking up papers with a spoke. But now he was helping some inmates prepare for their high-school equivalency exams, and he was doing aerobics and lifting weights. And he'd gotten to know many of the prisoners, heard their stories, met their families—he told me that unlike the press, which kept calling him 'the disgraced Sol Wachtler,' the prisoners called him 'Judge' and 'Your Honor.' He felt comfortable. He had adjusted."

But some of Sol's friends accepted the FBI's theory, seeing in it evidence that Sol was irrational, an idea that confirmed their loyal conviction that some form of madness had made him harass Joy Silverman in the first place. "Maybe he was just crazier than any of us ever knew," one friend, a judge, said.

After the stabbing, Sol was kept for a month in what prison authorities call "administrative detention," and prisoners call "isolation" or "the hole," a locked cell where food is passed in through a slot in the door. Alone, he became noticeably depressed and seemed to lose track of time. Then, wearing leg irons and handcuffs, he was sent to a different prison, one with a full-service psychiatric wing. It was the Federal Medical Center in Rochester, Minnesota, where he was given extensive psychiatric attention, treated with Prozac, and at last pronounced well enough to join the general prison population. He began living in an eight-by-fourteen-foot cell, sharing the limited space with three other inmates. And he began working, collecting a salary of twelve dollars a month. Ironically, the job he was given was to teach creative writing.

Occasionally, he would communicate with friends, writing letters in which he sometimes adopted a breezy, offhand style that seemed to make fun of all that had happened. "There isn't a murderer, rapist, arsonist, or major drug dealer who doesn't think of you as a great man," he wrote to lawyer William Kunstler.

"That includes the harasser of Joy Silverman." "Here I am with murderers, rapists, bank robbers, drug dealers," he wrote to columnist Cindy Adams. "Despite the stabbing, I have no fear of them. Of course, they're scared to death of me, the man who harassed Joy Silverman." He even told jokes in his letters. He was out of the psychiatric hospital, he wrote to Adams, and then, with an eerie allusion to the kidnap ad he had demanded Joy take, said, "I guess I'm just lucky—like the newspaper ad: 'LOST. BEAGLE. Left ear missing. Blind and castrated. Answers to the name "Lucky." ' "

But sometimes his tone turned dark. In another letter to a friend, he described a visit paid to him by U.S. Supreme Court Justice Harry Blackmun, shortly before he resigned his august office. "We had met on several occasions," Wachtler wrote, "and the summer before last, we both were given doctoral degrees at Claremont College in California. Blackmun was now honoring me by visiting me at a federal prison. We embraced on his arrival, and on his departure I wept, remembering what was—and will never be again."

POSTSCRIPT TO THE
NEW EDITION

Sol Wachtler was released from prison at the end of August, 1994, and was sent to a halfway house in Brooklyn, New York, just a few miles from where he had been born and where, heart brimming with romance, he had taken Joy on a tour of the haunts of his boyhood. As a result of his having behaved well in prison, his sentence had been reduced to thirteen months, so he had only two more months to serve on the morning he arrived at the shabby six-story halfway house and was shown to his sparsely furnished two-to-a-room bedroom. There, he was told the rules: He would have to sweep and mop his own room and some of the common areas; he would have to report to work at a job every day; he would have to return to the house no later than nine o'clock each night. And, he was informed, if he followed the rules, he might even be released in less than two months.

It seemed an easy enough regimen to Sol, and a day or two later he began his new routine. Every morning he reported to work at his job—a two-hundred-dollar-a-week desk job at a real-estate and property-management agency that was owned by his son's father-in-law, Fred Wilpon, who also owned New York's baseball team, the Mets. Evenings, he would dine with family members or friends. Then he would return to the halfway house and watch television with his fellow inmates.

But a part of him couldn't abide by the rules, and one night he defied them. He had requested permission to stay out late attending a five-hundred-dollar-a-plate dinner at Long Island University, where he had for so long been a member of the board of directors, but the permission had been denied. He went to the dinner and stayed out late anyway. As a result, his request to be released early from the halfway house was denied. But at last, late in October, he went home—home to Joan.

While he had been in prison, his and Joan's friends had gossiped constantly about the marriage, making bets that it wouldn't last. She'd leave him, they'd said. No, he'd leave her. But once he was out of the halfway house, it wasn't long before he was attending fashionable parties and benefits again, and always, she was at his side. Some people noticed that at these events, Joan looked downcast and tense. But there was no apparent rift in the relationship. Joan and Sol were once again, for good or ill, a couple.

Joy had been nervous about Sol's release. While he was in prison, she had received more threatening phone calls. The voice on the other end of the phone had been a woman's, and her words—spoken to Joy's secretary—had been ominous. "At this time next year, she'll be dead," the woman had said on one occasion. And on another: "It won't help, it won't help, she's dead."

Joy realized that the calls could have been made by people who had no connection to her or to Sol Wachtler, by crazies inspired to torment her simply because her name had been in the headlines, but she also feared that they might have been made by Wachtler loyalists, by friends or supporters of the former chief judge who blamed her for ruining his life. She went once again to the FBI, but this time, although they investigated the calls, they were unable to determine who might be threatening her.

She had other troubles, too. She and David Samson had broken up. The affair between them had proved to be but a passing thing. Moreover, her career as a prominent Republican fundraiser was also over—she'd been informed that she was a liability to the party. Additionally, her divorce from Jeffrey was proceeding acrimoniously. She had asked for a settlement package that included child support and alimony, as well as the title to both their apartment on Park Avenue, where Sol had come to call wearing his Stetson hat and string tie, and the house in Southampton, where she had entertained Barbara Bush. It was a settlement that would add up to more than ten million dollars, and Jeffrey, who had become engaged to another, younger woman, balked. The divorce case began moving at a snail's pace through the courts.

But despite all these unpleasantnesses, Joy began to put her life back together. She started dating again. And she became an active participant in the National Victim Center, an organization that lobbies on behalf of crime victims. At the center, her particular project became the development of an anti-stalking statute, a law that would be so detailed and complete that it could serve as a model and hopefully be enacted one day by every state in the union.

By the end of 1994, Sol, too, had begun putting his life back together. Still taking anti-depression medication and seeing his psychiatrist, Dr. Solomon, he had begun polishing a journal he had kept on his prison experiences, hoping to get it published as a book. And one cold December evening, he traveled to White Plains, New York, and gave a speech to the Westchester County Bar Association. It was his first public speaking engagement since the night he had addressed the New York State Bar Association in Albany and gone back to his chambers and written to Joy, "You stupid lousy cunt. I'm going back to Texas now. You better hope I die soon because if I don't you'll wish you were dead." Now, in a room hung with festive Christmas decorations and crowded with young, mostly male, attorneys, he sat on a dais, just as he had on so many occasions, and, looking suntanned and fit, he cheerfully accepted the handshakes and congratulations of those who had come to hear him. Then he rose to speak.

He began solemnly. "If someone asked me what the most difficult thing in the world to do is," he said, "it would be to compose an introduction to Sol Wachtler." But a moment later he turned on his famous wit. "As my prison term began coming to an end," he joked, "people kept asking me what I was going to do in the future. And I realized I had only two career choices.

I could either teach"—here he paused for just the right number of milliseconds—"or I could become mayor of Washington, D.C." At this allusion to the political resurrection of Mayor Marion Barry, who after being imprisoned on a drug charge had just been reelected to his former office, the audience began to guffaw and clap—and Sol knew he had them in his hands. He had lost none of his timing, his humor, his ability to charm. Encouraged, he turned to the subject of his talk, "Changes in the Criminal Justice System," and, citing some of his own experiences and many arcane statistics, he made an impassioned argument for rehabilitation and education, rather than stiff prison terms, for first-time drug offenders. The audience applauded all his recommendations, and when he finished talking, they gave him a lengthy standing ovation.

In January he started teaching law part-time at Pace University in Westchester. He wasn't sure if he'd continue to teach in the future, make it a full-time pursuit. He still had five hundred hours of community service to perform, and he decided he'd best get that out of the way before making a definite career plan. But in the meantime, teaching was satisfactory enough. He loved lecturing to the students, influencing them, making them laugh. At times, when he was in front of a class, he could even forget all that had happened to him in the past few years. But frequently when he watched television and saw New York's newly elected Republican governor George Pataki holding press conferences and making speeches, he would feel a sharp pang of sorrow, and afterward he would keep thinking how it could have been him standing up there, parrying those questions, giving that talk, receiving those accolades. And he knew that he had thrown it all away.

SOURCE NOTES

To create this narrative, the author interviewed over a hundred people who were either central figures in the story or whose lives intersected with those of the central figures. In addition, the author consulted various legal documents, books, and articles. She was unable to speak with Joy Silverman, who declined repeated requests for an interview.

ABBREVIATIONS

Unless otherwise noted, the interviews were conducted by the author. Frequently cited persons and court documents have been identified by the following abbreviations:

JS	Joy Silverman
SW	Sol Wachtler
Chertoff, Sent. Memo. of U.S.	Michael Chertoff, U.S. Attorney, Sentencing Memorandum of the United States, in re *USA* v. *Sol Wachtler* (U.S. District Court, Trenton, N.J., 1993).
Letter, Simring, Sent. Memo. of U.S.	Letter of Steven S. Simring, M.D., to Michael Chertoff, July 13, 1993 (Exhibit A, Sentencing Memorandum of the United States).
Letter, Miller, Sent. Memo. of S.W.	Letter of Frank T. Miller, M.D., to Judge Anne Thompson, May 12, 1993 (Exhibit C, Defendant's Exhibits to Sentencing Memorandum of Sol Wachtler, prepared by Charles Stillman and Theodore V. Wells, Jr.).
Stillman, Sent. Memo. of SW	Charles Stillman and Theodore V. Wells, Jr., Sentencing Memorandum of Sol Wachtler.
Add., Frosch and Miller, Sent. Memo. of SW	Addendum to Evaluation of Sol Wachtler, prepared by William A. Frosch, M.D., and Frank T. Miller, M.D. (Sentencing Memorandum of Sol Wachtler).
S. Wachtler, Prob. Proc., Wolosoff	Examination of the Honorable Sol Wachtler in Probate Proceeding, Will of Alvin B. Wolosoff, Deceased (Surrogate's Court, State of New York, County of Nassau, 1985).

Prologue

pp. 1–2 SW's telephone call to JS: Appendix to Chertoff, Sent. Memo. of U.S.

pp. 2–3 Conversation between Chertoff and Ashrafi: Interview with Michael Chertoff, Apr. 12, 1993.

pp. 3–4 SW's call: Appendix to Chertoff, Sent. Memo. of U.S.

pp. 4–5 "Joy was shaking": Interview with William R. Fleming, Jr., Oct. 21, 1993.

pp. 5–6 SW's call: Appendix to Chertoff, Sent. Memo. of U.S.

pp. 5–6 " 'There's been another call' " to "arresting the chief judge of the Court of Appeals of the State of New York": Interview with Michael Chertoff, Apr. 12, 1993.

p. 6 "When he landed in Denver": Interview with William R. Fleming, Jr., Oct. 19, 1993.

p. 6 SW's letter: Appendix to Chertoff, Sent. Memo. of U.S.

pp. 7–8 Joan Wachtler's experiences on Nov. 7, 1992: Interview with Joan Wachtler, July 16, 1993.

Chapter 1

pp. 13–14 SW's boyhood: Interview with SW, July 16, 1993.

pp. 14–15 SW at Milford: *The Milford Yearbook,* June 1947, and interviews with former teachers David Rosenbaum and Jerry Pepper, Mar. 25, 1993 (interviews conducted by Jack Bourque); "nose bobbed": interviews with two of SW's classmates, Apr. 6 and 7, 1993 (interviews conducted by Jack Bourque).

p. 15 "Where to go instead?": Interview with SW, July 16, 1993.

p. 15 "who hailed from Saranac Lake": Interview with Dick Simons, Mar. 21, 1993.

p. 15 "gave birth to a baby girl": Where? According to the *Daily News,* in an article dated Nov. 15, 1992, "Silverman has said she was born Apr. 8, 1947, in Newark, N.J., and has identified her father as Ben Fererh. But no record of either fact could be located there." The same was true of Saranac Lake.

p. 15 "Jeanette was a charmer": Interview with a friend of Jeanette's, May 5, 1993.

p. 16 Leon Wolosoff: "Funds for Queens Homes," *New York Times,* Oct. 18, 1931; "Goodyear Village Is Sold," *New York Times,* July 29, 1944; and obituary of Leon Wolosoff, *New York Times,* June 8, 1949.

p. 16 Max Blumberg's career: Obituary of Max Blumberg, *New York Times,* Nov. 10, 1938.

p. 16 Joan's nickname: Interview with a camp mate, Dec. 23, 1992.

pp. 15–17 SW's first dates with Joan: Interviews with Sol and Joan Wachtler, July 16, 1993.

p. 17 Washington and Lee University: Washington and Lee Catalogue for 1951–1952, and *Peterson's Guide to Four-Year Colleges,* 1992.

pp. 17–19 SW's career at Washington and Lee: Interviews with four frat mates of SW's, Mar. 10 and 17, 1993, and clippings from *The Ring-tum Phi, Washington and Lee Semi-Weekly Newspaper,* 1947–1952.

pp. 18–19 The Wolosoff brothers: Interviews with Robert Berne, Feb. 8, 1993, and Lester Brooke, Feb. 16, 1993.

p. 19 Nassau County: Stephen Birmingham, *The Rest of Us,* Little, Brown, 1984. John Clements, *New York Facts: A Comprehensive Look at New York Today, County by County,* Clements Research II, Inc., 1989. Arturo Gonzalez, *Eugene H. Nickerson: Statesman of a New Society,* James H. Heineman, Inc., N.Y., 1964. Edward J. Smits, *Nassau: Suburbia, U.S.A.,* Friends of the Nassau County Museum, n.d.

p. 19 Leon Wolosoff's death: Interview with Lester Brooke, Feb. 16, 1993.

p. 19 real estate "that would one day be worth many millions of dollars": How many? The *New York Times* reported in Catherine S. Manegold's "Judge and Heiress: The Rise and Fall of a Private Affair," Nov. 15, 1992, that Joan Wachtler became "heir to a $90 million fortune." Joan Wachtler told the author the figure was vastly exaggerated, but did not provide an alternative figure.

p. 19 " 'Elsie, the delivery boy is here!' ": Interview with Lauren Wachtler, Apr. 9, 1993.

p. 20 " 'She was one of those perfect girls' ": Interview with one of SW's frat mates, Mar. 17, 1993.

pp. 20–21 SW's story about "J.C.W." and the dream: *The Ring-tum Phi,* Oct. 2, 1951.

p. 21 SW's story about the kiss: *The Ring-tum Phi,* Oct. 30, 1951.

p. 21 "he and Joan had not yet had sex together": Letter, Simring, Sent. Memo. of U.S.

pp. 21–22 The wedding and its antecedents: Interview with Joan and Sol Wachtler, July 16, 1993.

p. 23 "the scholarship drive and her husband": *Sarah Lawrence Yearbook,* 1952.

pp. 23–25 The early days of the marriage: Interview with Joan and Sol Wachtler, July 16, 1993.

CHAPTER 2

p. 26 Great Neck: *Great Neck Circle* magazine, 1950–1952. Dr. Jay Schulman, "The Jews of Great Neck: A Heritage Reaffirmed," in *Ethnicity in Suburbia: The Long Island Experience,* ed. by Salvatore J. La Gumina, copyright 1979. *This Is Great Neck,* published by the League of Women Voters of Great Neck, 1975. Helene Herzig, *A Family of Families: Temple Beth-el 1928–1978,* Temple Beth-el of Great Neck, 1978.

p. 26 Sylvia Wolosoff: Interview with Amy Osler, Jan. 31, 1993.

p. 27 Bibbs's dream house: Interviews with Lester Brooke, Feb. 16, 1993, and Dick Simons, Mar. 21, 1993.

p. 27 Parties at the Wolosoff mansion and breakup of the couples: Interviews with Gail Rothstein, Feb. 2, 1993, and Dick Simons, Mar. 21, 1993.

pp. 27–28 "didn't . . . contribute financially" and "had to help him out with money": Interview with Dick Simons, Mar. 21, 1993.

p. 28 Jeanette's marriage to Germont: Interview with Dick Simons, Mar. 21, 1993.

p. 28 "could barely meet the mortgage payments": Interview with Helen Cox, Sept. 4, 1993.

p. 28 "working on a contractual basis, she did public relations for the city of Newark": Interview with Emma Garcia, Dec. 17, 1993 (interview conducted by Jack Bourque).

pp. 28–29 "It was at one of her functions that Bibbs had met her" to " 'I'm all she's got' ": Interview with Dick Simons, Mar. 21, 1993.

pp. 29–30 "They'd done it largely at Bibbs's urging": Interview with Joan and Sol Wachtler, July 16, 1993.

p. 30 "One of his favorite sayings was": Interview with Dick Simons, Mar. 21, 1993.

p. 30 FHA investigation of Wolosoff brothers: "Frauds in Selling Home Repair Jobs Under F.H.A. Cited," *New York Times,* Aug. 27, 1954.

p. 30 " 'They wanted houses' ": Interview with William Koeppel, Feb. 24, 1993.

pp. 30–32 "Once, Sol even negotiated a land deal for him": Interview with SW July 16, 1993.

p. 32 "he'd begun to try his hand at politics": Interview with Joseph P. Carlino, Mar. 10, 1993.

pp. 32–33 " 'Jeanette! Good God, what happened to you?' ": Interview with a friend of Jeanette's, May 5, 1993.

pp. 33–35 Bibbs and Jeanette: Interviews with Dick Simons, Mar. 21, 1993, Alexander Simons, Mar. 23, 1993, and a friend of Jeanette's, May 5, 1993.

p. 34 Bibbs "spent over a million and a half dollars on them": S. Wachtler, Prob. Proc., Wolosoff.

p. 34 Van Wolosoff: Interview with Dick Simons, Mar. 21, 1993.

pp. 34–36 " 'You must be the new Mrs. Wolosoff's daughter' " to "trying to be just like her mother": Interview with Dick Simons, Mar. 21, 1993.

pp. 36–37 SW as a father: Interview with Lauren Wachtler, Apr. 9, 1993.

pp. 37–38 SW and the North Hempstead Town Council seat fight: Interviews with Joseph P. Carlino, Mar. 10, 1993, and Sol Wachtler, July 16, 1993.

pp. 38–39 "he needed some land rezoned": Interview with Dick Simons, Mar. 21, 1993.

pp. 38–39 "the boy, Bruce, was rumored to be part of a fast crowd": Interview with Alison Wachtler, May 15, 1993.

p. 39 " 'had this *reputation*' ": Interview with Joan Wachtler, July 16, 1993.

pp. 39–40 Van and Jeanette: Interview with Dick Simons, Mar. 21, 1993.

p. 40 Bibbs's molestation of Joy: Interview with Phil Friedman, Aug. 19, 1993.

p. 40 "he and Joy had become lovers": Interview with Dick Simons, Mar. 21, 1993.

pp. 40–41 The relationship between Dick and Jeanette: Interview with Dick Simons, Mar. 21, 1993.

pp. 41–42 The meeting between Clint Martin and David Holman: Interview with a Long Island politician, Apr. 13, 1993.

pp. 42–43 Joy's relationship with Van: Interviews with Dick Simons, Mar. 21, 1993, and Sol Wachtler, July 16, 1993.

p. 43 Jeanette's feelings about Van and Jimmy: Interview with Dick Simons, Mar. 21, 1993.

p. 43 Bruce's adoption: Interview with Richard L. Gold, June 28, 1993.

p. 43 SW's victory: Interview with Joseph P. Carlino, Mar. 10, 1993.

CHAPTER 3

pp. 44–45 " 'Why didn't Bibbs adopt *you?* ' " to "seduction was second nature to her": Interview with Dick Simons, Mar. 21, 1993.

pp. 45–46 SW decides to run against Nickerson: "G.O.P. in Nassau Picks Candidate," *New York Times,* Feb. 24, 1967, "G.O.P. Nominates Its Nassau Slate," *New York Times,* Mar. 2, 1967, and interviews with Joseph P. Carlino, Mar. 10, 1993, and another Long Island politician, Apr. 13, 1993.

pp. 46–47 SW at the convention, and Don Kellerman's advice to him and Joan: *CBS Reports: Campaign American Style,* CBS television network, 1968.

p. 47 Joan's activities during the campaign: Interview with Joan Wachtler, July 16, 1993.

p. 47 "she'd made no impression on him": Interview with SW, July 16, 1993. SW reported to the author that although he didn't recall the first time he met Joy, she well recalled the first time she met him, and even remembered what he was wearing—a suede jacket.

p. 48 "she was impressed with *him*": Interview with Dick Simons, Mar. 21, 1993.

p. 48 " 'Are you Wachtler?' " Interview with Joan Wachtler, July 16, 1993.

p. 48 " 'It's a great embarrassment to have to ask friends for money' ": *CBS Reports: Campaign American Style,* op. cit.

p. 48 SW adept at raising money: "G.O.P. Fund Dinner Held for Nassau Candidate," *New York Times,* May 18, 1967.

p. 48 " 'He was the Great White Jewish Hope' ": Interview with Arlene Stang, Feb. 18, 1993.

pp. 48–49 "Sol was using dirty tricks": "Nickerson Says Rival Uses Fake Campaign Photo," *New York Times,* Sept. 29, 1967.

p. 49 " 'a slick, scurrilous campaign' ": "Lefkowitz Asks Poll Fraud Law," *New York Times,* Sept. 28, 1967.

p. 49 "One autumn day, he crisscrossed Nassau County with Sol": "Governor Stumps with Wachtler," *New York Times,* Oct. 11, 1967.

p. 49 "he came to a party at Sol's house": Interview with Alison Wachtler, May 15, 1993.

p. 49 "accused one of Sol's chief aides": "Nassau Democrats Accuse Republican of Attempt to Spy," *New York Times,* Oct. 27, 1967.

pp. 49–50 Events on election night: *CBS Reports: Campaign American Style,* op. cit.

p. 50–51 "She was a receptionist" to "marrying Dick": Interview with Dick Simons, Mar. 21, 1993.

p. 51 " 'Take on Wolf' ": Interview with Joseph P. Carlino, Mar. 10, 1993.

pp. 51–52 " 'After three years, you'll be bored or alcoholic' ": Interview with SW, July 16, 1993.

p. 52 " 'I'm not going to be deputy anything' ": Interview with Long Island politician, Apr. 13, 1993.

pp. 52–53 SW and the Nassau Bar Association: "Wachtler to Seek Nassau Judgeship," *New York Times,* Dec. 2, 1967; "Wachtler Facing a Judgeship Snag," *New York Times,* Dec. 31, 1967; "Wachtler Fails in Nassau Appeal," *New York Times,* Jan. 7, 1968.

p. 53 "Up in Albany, Rockefeller was enraged": Interview with Long Island politician, Apr. 13, 1993.

p. 53 "the question of Sol's endorsement was sent to the bar association's board of directors": Actually, SW had tried to get the board to bypass the judiciary committee earlier, but the board members at first refused. It was only on SW's second try that they overruled their committee. Interview with Long Island politician, Apr. 13, 1993.

p. 53–54 " 'I'm not Joy's father' " and engagement presents: Interview with Dick Simons, Mar. 21, 1993.

pp. 54–55 The engagement party: Interview with Dick Simons, Mar. 21, 1993. Simons thought the incident in which Jeanette teased him about SW's attraction to Joy occurred at his wedding party, but SW told the author he did not attend the wedding, only the engagement party.

p. 54 " 'No one had the right to be that tall' ": Interview with Dottie Bernstein, Feb. 12, 1993.

p. 54 "he would date his first encounter with her to this festive evening": S. Wachtler, Prob. Proc., Wolosoff.

p. 55 The Florida land: Interview with Dick Simons, Mar. 21, 1993.

pp. 55 "he hadn't given them legal title" to " 'you go ahead and do it' ": Court documents filed in the case of *James K. Wolosoff* v. *Alvin B. Wolosoff et al.*, dated Aug. 20, 1975, and Apr. 21, 1976.

pp. 55–56 Joy and Dick Simons's honeymoon: Interview with Dick Simons, Mar. 21, 1993.

pp. 56–57 Madame Germont: Interview with Dick Simons, Mar. 21, 1993.

p. 57 " 'I used to send him a hundred dollars here, fifty dollars there' ": Interview with Dick Simons, Mar. 21, 1993.

pp. 57–58 "The poor kid, he would tell himself" to "she never spoke to her father again": Interview with Dick Simons, Mar. 21, 1993.

CHAPTER 4

pp. 59–60 The stenographer: Interview with court stenographer Arnold Cohen, Mar. 15, 1993.

p. 59 SW's career as a trial judge in Mineola: Interview with Judge Joseph Bellacosa, May 18, 1993.

pp. 60–63 "asked Bibbs to set up Dick" to "one of the most fashionable apartment buildings in Palm Beach": Interview with Dick Simons, Mar. 21, 1993.

p. 63 "The kids had always come to him, not Joan": Interviews with Lauren Wachtler, Apr. 9, 1993, and Joan and Sol Wachtler, July 16, 1993.

pp. 63–64 Margiotta: "Nassau Republicans March to Beat of Powerful Drumming by Margiotta," *New York Times,* Dec. 8, 1972.

p. 64 "The party needed help": Interviews with Victor Kovner, Feb. 1, 1993, and Judge Milton Mollen, Feb. 19, 1993. "Feud of Esposito and Troy Annuls Judgeship Pact," *New York Times,* Mar. 3, 1972.

p. 64 "Generally, court of appeals seats weren't contested": Today in New York State, court of appeals judges are appointed by the governor. SW's campaign was an important factor in the change.

p. 64 SW would have four hundred thousand dollars to spend on television ads: "Nassau Republicans March to Beat of Powerful Drumming by Margiotta," *New York Times,* Dec. 8, 1972.

pp. 64–65 Palm Beach: Charlotte Curtis, *The Rich and Other Atrocities,* Harper & Row, 1976; Murray Weiss and Bill Hoffman, *Palm Beach Babylon,* Birch Lane Press, 1992.

p. 65 "as one writer put it": Tom Buckley, "Palm Beach Is . . . ," *The New York Times Magazine,* Mar. 21, 1971.

p. 65 " 'found out finally what was expected of her' ": Ibid.

p. 66 JS tears up a gown: Interview with an old family friend, Feb. 12, 1993.

pp. 66–68 "But gradually, after Joy met and became friendly with several young women" to "Once, a Steuben-glass vase": Interview with Dick Simons, Mar. 21, 1993.

p. 68 "dialed Gucci in Milan": Interview with Alexander Simons, Mar. 23, 1993.

p. 68 SW "needed to do something to focus attention on himself": Interview with Bob Kaufman, Feb. 24, 1993.

p. 69 "a different direction for his commercials": Interview with Sheila Kelley, May 6, 1993.

p. 69 "When the commercial was aired": "Guides Set Forth on Judicial Race," *New York Times,* Apr. 15, 1972.

p. 69 "he began to have second thoughts": "Wachtler Drops a TV Commercial," *New York Times,* Oct. 30, 1972.

pp. 69–70 " 'Sol has to sit there in that judgeship' ": "Nassau Republicans March to Beat of Powerful Drumming by Margiotta," *New York Times,* Dec. 8, 1972.

pp. 70–72 " 'We should never have left St. Pete' " to "leaving all their financial obligations in his lap": Interview with Dick Simons, Mar. 21, 1993.

p. 72 " 'My childhood growing up' " and " 'My life is like a soap opera' ": Brian Kates, "Joy's Search for Happiness," *Daily News,* Nov. 15, 1992.

pp. 72–73 "Joy was on Bibbs's side in the disputes" to " 'May the man who's right win' ": Interview with Dick Simons, Mar. 21, 1993.

p. 73 SW "cast an enormous shadow": Interview with Alison Wachtler, May 15, 1993.

pp. 73–74 Joan gives up political work, decides to study social work: Interview with Joan Wachtler, July 16, 1993.

p. 74 "the abortion required an operation" to "he was busy with his litigation with Bibbs": Interview with Dick Simons, Mar. 21, 1993.

p. 74–75 David Paul: "More Crimes of the '80s," *Newsweek*, Dec. 6, 1993. Myra MacPherson, "David Paul and his CenTrust S&L," *Washington Post*, Mar. 19, 1990. Peter Becker, "David Paul Had a Great Fall," *M, Inc.*, Mar. 1991. Interview with Larry Weisman, May 23, 1993. Note: Paul was convicted in late 1993 of more than sixty counts of fraud.

pp. 75–76 Paul's deposition: Interview with Dick Simons, Mar. 21, 1993.

p. 76 JS marries David Paul in a Las Vegas wedding parlor: "Joy's Search for Happiness," Kates, *Daily News*, Nov. 15, 1992. The description of the parlor is drawn from "Marrying Absurd," in Joan Didion's *Slouching Towards Bethlehem*, Simon & Schuster, Touchstone ed., 1979.

pp. 76–77 JS's call to Simons from Las Vegas: Interview with Dick Simons, Mar. 21, 1993.

CHAPTER 5

p. 78 "Whatever passion had once existed between them had begun to evaporate": Letter, Simring, Sent. Memo. of U.S.

p. 78 "sex was apparently not a high priority" to "passion for worldly success": Interview with a longtime friend of SW's, Mar. 29, 1993.

p. 79 SW's most important early decisions on court of appeals, and SW's behavior toward friends and lawyers: Interview with Mike Traynor, June 12, 1993.

pp. 79–81 "He especially liked tricking Jacob Fuchsberg" to "never gave adultery a thought": Interview with a member of SW's staff, June 8, 1993.

p. 81 " 'If I'd lived with him two days, I'd never have married him' ": Interview with an intimate of JS's, Oct. 28, 1993.

p. 81 "within two months of the wedding ceremony, they got an annulment in the Dominican Republic": *Daily News,* Nov. 15, 1992, and interview with Helen Cox, Sept. 4, 1993.

p. 81 "Six months later, Joy began to be seen with a friend of Paul's": *Daily News,* Nov. 15, 1992.

p. 82 Jeffrey Silverman's early career: Ibid.

p. 82 "haggle over the terms of a divorce": Ibid.

p. 82 Joan Wachtler goes back to school: Letter from Joan Wachtler to Judge Anne Thompson, n.d., and interview with Joan Wachtler, July 16, 1993.

p. 82 Joan's internship: "Joan Wachtler to Head Women for Purcell," *Great Neck News,* 1981.

pp. 82–83 Dick Simons wins lawsuit: Interviews with Dick Simons, Mar. 21 and June 3, 1993.

pp. 83–84 James Wolosoff sues Bibbs: Court documents filed in the case of *James K. Wolosoff* v. *Alvin B. Wolosoff, et al.,* dated Aug. 20, 1975, and Apr. 12 and 21, 1976.

pp. 84–85 Allen H. Weiss tries to settle the suit: Interviews with Allen H. Weiss, Feb. 9 and Mar. 4, 1993.

p. 85 Bibbs "rued the day that Jimmy had ever been conceived": Probate Proceeding, Will of Alvin B. Wolosoff, Nov. 8, 1985.

p. 85 Bibbs cuts Jimmy out of his will: Interviews with Allen H. Weiss, Feb. 9 and Mar. 4, 1993.

p. 86 SW considers running for governor in 1978 to "He had so many IOUs out around the state": "Judicious Reluctance," *New York Times,* Apr. 10, 1977.

pp. 86–87 "He has to be fed constantly with applause and admiration": Interview with a member of SW's staff, June 8, 1993.

p. 87 " 'the computer baby' ": Interview with an intimate of JS's, Oct. 28, 1993.

pp. 87–88 "he and Joy talked for a while" to "let her know, in no uncertain terms, that she wasn't his type": Interview with an acquaintance of JS's, Aug. 1, 1993.

p. 88 " 'There's always Macbeth' ": "Judge Tries Anew to Spell Out Initial Protest," *New York Times,* Mar. 31, 1979.

p. 88 " 'They know you, and they *still* want you' ": Interview with a longtime friend of SW's, Mar. 29, 1993.

pp. 88–89 Bontscha Schvaig: Interview with Mike Traynor, June 12, 1993.

p. 89 "threaten to report him to the IRS": Interview with SW, July 16, 1993.

p. 89 " 'too bad we can't kill Bibbs' ": Interview with a friend of JS's, July 29, 1993.

p. 89 "Joy put a memorial announcement in the *Times:"* Deaths column, *New York Times,* Oct. 13, 1980.

p. 89 "every year afterward on the anniversary of her death": Interview with Gail Rothstein, Feb. 3, 1993.

p. 90 "played poker together" to "good candidate": Mario Cuomo, *The Diaries of Mario M. Cuomo,* Random House, 1984, pp. 65–66.

pp. 90–91 SW's judicial opinions: Interview with Mike Traynor, June 12, 1993.

p. 91 " 'It grows in slums' ": Speech given by SW before the Albany Bar Association in Dec. 1980.

p. 91 " 'The greatest responsibility for our national welfare' ": Speech given by SW before the Judicial Section of the New York State Bar Association, Jan. 24, 1981.

p. 91 "They had stopped altogether": Letter, Simring, Sent. Memo. of U.S.

p. 91 " 'made a play for me' ": Interview with SW, July 16, 1993.

p. 92 "Albany waitress named Dorothy": Interview with an intimate of JS's, Oct. 28, 1993.

pp. 92–93 Fuchsberg and the Century Club: Interview with a member of SW's staff, June 8, 1993.

p. 93 SW didn't want the stress and strain of running: Interview with SW, July 16, 1993.

p. 93 "The old Nassau power broker had been indicted": "Margiotta and Ex-Judge Indicted in Alleged L.I. Insurance Fraud," *New York Times,* Nov. 25, 1980. Margiotta was eventually convicted and served one year of a two-year jail term.

p. 93 " 'Why does my high-minded friend' ": Interview with a longtime friend of SW's, Mar. 29, 1993.

p. 93 "no intention of running": "Four Judges Take the Stand as Witnesses for Margiotta," *New York Times,* Apr. 17, 1981.

pp. 93–94 "the gossip in Albany": Interview with a New York politician, Feb. 19, 1993.

p. 94 Honey Wolosoff: Interview with Lauren Wachtler, Apr. 9, 1993.

CHAPTER 6

p. 95 Bibbs's will: The Last Will and Testament of Alvin B. Wolosoff, July 14, 1982.

p. 95 " 'Did he love my mother?' " Interview with Helen Cox, Sept. 4, 1993.

p. 95 Bibbs lent Jeffrey money for stocks: Interview with SW, July 16, 1993.

p. 96 Ply-Gem becomes a major company: "Strong Finish in '85," *Barron's Investment News & Views,* Sept. 9, 1985. "A Do-It-Yourself Supplier That's Built a Following," *Business Week,* July 11, 1988. "Improving Homes, Improving Minds," *Management Review,* Dec. 1988.

p. 96 "Sol, inviting Van to his chambers" to " 'all I want' ": S. Wachtler, Prob. Proc., Wolosoff.

p. 96 " ' If you give her a million dollars today' ": Interview with SW, July 16, 1993.

pp. 96–97 Bibbs's death: Interview with Dick Simons, Mar. 22, 1993.

p. 97 Bibbs's funeral and Sol's subsequent conversation with Joy: Interview with SW, July 16, 1993.

p. 97 "small talk . . . about her astrologist": Interview with Alison Wachtler, May 15, 1993.

pp. 97–98 Serious consideration given to only SW and Milton Mollen (recently the head of the Mollen Commission, investigating police corruption in NYC): "The Making of a Chief Judge," *New York Times,* Jan. 6, 1985, and interview with a former adviser to Governor Cuomo, Feb. 25, 1993.

p. 98 "choosing Sol would make Cuomo look good": Interview cited in preceding note.

p. 98 Governor Cuomo's explanation of why he selected SW as chief judge: Radio interview on the show "Capitol Connection," Jan. 2, 1985.

pp. 98–99 Joy's activities: Interviews with Phil Friedman, Aug. 19, 1993, and a Nightingale-Bamford mother, Aug. 20, 1993. "Envoys Without Experience," *Washington Post,* July 18, 1989.

p. 99 " 'There are a lot of things I want that I don't have' ": Interview with Kathryn O. Greenberg, Aug. 2, 1993.

pp. 99–100 Joy's reluctance to have Honey be cotrustee of her trust: Interview with SW, July 16, 1993.

p. 100 " 'I think Jeffrey's fooling around' ": Interview with Kathryn O. Greenburg, Aug. 2, 1993.

p. 101 "dreamed up a way to make Joy even happier": Interview with SW, July 16, 1993.

p. 101 Joy asks for assistance and advice: Interview with SW, July 16, 1993.

p. 101 "her darling little bichon frise": Interview with SW, July 16, 1993. Interestingly, at one point during the interview, when SW mentioned the bichon frise, Joan Wachtler said wryly, "We always had dogs. But we had a beagle and a St. Bernard."

pp. 101–02 SW makes suggestions to Joy about her future: Interview with SW, July 16, 1993.

pp. 102–03 "Weiss thought they had a chance" to "any litigation in the state could potentially end up there": Interviews with Allen H. Weiss, Feb. 9 and Mar. 4, 1993.

p. 103 SW volunteered that he'd not only checked the law but asked his colleagues on the court of appeals whether they thought he ought to disqualify himself: *Newsday,* which investigated this assertion after SW's arrest, reported that "five of six colleagues" said that "he had never mentioned it to them." Cited by Eric Pooley in "Crazy for You," *New York Magazine,* Dec. 14, 1992.

p. 103–04 "Wachtler was using the politically powerful firm Shea and Gould" to "they would be based on monomania": Interviews with Allen H. Weiss, Feb. 9 and Mar. 4, 1993. S. Wachtler, Prob. Proc., Wolosoff.

pp. 104–05 " 'Evan! Hey, Evan!' " to "Made him stop running": Interview with Dick Simons, Mar. 21, 1993.

p. 105 "received a call from Judge Radigan" to "not as completely as he had planned": Interviews with Allen H. Weiss, Feb. 9 and Mar. 4, 1993.

pp. 105–06 Joy and Sol discuss her getting a job with the mayor: Interview with SW, July 16, 1993.

p. 106 SW's house in Albany: Interview with Alison Wachtler, May 15, 1993. Letter from Joan Wachtler to Judge Anne Thompson, n.d.

p. 106 "Gardening became his passion": Interview with Phil Friedman, Aug. 19, 1993.

pp. 106–07 Joy sends gift basket to SW: Interview with Joan Wachtler, July 16, 1993.

CHAPTER 7

pp. 111–13 SW speaks at a luncheon held by the Long Island Association to "He gave her his . . . credit card number": Interview with SW, July 16, 1993.

p. 113 "It's as if . . . Joy's a little girl playing dress-up": Interview with the wife of a close friend of George Bush, Mar. 16, 1993.

p. 113 JS visits the court of appeals: Interview with SW, July 16, 1993.

pp. 113–14 " 'I never—never with one exception, [that] woman in upstate New York' ": Interview with SW, July 16, 1993. It is possible that the woman in question was a waitress in Albany named Dorothy. The author was told during an interview with a person close to JS that while Jeanette was still alive, SW had had some sort of sexual or romantic relationship with an Albany waitress named Dorothy and that Elsie Wolosoff had passed the news along to Jeanette, who had gossiped about it with JS.

pp. 114–18 " 'I thought we were going to have dinner alone' " to "he let Joy and Paola check out of the Susse Chalet and move into his farmhouse": Interview with SW, July 16, 1993. Note that Dr. Simring, the psychiatrist who examined SW for the prosecution, dates the first kiss to Oct. 4, 1987, whereas the author dates it to early in 1987. This is because SW remembered firmly during the author's interview with him that the first time he and JS touched was at his Long Island Association appearance during the blizzard, which occurred on Jan. 22, 1987, and said that Joy's trip to Albany came "shortly afterward," and their first night together "about two weeks later." The author believes her date is more accurate than Dr. Simring's because at the time SW was interviewed by Simring, he was, according to his own psychiatrist, confused about time and became more accurate as the months passed.

p. 118 "Joy introduced Sol to a whole new world of sexuality ... that made intercourse seem dull and pedestrian": Letter, Simring, Sent. Memo. of U.S.

p. 118 "A state commission on judicial conduct had recommended to Sol that the judge ... be removed from the bench" to "Gelfand announced that he would appeal": "Bronx Judge Vows He'll Fight Panel's Verdict for Removal," *Newsday*, Mar. 27, 1987. "State Court Suspends Gelfand—With Pay," *Newsday*, Apr. 28, 1987.

pp. 118–20 Gelfand's meeting with SW: Interviews with Judge Bertram Gelfand, Sept. 22 and Nov. 14, 1993.

p. 120 "They saw each other once every other week" to "one weekend a month together": Cindy Adams, "Dad Gets the Rap for the Way Joy 'Destroys' Men," *New York Post*, Sept. 10, 1993.

p. 120 Joan's resentment: Letter of Joan Wachtler to Judge Anne Thompson, n.d.

pp. 120–21 "She's got *some* temper" to " 'There's a lot of history there' ": Interview with a member of SW's staff, June 8, 1993.

p. 121 " 'Go over to the Bush for President headquarters' " to " 'Bush supporter' ": Interview with SW, July 16, 1993.

pp. 121–22 JS's activities at campaign headquarters: Pooley, "Crazy for You," *New York Magazine,* Dec. 14, 1992.

p. 121 " 'She's a snake' ": A Bush campaign staffer quoted in "Joy's Search for Happiness," *Daily News,* Nov. 15, 1992.

pp. 121–22 " 'She's pushy ... eye toward an appointment' ": Interview with the wife of one of Bush's financial advisers, Mar. 8, 1993.

p. 122 " 'She sucked him up for one thousand dollars' ": Julie Wadler, as quoted in Pooley, "Crazy for You," *New York Magazine,* Dec. 14, 1992.

p. 122 " 'It was a pleasure to meet you at lunch' " to " 'It's always a delight to talk to someone who's so well informed' ": These are prototypical letters. The quotations are based on those in actual letters shown to the author by SW on July 16, 1993.

p. 122 " 'I read your interesting and inspiring closing statement' ": From a letter written to Angier Biddle Duke by SW and signed by JS. Interview with SW, July 16, 1993.

pp. 122–23 The "You done good" letter: Interview with SW, July 16, 1993.

p. 123 JS's meeting with Lawrence Bathgate: Interviews with Lawrence Bathgate, Mar. 2 and 3, 1993.

p. 123 " 'How much do you love me?' ": Interview with SW, July 16, 1993.

p. 124 "training in such fields isn't necessary. Nor is a license": Note that the state of New York has held numerous hearings in an attempt to establish legislative licensing procedures for psychotherapists, but the effort has not proved successful.

p. 124 JS leaned on Eleanor Sloan: Interview with Phil Friedman, Aug. 19, 1993.

pp. 124–25 SW goes to see Sloan: Interview with SW, July 16, 1993.

p. 125 "She had told him the sexual predilections of all her husbands": Interview with SW, July 16, 1993.

pp. 125–26 "She told him, too, about her relationship with her stepbrother" to "getting close to five million dollars for it": Interview with SW, July 16, 1993.

p. 126 The LIU dinner: Interview with Joan Wachtler, July 16, 1993.

pp. 126–27 SW addresses a group of businessmen in Albany: " 'The Wachtler-Cuomo Show' Knocks 'Em Dead in Albany," *New York Law Journal,* Mar. 28, 1988.

p. 127 JS holds fund-raiser in Southampton: Interview with one of the guests, Mar. 8, 1993.

pp. 127–28 " 'It was intimate, that was the wonderful part of it' " and " 'It was the single most successful party' ": "In New Orleans, the Grand Old Parties," *Washington Post,* Aug. 15, 1988.

p. 128 JS makes speech at the Harmonie Club: Interview with William Koeppel, Feb. 24, 1993.

pp. 128–29 SW suggests to JS that she try for an ambassadorship: Interview with SW, July 16, 1993.

p. 129 "afraid that being identified as pro-choice would harm her chances ... both financially and ideologically": Interviews with Tania Melich, Feb. 18 and Dec. 10, 1993.

pp. 129–30 JS promotes SW for Supreme Court: Interview with William Koeppel, Feb. 24, 1993.

p. 130 SW writes sample questions: Interview with SW, July 16, 1993.

pp. 130–31 Jeffrey Silverman visits Barbados: "Envoys Without Experience: Bush Favors GOP Donors as Ambassadors," *Washington Post,* July 18, 1989.

pp. 131 JS in Albany: Interview with a member of SW's staff, June 8, 1993.

pp. 132–33 "Was Joy in love with him?" to "the pinnacle of their love": Interview with SW, July 16, 1993.

CHAPTER 8

p. 134 " 'I *love* George Bush' ": Interview with a Nightingale-Bamford mother, Aug. 20, 1993.

p. 134 "a 'major exhibit . . . wealth given freely to the GOP' ": "Envoys Without Experience: Bush Favors GOP Donors as Ambassadors," *Washington Post,* July 18, 1989.

pp. 134–35 " 'I'm caught in a web in Washington' " to "deeply touched by her predicament": Interview with Phil Friedman, Aug. 19, 1993.

pp. 136–37 "I'm lying here in a pool of blood" to "guilt and self-loathing": Interview with SW, July 16, 1993.

p. 137 "blamed Sol for her defeat": Interview with a friend of JS's, July 29, 1993.

p. 137 " 'It's absolutely untrue' ": Interview with Jeffrey Silverman, Mar. 24, 1994.

p. 138 "She said to Sheresky": Interview with Norman Sheresky, Mar. 26, 1993.

p. 138 "Joy began to urge Sol to marry her": Interview with SW, July 16, 1993.

p. 138 Bush's Jan. 2, 1990 letter to JS: Interview with SW, July 16, 1993.

pp. 138–39 " 'The courts are not for raising revenue' ": "Judge Assails Cuomo," *Newsday,* Feb. 22, 1990.

p. 139 " 'I differ with the chief judge on fees' " to " 'can't do it this year' ": Gary Spencer, "Cuomo, Wachtler See Improved Dialogue," *New York Law Journal,* Mar. 14, 1990.

p. 139 "The scuttlebutt in Albany": Interview with Phil Friedman, Aug. 26, 1993.

p. 139 " 'There are differences' ": Gary Spencer, "Cuomo, Wachtler See Improved Dialogue," *New York Law Journal,* Mar. 14, 1990.

p. 139 Joy "expected gems" to "gone to Morty to make his purchases": Interview with SW, July 16, 1993.

p. 140 Dinner in Greenwich Village: Interview with Phil Friedman, Aug. 19, 1993.

p. 140 Dinner at Elaine's: Interview with Norman Sheresky, Mar. 26, 1993.

pp. 140–41 "There was someone else who knew" to "didn't

know what to believe'': Interview with Lauren Wachtler, Apr. 9, 1993.

pp. 141–42 " 'The cases on Tuesday were pretty good' ": SW, "Yes, Jessica, There Are 'Good' and 'Bad' Lawyers," *New York Law Journal,* May 1, 1990.

p. 142 "She was an easy child to be fond of" to "tranquil as a summer's day": Interview with Phil Friedman, Aug. 19, 1993.

p. 142 "Sol sometimes daydreamed" to "wavered about their summer plans": Interview with SW, July 16, 1993.

p. 142 "fears of ending up husbandless": Interview with a friend of JS's, July 29, 1993.

p. 142 "promised her that he would leave Joan on Labor Day weekend": Chertoff, Sent. Memo. of U.S.

pp. 142–44 "Joan Wachtler went to the wedding" to " 'Not nearly as pretty as she used to be' ": Interview with Joan Wachtler, July 16, 1993.

pp. 144–45 SW's supposed brain tumor: Information about the brain tumor is drawn from the Sentencing Memorandum prepared by Michael Chertoff in *USA* v. *Sol Wachtler,* and from interview with SW, July 16, 1993. Note that SW eventually learned that the cause of his symptoms was a herniated disk.

p. 145 Elizabeth Racine: Interview with SW, July 16, 1993.

pp. 145–46 "Sol's reports to Joy about his brain tumor" to "medical problems alone anymore": Chertoff, Sent. Memo. of U.S.

p. 146 "the sex between them was still intense": Letter, Simring, Sent. Memo. of U.S.

p. 146 " 'I cannot escape the feeling ... any given time' ": Letter written by SW to a Yale student, quoted in Manegold, "Judge and Heiress: The Rise and Fall of a Private Affair," *New York Times,* Nov. 15, 1992.

pp. 146–47 "Tenuate could produce" to " 'indistinguishable from schizophrenia' ": *Physicians' Desk Reference,* 47th edition, Medical Economics Data, 1993.

p. 147 " 'You gotta find me a woman' " to " 'I'll look around' ": Interview with Lawrence Bathgate, Mar. 3, 1993.

p. 147 "He seemed present but not present" to " 'He isn't *with* the rest of us' ' ": Interview with Republican party contributor, July 11, 1993.

p. 148 " 'It's not so much fun to travel with him' " to " 'killing myself at work' ": Interview with John Maguire, Mar. 30, 1993.

p. 148 JS at White House dinner: Interview with the theatrical agent who accompanied her, July 6, 1993.

p. 149 "girlfriend of . . . George Bush" to " 'I'm not his social secretary' ": Interview with William Koeppel, Feb. 24, 1993.

pp. 149–50 " 'You've got to find me a man' " to "put her number aside": Interview with Lawrence Bathgate, Mar. 3, 1993.

p. 150 " 'I can't leave your mother' " to " 'make your own decision' ": Interview with Lauren Wachtler, Apr. 9, 1993.

p. 151 " 'I had the feeling you were going to dump me' ": Letter, Simring, Sent. Memo. of U.S.

p. 151 "had the idea that Joy hated him" to " 'love anyone the way I love you' ": Interview with SW, July 16, 1993. Letter, Simring, Sent. Memo. of U.S.

p. 151 "presumably a few days after Joy's night in Philadelphia with Sol": The author was unable to establish the exact date. It could have been before or after the night in Philadelphia.

p. 151 " 'You're probably already busy' " to " 'they were in love' ": Interview with Lawrence Bathgate, Mar. 3, 1993.

p. 152 " 'Tough duty!' " to "made the President guffaw": Interview with Lawrence Bathgate, Mar. 3, 1993.

p. 152 "They met for dinner" to "his loss seemed immeasurable": Interview with SW, July 16, 1993. Letter, Simring, Sent. Memo of U.S.

p. 153 "the last time he'd tried to reach him, Cuomo had directed": "Gov, Chief Judge Face Off," *Daily News,* Sept. 26, 1991.

p. 153 "That afternoon, he filed his lawsuit": Note that the lawsuit was dropped in January 1992 when Governor Cuomo promised an extra $19 million for the state's courts in the next year. Wachtler rehired the people who'd been fired and reopened the closed courts. "Top Judge Ends Feud with Gov.," *Newsday,* Jan. 17, 1992.

p. 153 "he seemed manic": This was the author's reaction to his televised appearances at the time of the suit.

pp. 153–54 " 'He could not stay seated' " to " 'pound law books' ": Robin Pogrebin, "Cuomo Against Wachtler: A Feud Among Friends," *New York Observer,* Oct. 21, 1991. Interestingly, Pogrebin also observed that "When discussing the current dispute, Judge Wachtler sounds somewhat like a spurned lover, forced to wait by the telephone."

p. 154 "Joan was different" to "cuddle the baby": Interview with Randa Pittel, Mar. 8, 1993.

pp. 155–56 " 'Where are you?' " to "She didn't want to see him again": Interview with SW, July 16, 1993, and Chertoff, Sent. Memo. of U.S.

p. 156 " 'David's handsomer than you' " to " 'earns five times as much money as you' ": Interview with SW, July 16, 1993.

p. 156 SW stopped eating: Letter of Joan Wachtler to Judge Anne Thompson, n.d.

CHAPTER 9

p. 159 " 'Something is terribly wrong [with Sol]' " to " 'drug-related?' ": Joan Wachtler's diary, as quoted in Stillman, Sent. Memo. of SW.

p. 159 "He'd be stigmatized, like poor Tom Eagleton": Interview with SW, July 16, 1993. In 1972, Senator Thomas Eagleton was dropped as the Democrats' vice presidential candidate after word leaked out that he'd been treated for manic-depressive illness.

p. 160 " 'He's done bad, bad things' " to "mortgage had recently been paid off": Chertoff, Sent. Memo. of U.S. and interview with SW, July 16, 1993.

p. 161 " 'Sol's harassing me' " to " 'She's crazy' ": Interview with Norman Sheresky, Mar. 26, 1993.

pp. 162–63 "The first person to whom he pretended" to "Elaine wouldn't do it": Chertoff, Sent. Memo. of U.S.

pp. 163–64 Joan calls Dr. Lanman: Letter, Miller, Sent. Memo. of SW.

pp. 164–65 " 'Where did Jessica spend her Thanksgiving?' " to " 'I wonder how long *that* will last' ": Interview with SW, July 16, 1993.

p. 165 " 'five years ago a friend' ": Letter of SW dated Dec. 18, 1991. Appendix to Chertoff, Sent. Memo. of U.S.

p. 166 SW gives tribute to Charles Breitel: Videotape of opening session of the court of appeals, Jan. 7, 1992.

pp. 166–67 SW's cards and calls: Chertoff, Sent. Memo. of U.S. and Appendix.

pp. 167–68 SW's trip to Florida: Letter, Miller, Sent. Memo. of SW.

pp. 168–70 SW's cards: Chertoff, Sent. Memo. of U.S. and Appendix.

p. 170 SW's call to Sheresky: Chertoff, Sent. Memo. of U.S.

pp. 170–71 SW's cards: Chertoff, Sent. Memo. of U.S.

p. 171 "Joy had intercepted this perversion": Interview with William R. Fleming, Jr., Oct. 21, 1993.

pp. 171–72 SW's letters: Chertoff, Sent. Memo. of U.S.

p. 172 "Joy, when she heard about the letter": Interview with Norman Sheresky, Feb. 8, 1994.

p. 172 SW tells jokes at the LCA dinner: "The Talk of the Town," *The New Yorker*, Apr. 26, 1993.

pp. 172–75 SW and JS's telephone conversation: Stillman, Sent. Memo. of SW and interview with SW, July 16, 1993.

pp. 176–77 SW's letter: Appendix to Chertoff, Sent. Memo. of U.S.

p. 177 "talked to Sheresky and consulted private investigators": Interview with Norman Sheresky, Oct. 4, 1993.

p. 177 "A colleague" to "pharmaceutical manufacturer": Add., Frosch and Miller, Sent. Memo. of SW.

pp. 177–79 SW's letters: Appendix to Chertoff, Sent. Memo. of U.S.

p. 179 Eleanor Sloan calls SW: Chertoff, Sent. Memo. of U.S.

pp. 179–80 "she'd go to the FBI" to "He seemed as genial as ever": Interviews with Norman Sheresky, Mar. 26 and June 13, 1993.

pp. 180–81 "He had called the information operator in Linden" to " 'give the letter all the right meaning' ": Interview with SW, July 16, 1993.

pp. 181–85 SW's letters: Appendix to Chertoff, Sent. Memo. of U.S.

p. 185 "Joan Wachtler, who knew nothing" to "call the guests and apologize": "Attorney Work Product" prepared by the office of Charles Stillman.

pp. 185–86 SW's card and letter: Appendix to Chertoff, Sent. Memo. of U.S.

p. 186 " 'I've *got* to dispel this notion' ": Interview with SW, July 16, 1993.

pp. 186–87 SW dresses as "Purdy": Chertoff, Sent. Memo. of U.S., and Letter, Miller, Sent. Memo. of U.S.

pp. 187–88 "By the end of August" to " 'get me out of your life' ": Appendix to Chertoff, Sent. Memo. of U.S. and interview with SW, July 16, 1993.

p. 188 "advised all her friends" to "did not make him rethink his plan": Interview with SW, July 16, 1993.

p. 189 " 'Sessions got the call [to see her] from Bush' ": Interview with SW, July 16, 1993.

CHAPTER 10

pp. 190–91 "Carrie Brzezinski, special agent" to "private investigator anywhere in Texas with the name David Purdy": Interview with Carrie Brzezinski and William R. Fleming, Jr., Mar. 31, 1993, and interview with William R. Fleming, Jr., Oct. 19, 1993.

p. 191 " 'You could set a bomb off in the courtroom and I might not know it' ": Gay Jervey, "An Off-Broadway Star," *The American Lawyer*, Oct. 1992.

pp. 191–92 "Chertoff already had a glancing familiarity" to

" 'trap and trace the calls' '': Interviews with Michael Chertoff, Apr. 12 and Oct. 20, 1993.

pp. 192–93 "Brzezinski and Fleming had already begun following up" to "becoming tearful or angry": Interviews with William R. Fleming, Jr., Oct. 19 and 21, 1993.

pp. 193–94 SW's call: Appendix to Chertoff, Sent. Memo. of U.S.

pp. 194–95 "Chertoff sat down with Ashrafi" to " 'would I agree to arrest him' '': Interview with Michael Chertoff, Apr. 12, 1993.

p. 195 "One day, his clerks insisted on a briefing": Add., Frosch and Miller, Sent. Memo. of SW.

pp. 195–96 " 'How long were you on the phone with Daddy' '' to " 'Okay, gotta go' '': Interview with Lauren Wachtler, Apr. 9, 1993.

p. 196 SW hears his last case: Videotape of court of appeals, Oct. 22, 1993 and interview with Mike Trainor, June 8, 1993.

pp. 196–97 "He was at the Harmonie Club that night" to "left the club": Interview with Matthew Crosson, Oct. 12, 1993.

p. 197 SW's call: Appendix to Chertoff, Sent. Memo. of U.S.

p. 197 " 'Do you think I should take the mike?' '' to " 'usual warm and witty way' '': Interview with Judge Milton Mollen, Feb. 19, 1993.

p. 198 SW's call: Appendix to Chertoff, Sent. Memo. of U.S.

pp. 198–99 "Joy was jumpy" to "FBI headquarters in Newark": Interview with William R. Fleming, Jr., Oct. 22, 1993.

p. 199 SW's call to Yesim Oklu: Chertoff, Sent. Memo. of U.S.

p. 200 " 'Wachtler used that phone' '': Interview with William R. Fleming, Jr., Oct. 22, 1993.

p. 200 "Chertoff changed his mind": Interview with Michael Chertoff, Oct. 20, 1993.

pp. 200–01 " 'With this guy's family' '' to "Sol got up to go": Interview with Joseph P. Carlino, Mar. 10, 1993.

pp. 201–03 SW's call: Appendix to Chertoff, Sent. Memo. of U.S.

pp. 203–04 "five FBI agents in five separate cars" to "Sol reached the airport": Interview with William R. Fleming, Jr., Oct. 25, 1993.

pp. 204–05 "Sol's in top form": Interview with Judge Edwin Torres, Feb. 5, 1993.

p. 205 "Sol had proposed to Long Island University": Interview with Judge Milton Williams, Feb. 9, 1993.

p. 205 " 'Vintage Sol Wachtler' ": Interview with William R. Fleming, Jr., Oct. 25, 1993.

pp. 205–06 "gave an interview over his car phone": Fredric Dicker, " 'Brilliant' Jurist Was Seen as a Class Act," *New York Post,* Nov. 9, 1992.

pp. 206–08 SW's letters: Appendix to Chertoff, Sent. Memo. of U.S. Note: "Val's house" is a reference to the house David Samson rented in Water Mill, and "the Sutter house" is a reference to a nearby neighbor's home.

p. 207 "your hotel": Here, SW has "Purdy" refer to JS's apartment building as a "hotel," perhaps in order to indicate the detective's ignorance, as he does with "Purdy's" frequent misspellings and grammatical errors.

pp. 208–10 "Michael Chertoff drove from New Jersey" to "drank coffee, chewed a bagel": Interview with Michael Chertoff, Oct. 27, 1993.

p. 210 "Joy was hearing the radioed reports too" to "spectator watching events play out": Interview with William R. Fleming, Jr., Oct. 27, 1993.

pp. 210–12 "Ramón reached Shanley's" to "was now overwhelming": Interview with Michael Chertoff, Oct. 27, 1993.

pp. 212–13 " 'What's bothering you?' " to " 'I don't know what it is' ": Interview with Lauren Wachtler, Apr. 9, 1993.

p. 213 "Was Lauren 'Miss Heather'?" to " 'string tie' ": Interview with Michael Chertoff, Oct. 27, 1993.

pp. 213–14 " 'He's putting on a *what?*' " to "gave her the envelope": Interview with William R. Fleming, Jr., Oct. 28, 1993.

pp. 214–16 "Back at the command post" to " 'let's take him down!' ": Interview with Michael Chertoff, Oct. 27, 1993.

pp. 216–17 "Sol was nearly home" to "until much later": Interview with SW, July 16, 1993.

p. 217 " 'Do you know what the worst part is?' " to " 'I could have been governor' ": Chertoff, Sent. Memo. of U.S.

CHAPTER 11

p. 218 " 'It can't be! It's bizarre' ": Interview with Matthew Crosson, Mar. 24, 1993.

p. 218 " 'It's beyond bizarre. . . . realm of the fantastic' ": Interview with Judge Edwin Torres, Feb. 5, 1993.

p. 218 " 'It's an aberration. . . . brain tumor' ": Interview with Judge Milton Williams, Feb. 9, 1993.

p. 218 " 'It's as if somebody else invaded his body' ": Interview with Fern Sussman, Apr. 2, 1993.

p. 219 " 'Send him to a hospital. . . . Federal marshals guarding him' ": Interview with Michael Chertoff, Nov. 19, 1993.

p. 219 " 'It's like one of Daddy's Bad-Boy George Raft stories' ": Interview with Lauren Wachtler, Apr. 9, 1993.

pp. 219–20 "She refused to let his confession crush her" to "finding a psychiatrist for her husband": Interview with Joan Wachtler, July 16, 1993.

pp. 220–21 "Dr. Solomon was in bed and asleep" to "no medications except Valium, to calm him": Interview with Sanford Solomon, M.D., Sept. 26, 1993.

pp. 222–23 "Sol was dressed, that morning" to "tears flooded his eyes": Jim Dwyer, "No Jail, But 'Tears' at Fall From Grace," *Newsday,* Nov. 11, 1992.

p. 223 " 'When the deal is done' ": Ibid.

pp. 223–24 " 'For approximately forty-five minutes' " to " 'not able to appreciate or grasp it' ": Letter, Miller Sent. Memo of SW.

p. 224 "Sol's was a 'toxic mania' ": Interview with Sanford Solomon, M.D., Sept. 26, 1993. To test his hypothesis, Dr. Solomon took Wachtler off lithium. His mania did not return.

p. 224 " 'I feel as though I'm already dead' " to " 'people I've already hurt' ": New York Hospital Cornell Medical Center "Nurses' Rating Summary 12/07/92 to 12/14/92." Appendix to Chertoff, Sent. Memo. of U.S.

p. 224 "He *missed* her": Interview with SW, July 16, 1993.

p. 224 " 'I'd rather go to jail . . . all in one day' ": New York Hospital–Cornell Medical Center "Nurses' Rating Summary 12/07/92 to 12/14/92." Appendix to Chertoff, Sent. Memo. of U.S.

p. 225 " 'Who is she?' " to " 'special treatment' ": Interview with woman editor, March 15, 1993.

pp. 225–26 "Early in their first session" to " 'clear psychopathic streak to Wachtler' ": Interviews with Dr. Louis B. Schlesinger, Mar. 16 and Mar. 19, 1994.

pp. 226–27 " 'no small matter' " to " 'observing the effect on Joy Silverman of his threats and coarse language' ": Letter, Simring, Sent. Memo. of U.S.

pp. 227–28 "it better be something serious" to " 'that's what we've got the criminal law for' ": Interviews with Michael Chertoff, Apr. 12 and Nov. 12, 1993.

pp. 228–30 SW's appearance at U.S. District Court in Trenton: Observations and quotations from author's attendance at the arraignment, Feb. 17, 1993.

p. 230 " 'Maybe . . . But even if we do, Wachtler's going to have to do jail time' " to "doing sound work handling the trust money?": Interview with Michael Chertoff, Nov. 19, 1993.

p. 231 "Joy felt": "Memorandum in Support of Answer and Objections of Joy Silverman to Petitions of Trustee to Resign," in re *In The Matter of the Applications Pursuant to SCPA 715 of Sol Wachtler Trustee of the Trusts for the Benefit of Bruce Wolosoff, Joy Silverman, Honey Wolosoff, and Van Warren Wolosoff, under the Last Will and testament of Alvin B. Wolosoff, Deceased* (Surrogate's Court, State of New York, County of Nassau, 1993).

p. 231 "Sol felt": Interview with SW, July 16, 1993.

p. 231 " 'I wonder whether she ever really cared for me. . . . controls my money' ": Interview with SW, July 16, 1993.

p. 232 " 'Isn't David wonderful?' " to " 'divine?' ": Interview with the wife of a close friend of George Bush, Mar. 16, 1993.

pp. 232–34 " 'Do you promise to tell the truth' " to " 'going around like a screaming banshee' ": Observations and quotations from author's attendance at plea hearing, Mar. 31, 1993.

p. 235 " 'I am a licensed certified social worker' " to " 'out-of-control raving maniac' '': Joan Wachtler, "To Be Mentally Ill Doesn't Mean Raving," *New York Times,* Apr. 8, 1993.

p. 235 " 'Whatsa matter, David? You didn't like my taste?' " to " 'You still believe everything you read in print?' '': Interview with Lawrence Bathgate, Nov. 12, 1993.

p. 236 "he wondered if he would always have a lingering sense of loss": Interview with SW, July 16, 1993.

p. 236 " 'Joy's not that young!' " to "murder her": Interview with Joan Wachtler, July 16, 1993.

p. 236 " 'How could someone as intelligent as you fall for that crap?' '': Interview with Joan Wachtler, July 16, 1993.

p. 236 "maybe he'd enjoyed seeing someone who could be such a bitch": Interview with SW, July 16, 1993.

pp. 236–37 "Dr. Solomon was still seeing Sol twice a week" to "You bet there was": Interview with Sanford Solomon, M.D., Sept. 26, 1993.

p. 238 The party at Tavern on the Green: "To State Judges, He's Sol Right," *New York Post,* June 30, 1993.

p. 238 "What's the *matter* with those guys?" to "effectively done violence to a mother and a daughter": Michael Chertoff, remarks before Judge Anne Thompson at the sentencing of SW, Sept. 9, 1993.

pp. 238–39 "thick packet of materials" to " 'highest aspirations of our Judeo-Christian culture' '': Stillman, Sent. Memo. of SW.

p. 239 "Stillman wasn't sure it was a good idea": Interview with Charles Stillman, Aug, 17, 1993.

p. 240 *"The New York Times* ... pointed out": "Seeking Leniency Ex-Judge Wachtler Blames Adversaries," *New York Times,* Sept. 5, 1993.

pp. 240–47 "On September 9, a dank and gloomy day" to "federal correctional institution in Pensacola": Observations and quotations from author's attendance at sentencing, Sept. 9, 1993.

p. 247 " 'It'll be all right' " to "grabbed a handkerchief": Interview with Sanford Solomon, M.D., Sept. 26, 1993.

p. 247 " 'With Sol Wachtler's sentencing today ... victimize women and children' '': "Silverman: 'Message Has Been Sent,' " *Newsday,* Sept. 10, 1993.

p. 248 " 'Joy's an avaricious person. . . . And she wanted more, from *my* husband' ": Cindy Adams, "Dad Gets the Rap for the Way Joy 'Destroys' Men," *New York Post*, Sept. 10, 1993. Interestingly, Joan Wachtler makes an error about the number of JS's husbands—there have been three, not two.

p. 248 " 'Joy never knew her father. . . . One by one' ": Ibid.

p. 248 " 'Teach?' " to " 'be a hero again!' ": Interview with Dick Lavinthol, Nov. 19, 1993.

p. 249 " 'It's dangerous' " to " 'people with grudges against judges' ": Interview with Sanford Solomon, M.D., Sept. 26, 1993.

EPILOGUE

p. 251 "Sol had been stabbed" to "middle tines removed": Interview with FBI office in Raleigh. N.C., Nov. 29, 1993 (interview conducted by Jack Bourque).

p. 251 "According to Sol" to "attacked him": Interview with Sanford Solomon, M.D., Nov. 24, 1993.

pp. 251–52 "the injury appeared to be self-inflicted": *Daily News*, Dec. 22, 1993.

p. 252 "Why would he have wanted to hurt himself?" to "He had adjusted": Interview with Sanford Solomon, M.D., Nov. 24, 1993.

p. 252 "After the stabbing" to "creative writing": Letter from SW to a friend, dated Apr. 15, 1994.

pp. 252–53 Letter to William Kunstler: "Kunstler's Fan Mail," *Newsday*, Feb. 2, 1994.

p. 253 Letter to Cindy Adams: "Marla Reminisces About Past; Wachtler Leading a Dog's Life," *New York Post*, Apr. 4, 1994.

p. 253 " 'We had met on several occasions' to 'will never be again' ": Letter from SW to a friend, dated Apr. 15, 1994. Note: the honorary degree to which SW refers was given not "the summer before last," which would have been 1992, but in 1991.